Barrie Mahoney worked as a teacher and head teacher in the south west of England, and then became a school inspector in England and Wales. A new life and career as a newspaper reporter in Spain's Costa Blanca led to him launching and editing an English language newspaper in the Canary Islands.

Following the successful publication of his first novel, 'Journeys and Jigsaws', he is still enjoying life in the sun and writes regular columns for newspapers and magazines in Spain, Portugal, Ireland, Australia, South Africa, Canada and the USA.

Visit the author's website: www.thecanaryislander.com

Books by same author

Journeys and Jigsaws (Vanguard Press) 2009
ISBN: 978 184386 538 4

LETTERS
FROM THE ATLANTIC

I would like to thank all those people that I have met on my journey to where I am now.

To supportive friends who helped me to overcome the many problems and frustrations that I faced and taught me much about learning to adapt to a new culture. Also, to friends in the UK, or scattered around the world, who kept in touch despite being so far away.

To people that I met through working as a newspaper reporter and editor in Spain and the Canary Islands and the privilege of sharing their successes and challenges in life.

To my publishers, Pegasus Elliot MacKenzie, for their professional help and support and the peace of mind that comes with knowing that you are in the right hands.

Barrie Mahoney

LETTERS
FROM THE ATLANTIC

Vanguard Press

A CIP catalogue record for this title is
available from the British Library.

ISBN 978 184386 6459

Vanguard Press is an imprint of
Pegasus Elliot MacKenzie Publishers Ltd.
www.pegasuspublishers.com

First Published in 2011

Vanguard Press
Sheraton House Castle Park
Cambridge England

Printed & Bound in Great Britain

This is a book about real people, real places and real events, but names of people and companies have been changed to avoid any embarrassment.

To my life partner, David, for his love and support and for travelling the journey together.

Contents

Preface

The people of Britain have always been adventurers. Despite being an island people, many of our forefathers felt the urge to leave its shores and to explore the world beyond. Our national history is full of exciting accounts of explorers and adventurers. The days of Empire made travel to far off lands even easier and the Victorians, in particular, took full advantage of the increasing ease of travel throughout Britain, Europe and beyond.

In modern times, with the arrival of the aeroplane and fast ferries, affordable overseas travel became more accessible to many more people. In recent years, the UK's entry into the European Union has made it much easier for those with the spirit of adventure inside them to live and work overseas. In the last twenty years, the rapid increase in UK house prices has left many owner occupiers in the fortunate position of having sufficient equity in their property to make their wish to travel a real possibility. Second homes in France, Spain and Italy are no longer the province of the fortunate few and, for many others, the opportunity to leave the UK and make a permanent move to another country within the European Union, had become too tempting to ignore.

'Letters from the Atlantic' is the account of the adventures that my partner, David, and myself have experienced since our move to Spain and the Canary Islands. We were both primary school head teachers for many years, with myself becoming a school inspector and education consultant, working in schools throughout England and Wales. We felt that we done our bit for Queen and Country, and that now it was time for something completely different. I thoroughly enjoyed my time in the education service, but I have always believed that the recognition of one's own 'sell by date' is important for personal sanity, as well as for future happiness.

Like so many who had gone before us, often tempted by the warmer climate and lower cost of living, we decided to sell up and move to a country that we both already loved. Spain's Costa Blanca was to become our new home, together with our loveable yet self-willed corgi, Barney, and later to be joined by a 'fruit bat' called Bella.

'Letters' begins with my experiences of leaving the education service and starting a part-time job as a newspaper delivery 'boy' in the Costa Blanca. A period as a newspaper reporter and photographer led to being sent to the Canary Islands to launch and edit a new English language newspaper in the small Atlantic island of Gran Canaria.

I hope that 'Letters' give readers an insight into our many experiences during this challenging and exciting period of our lives. Looking back, I am not quite sure how we overcame all of the problems, but we did and have enjoyed most of it in the process! Little did we know that when we left the UK on that cold and wet February morning that this was only the beginning of our adventures and that I would be writing letters to friends and family from a small island off the west coast of Africa.

I also hope that this book will serve as an inspiration to those of you who are tempted by a new life in the sun. If you feel that you have a sufficiently flexible approach to life and have the will to succeed, despite the odds, you will achieve your goals. Don't let others, who may be less adventurous than yourselves or have their own agendas, put you off. Grasp your new opportunity and challenge with determination and make it happen!

Barrie Mahoney

Part 1

The Costa Blanca Years

Letter 1
All Change

"You boys alright over there?" came a voice from the desk at the far end of the showroom. The short dumpy woman, who had been chatting on the telephone when we entered the showroom, came waddling over to us. "How may I help you?" she added, in a voice that sounded as if it were normally reserved for telephone clients.

"Well, we are just looking really. We saw the advertisement and the photos in the window and thought we would find out a little more about what you have to offer," I replied, trying not to sound too interested.

The short dumpy woman standing in front of us was typical of those who have spent either too long in the sun or cooking in a tanning parlour at too high a setting – or maybe both. Her skin had turned into a kind of wrinkled, leathery brown material, its suppleness and natural sheen had long gone due to the effects of too much sun and, possibly, too much alcohol and dehydration.

"Is there any property that you particularly like the look of?" beamed Sally Hedges – her name badge was a certain give-away.

"Yes, the Alhambra looks very nice. It's er very…" I replied, trying to find the right word to describe the style of the property that I had fallen in love with in the window display.

"Roman?" interrupted Sally, briskly. "Yes, I like it too, but they are not building many of those. In fact I don't think there are any available at the moment." Noting my obvious disappointment she quickly added, "What about the Mimosa, they are really good value."

I shook my head, "No, I don't think so. We're only having a general look. Thank you anyway."

With that we prepared to leave, but Sally stood between us and the doorway.

"Tell you what. I don't usually do this for clients, but give me your telephone number and I'll contact you as soon as an Alhambra becomes available. No obligation, of course. Do you know that we fly you out to the Costa Blanca, three nights in a hotel, all meals and drinks and the services of our own guide for just forty-nine pounds each?"

"Only forty-nine pounds," I gasped. "I guess that means we are committed to buying something."

"No, not at all. If you do, then that's great and I get my commission. If not, it doesn't matter. All you pay is forty-nine pounds each. You do have to get to Gatwick yourself though," she added, as an afterthought.

This is how our Spanish adventure began and two weeks later we were heading for the sun and, little did we know at the time, that our lives would never be the same again!

It had been a difficult year for both of us, and my partner, David and I had finally decided that we had had enough of the UK and that a new life in Spain would be good for our general health, and our sanity. A number of years working as a school inspector in England and Wales had been challenging as well as a great privilege, but had begun to take its toll.

Seven years 'on the road' with every second week spent in a Travel Inn or similar accommodation tends to wear one down, particularly in the depths of winter when trying to find a village school in the Welsh valleys or Yorkshire Dales at night or on miserable, dark winter mornings. I have always maintained that one of the secrets of life is recognising your own 'sell by date' and that it is always best to leave on a high note, rather than be pushed out by either poor performance or ill health. As soon as we cease to enjoy our work then maybe it is time to stand aside and move on. Certainly, children deserve the very best and tired teachers, as well as tired school inspectors, are not conducive to their well-being. Although seven years as a school inspector had its fair mix of highs and lows, I shall never forget that special tingling in the spine that I always felt when watching a gifted teacher at work in the classroom or witnessing a young child experiencing something new and wonderful in their learning. It had been a huge privilege to be part of.

Little did I know at the time of inspecting a particularly good primary school in South Wales that it would be my last. It was one of those schools that was a pleasure to be in. The school was bright and attractive, overflowing with imaginative, time-consuming displays of children's work. The staff achieved a sense of wonder and excitement in the classroom, children were interested, lively and mostly well behaved in their lessons, and the head teacher was a gifted teacher and leader, as well as someone who went to great lengths to care about the pupils and staff in her school. As colleagues, Marion and I hit it off from the time of the first visit. A divorced woman in her late fifties, Marion had a great sense of humour – an essential quality in a successful head teacher, and which sometimes bordered upon the wicked. Indeed, it seemed to me that we both genuinely enjoyed our early morning and late afternoon meetings that were so often the dread of many head teachers and registered inspectors. Marion always prepared cups of delicious coffee as well as providing a plate of chocolate biscuits – the secret of many a successful school inspection. Goodness knows what the staff must have thought when they heard our hearty laughter. This head teacher listened carefully to the praise, criticism and advice that I had to offer, but was not afraid to challenge and to ask questions. Yes, this was a good school to be in and I was well aware that most children would do very well in its care.

Strangely enough, the school must have recognised that a significant change in my life was about to happen, as Marion presented me with an engraved glass bowl at the end of school assembly on my last day at the school. "For a job well done," the engraving had said and is something that I will always treasure. Gifts were also given to my colleagues on the team and I thought at the time that this was unusual as the offer and acceptance of gifts was rare, and certainly not the 'done thing' for a school inspector. However, the staff had obviously gone to a great deal trouble in preparing the gifts, as well as getting the glass bowl engraved and it would have seemed churlish not to gratefully accept their kindness in the spirit of which it was intended. As it turned out, it was to be a gift marking my retirement as a school inspector. It was the end of one chapter and the beginning of the next.

David and I had often talked about moving to a warmer and sunnier climate and starting a new life, possibly in Spain, a country that we had already explored and loved. We had considered all the usual possibilities of opening a bar, but quickly realised that although maybe twenty years earlier Joan and Bert from Wigan would have made a great success from opening a British bar in the Costas, times had changed and it was no longer a guaranteed success. It was also pointed out to me that I as have an intense dislike of smoking, loud music and too many late nights, maybe I was not the best person to run a bar anyway!

It was after attending yet another 'New Framework' meeting following the appointment of a new Chief Inspector for Schools that I finally realised that I didn't want to play that particular game anymore. My view has always been that inspection is a powerful tool for school improvement, if used wisely. Sensitively implemented it was possible to improve the quality of teaching and pupils' learning, yet within the context of what was possible given social, community and financial pressures. The inspection process could be, at times, a blunt and cruel instrument, but was in my view, a necessary yet imperfect process to ensure that children were given the best education possible. It was also my experience that most inspections were usually carried out by experienced and compassionate people who also knew what was achievable. Apart from the inspection reports themselves, in the early days of school inspection much was achieved unofficially by a professional, constructive dialogue between professionals doing a very difficult job. Times were changing and the new inspection framework was something that I no longer wished to be part of. Yes, it was time to hang up the badge and throw away the briefcase for ever.

Two weeks after my last inspection in Wales, David and I found ourselves on an inspection trip to the Costa Blanca in Spain. As Sally had correctly told us, it was one of those very heavily subsidised affairs where one basically pays a nominal fee for the flight and the company, estate agents in all but name, bear the cost of hotel accommodation and meals, as well as excursions to a number of available properties in the area. Usually the buyer eventually pays an inflated price for the property if they decide to purchase, to offset the cost of all this hospitality. However, in their defence, a number of these property companies and agencies do provide a valuable service and make it possible to easily purchase an overseas property, giving all the necessary support during the sale and beyond. David and I had already agreed that this was only a preliminary visit and, at this stage, we had no intention of buying anything. Unfortunately, it was during one of my visits to the company's offices that I had already fallen in love with a particular design of a villa. It was of Romanesque design, with tall pillars adorning its fabulous sun terrace and was called an Alhambra. How impressive it looked in the photo when set against a bright blue and cloudless sky. No, we would not be buying anything on our four-day inspection visit, and I had made this perfectly clear when Sally had arrived at our home one afternoon clutching the tickets.

Upon our arrival at Alicante airport, we were met by an amiable middle-aged Welshman, somewhat predictably known by the name of Taffy. The stocky Welshman quickly gathered together the small group of would-be buyers and we were whisked away in a small brightly coloured minibus to a very pleasant seaside hotel in a small town near Torrevieja. After giving us an hour or so to change and freshen up, we met together in the hotel lounge for drinks before dinner. We soon got talking to a retired couple, Anne and Peter. The couple lived in Brighton and they were looking to buy a property for investment, but with a plan that sometime in the future they themselves would move to Spain. It was clear from our very first meeting that it was Peter who was the driving force in the relationship, and that it was he, and not Anne, who would like to move to Spain. There was certainly an 'awkwardness' between the couple.

"It's the kids," Anne had confided to me over dinner. "I want to be near them. We have grandchildren and I don't want to miss seeing them grow up."

"We can always fly back," Peter had interrupted. "Flights from Alicante are cheap and frequent. Anyway, think of all that sunshine and golf! The kids can come out and stay with us in the sun. It will do them the world of good to get out of London."

"Yes, it's just the golf that Peter's interested in! He seems to forget that we have family responsibilities at home. Besides, I don't want to leave our friends either. They mean a lot to me."

"My God, woman," Peter had snapped. "Anyone would think that we were moving to the Far East!"

I quickly changed the subject, correctly recognising that I had unwittingly become involved in a long running dispute

32

between the couple. I turned to my left where a very jovial conversation was taking place between David and a sprightly elderly woman, wearing a very smart tweed suit, inappropriate for the climate, and whose slim body was dripping with gold bracelets, rings and broaches.

The elderly woman turned to me and beamed a toothy smile, "Hello, I'm Alice," she announced, promptly spitting out the tiniest piece of tuna upon my bare, white arm that for the first time in many months had found itself exposed in a short sleeve shirt.

"Oooh, I'm so sorry about that," continued Alice, flicking my arm with a blue paper napkin. "It's my new teeth. Teeth give you so much trouble right from the cradle to the grave, don't they? I didn't mean to spit at you, we have only just met. You look after yours, young man."

I couldn't help but roar with laughter at this response and declined to reply with the comment that I was bursting to make when a plump, much younger woman popped her head between Alice and her tuna salad.

"You must forgive my friend, Barrie. It is Barrie, isn't it?" beamed the younger woman. "Alice gets a bit carried away, don't you dear? I have just been talking to your friend. It sounds as if you really are on an adventure! I'm Joy," Joy beamed and followed up with the predictable and, no doubt, well-rehearsed line, "Joy by name and Joy by nature."

I shook the clattering, bracelet-adorned chubby hand that was firmly pushed towards me, somewhat rudely, in front of Alice and her tuna salad. However, I could see that these two ladies were going to be great fun.

"Good to meet you, Joy. So you and your mother are looking for a place in the sun as well?"

Joy giggled, "Oh, I can see that you are a one, darling!" she exclaimed. "Alice isn't my mother, we are just good friends, and no, we are not lesbians, darling," she added, reading my mind.

"No, I didn't think you were for one moment," I quickly replied, realising that I may have seriously misjudged the relationship.

"Now, what are you two gorgeous boys up to, darling," flirted Joy, fluttering her eyelashes.

"Well, we are just exploring the area, just looking at this stage," I replied firmly, knowing that Taffy, Villa Sun's representative, was listening to every word that was being said and, at the same time, was plying us all with as much alcohol as we could drink. "I doubt we will find what we are really looking for on this trip."

"So what is it you are looking for, Barrie?" interrupted Taffy, his Welsh lilt gently flowing across the endless babble of sound that was coming from Alice and Joy.

"Er, well I like the look of the Alhambra, but I doubt you have any in our price range," I added quickly, catching just the beginnings of a glare from David seated at my side.

"I wouldn't be so sure about that, Barrie," Taffy replied thoughtfully. "You will be surprised at what I will be showing you tomorrow. We have a huge range of properties, something for everyone. You just wait and see."

It was certainly a fun-filled evening. Taffy, to his credit and no doubt to that of his company, wined and dined us perfectly. Endlessly flowing wine, delicious food and good company did exactly what was intended. By the time that coffee and liqueurs were ordered, as well as yet another generous gin and tonic for Alice, Taffy knew exactly what we were all looking for as well as our price range. Indeed, it could be said that Taffy was grooming us all for a hefty commission bonus to his salary cheque at the end of the month.

By the end of the evening and once we had all retired to the hotel lounge for yet more drinks, we all seemed to know each other very well. The evening was alive with the sound of shrieks from Alice as she regaled us with yet another blue joke, which

34

got bluer with each gin and tonic. Her companion, Joy, was indeed true to her name and although the volume of her shrieks was a little less than Alice, she too seemed to get louder with each generous measure of vodka that was put before her. Taffy had left the group after dinner, reassuring us that he had a wife and dog to get home to and warned us to get a good night's sleep and to be up 'bright and early' for the following day's adventures. Anne and Peter too had also decided to retire when Taffy left. Certainly those early tensions between the couple had almost disappeared, and both were now looking far more relaxed than when we had first met. It was clear that Anne was not at all happy about the possible purchase of a property, and was doing her best to curb Peter's obvious enthusiasm for a move to the sun and his favourite golf course.

"Come on boys, I'm having another! Taffy says that we can order what we like and just put it on the tab. Let's make the most of it," slurped Alice, her new teeth still giving her some problems. "I'll go and get 'em. Same again everyone?"

Alice left her seat relatively gracefully and headed towards the bar. Meanwhile Joy was by now looking much the worst for wear as she sat with eyes half closed on the comfortable sofa, her ample form resting against David, who was doing his best to squeeze to the very edge of the sofa – as far away from Joy as was possible.

"I don't know how that woman does it, darling," mumbled Joy. "We drink about the same, indeed, she usually drinks far more than me, yet drinks me under the table every time. It just doesn't affect her. Her liver must be in a right old state. Just look at her chatting up that gorgeous Spanish barman."

Alice returned shortly afterwards and sat down with a sigh. "That barman's got a great bum," she announced loudly. "Wish I were a few years younger. I would soon show him a thing or two in the bedroom department."

Joy giggled and slumped further down the sofa whilst Alice sat, pert and upright, in the chair beside her, beaming broadly.

"Lovely men over here, boys, but then, I guess you two have already noticed."

Letter 2
The Villa

The following morning was difficult. Yes, I had drunk far too much, and my head was still spinning from the previous evening. However, as we commented together later, we had drunk nowhere near as much as Alice and Joy. We wondered how the two ladies were, and doubted that they would appear for breakfast. Indeed, it seemed highly unlikely that they would appear for the minibus viewing-trip with Taffy. Reasoning that a strong black coffee would be just the thing to get us moving, we headed to the well-stocked breakfast bar in the dining room.

We had only just sat down with our cups of coffee and croissants when there was a loud cry from the entrance to the dining room.

"The boys, it's the boys!" shrieked Alice as she headed towards us at an alarming speed. We stood to greet her and a very subdued Joy standing by her side. No, Joy was not a picture of good health this morning. We stood up to greet the pair and Alice hugged us and gave us each two wet kisses on each side of our cheeks.

"May we join you?" announced Alice, sitting down and waving Joy to the spare seat beside her. Joy didn't look at all well, but she managed a faint smile and sat down wearily. I smiled and nodded, and moved my croissant safely out of Alice's line of fire.

"Good night last night, boys, eh?" Alice giggled, pointing to the waiter whom we recognised as the barman from the previous evening. Alice cheerily waved to him and he headed to our table smiling at Alice.

"Good morning, Carlos," beamed Alice, "How are you today? Now, young man, may we have two teas, please? Do we serve ourselves or will you do it for us?"

"Ladies will go to the bar and get food they want," replied the friendly Carlos in broken English, pointing to the well-stocked tables adorned with a generous selection of food to suit all tastes.

"Ooh, I'm having bacon and eggs if they have any. I wouldn't also mind some of that delicious ham they have over here, as well. You coming, Joy?"

Joy, who was still looking very much the worst for wear, shook her head miserably. Alice nodded and determinedly strode off towards the breakfast bar.

"I just don't know how she does it," began Joy. "She can drink me under the table any time. She spends all night knocking back vodkas, wine and all manner of booze and can still get up early for a long walk and eats bacon and eggs for breakfast. You just watch what she comes back with. She is in her mid-seventies, you know."

We laughed with admiration. Certainly we couldn't see Joy heading out for a long walk before breakfast, nor ourselves for that matter after last night's revelries.

Alice returned shortly afterwards with a tray heaped with a selection of cheeses, hams, salad and bread rolls. A pot of yoghurt and a bowl of cereal completed the breakfast that Alice had planned for herself.

"Pity, no eggs and bacon," Alice grumbled. "Of course this is Spain, isn't it? I keep forgetting. They don't eat such things do they? I brought you a yoghurt as well, Joy. Thought you may fancy it."

"Oh no, thank you, Alice. I couldn't manage a thing," muttered Joy, who was anything but true to her name this morning. I don't know how you can eat that lot and still retain a figure."

"Exercise dear. Healthy eating and exercise is the secret," began Alice tucking in to her bowl of cereal. Alice's new teeth were fascinating to watch as they seemed to move from side to side rather than up and down – a little like a cow grazing, I thought wickedly, but grateful that I was not sitting directly in the line of fire this time, and my croissant was safe.

"You would never believe that I was such a sickly child, would you? Mother thought I wouldn't make it even to two years old. Thin and waif-like they said."

"Well, you proved them wrong, Alice. Joy tells me that you have already been out for a walk this morning?" began David.

"It is such a beautiful little town and we are so close to the sea. I wouldn't mind an apartment right here, Joy. What do you think?"

"I really don't mind that much, you know that, Alice. As long as I can get to the shops and it has somewhere for me to sunbathe. Anyway, you are the one that's paying for it."

Alice began to laugh, and a gentle spray of milk and mashed cereal shot across the table, narrowly missing David's arm.

"Damn, so sorry dear. I really must get these teeth looked at. No. It is George who is paying for it really, Joy. Lived with the bugger for all those years. I deserve some kind of reward. I'm owed it."

"You didn't live with him," protested Joy, "you threw him out years ago."

"Well, what I mean to say, is that I was still technically married to the man when he died. Not my fault that he forgot to change his will, is it? He was a nasty piece of work. I don't know what I ever saw in him."

"Well, he left you enough to buy a property in England and have a comfortable life in Spain," began Joy, "I say, good on him."

A short time later we gathered together to meet Taffy in the hotel entrance hall. There was no sign of Peter and Anne, nor had they appeared at breakfast. Alice and Joy came down the stairs just as Taffy arrived. Gone was Alice's suit and was replaced by a pretty summer dress that looked much more suitable for hot weather.

"Good morning all," began Taffy. "I trust you had a good night after I left you and that the hotel is looking after you well. These visits costs Villa Sun a lot of money and we want to make sure that you are treated really well."

We nodded appreciatively and followed Taffy out of the door to the brightly coloured minibus that was parked directly outside the main entrance to the hotel.

"Didn't we ought to wait for Anne and Peter, Taffy?" enquired Joy as she was taking her seat beside Alice.

"No, I had a call from them this morning. Apparently Anne isn't feeling well and they are giving today a miss. Pity really because these tours cost Villa Sun a lot of money, as I said, and we do expect clients to at least take a look at the properties we have on offer. It's a condition of the visit, but there's nothing we can do about it if someone is ill. You don't have to buy, but you must at least look."

Not an unreasonable request, I thought, bearing in mind that we had paid less than fifty pounds each for the four day visit, including flights, hotel accommodation, meals and the services of Taffy.

"I guess you get a few trying it on," enquired Alice.

"Yes, we do get a few folk out here who have no intention of buying. They come out for a free holiday and then head off to the beach. Not fair really. I get paid commission on sales and if I don't sell, I don't eat."

40

"Well, I'm buying, Taffy, assuming I find the right property," announced Alice grandly. Taffy smiled gratefully.

The following two days were filled with viewing endless properties in the locality. We saw so many that by the end of the visit they had all blurred into one concrete mass. Most were attractive apartments intended for the overseas buyer, complete with swimming pools, sun terraces and even jacuzzis. They were intended for the 'expat' who was retiring to Spain, with ease of maintenance being a high priority. These were not the kind of properties that the Spanish themselves would wish to live in, being well away from the towns, as well as being overpriced. Many of the developments were unfinished and, indeed, some had not been started. We were shown plots of barren land amidst endless fields of orange and olive groves where new developments would one day appear. Taffy quickly realised that neither the ladies nor we were interested in such long-term projects and modified his itinerary accordingly. Most of the properties that we saw were delightful, although the quality of build varied enormously, and there was certainly some poor workmanship on display.

"I just adore all those tiles, don't you boys?" chattered Alice, excitedly. "We get nothing like this at home. I do so love those pretty blue ones with the little yellow and white flowers."

It was towards the end of the second day that Alice and Joy had decided on a very attractive apartment in a small development close to the sea. For once, both women were very quiet when looking around the apartment and, as it was on the ground floor, it would suit their needs perfectly. Taffy delightedly pointed out all the benefits and features of the property, quickly recognising that he was close to achieving a sale and a fat commission cheque at the end of the month.

David and I remained quiet, leaving Alice and Joy to chat amongst themselves. It was an attractive apartment, overpriced, yet appeared to be what they were both looking for.

"Well, I think this is the one!" announced Alice as she sat in the coach with a contended sigh. "As it has a terrace and is on the ground floor, it will be ideal for Buster. My little Yorkie, you know," she added as an afterthought.

"Well, Alice, I will reserve it for you until the end of tomorrow, just so that no one else snaps it up, you understand. Let's carry on with the tour for Barrie and David and, who knows, you boys may also find something that you like."

I nudged David. Yes, we would look and keep an open mind, but we were certainly not buying, not at these prices anyway.

It was on the final day, when it became clear that Taffy was determined to sell us something, and David and I were equally determined not to buy anything, that Taffy made a surprise announcement.

"You guys not found anything you like yet?"

"We have seen some that we like Taffy, but none that we are really excited about. Not enough to buy anyway."

"Well. I may have a surprise for you," laughed Taffy as we drove into a small development of pretty white and blue villas. "Didn't you tell Sally back in the office you liked the Alhambra? Remember, the one that you saw in the showroom back home?"

"Yes, but I think she said that the company weren't building any more of that design," I began.

"Just look over there." Taffy drew the minibus to a sudden halt and pointed up a driveway to a beautiful white, detached villa with black railings and tall Romanesque pillars – it was an Alhambra!

"How did you manage that, Taffy? You saved it until last."

"Well, I called my boss last night and explained that you were looking for this design and he told me that this one was back on the market. It had been sold once before a year or so ago, but the buyers backed out yesterday because of family

42

illness. They cannot move to Spain after all. It has just been finished and has never been lived in."

"And the price?" I enquired.

"Same as when it was being built two years ago. We have already been paid a deposit for it, which we get to keep to cover our expenses, and this means that we can pass it on to you at the original price to get rid of it quickly, but you will need to decide by the end of the visit. Do you want to have a look inside?"

We both knew when we walked up to the large sun terrace and into the villa that it was for us. Now it was our turn to be silent whilst Alice and Joy chattered excitedly, doing Taffy's job for him. They pointed out the large windows, a large space sufficient for a swimming pool as well as pretty blue floor tiles on the sun terrace.

"I can see you two boys here. This is just perfect for you both," exclaimed Alice.

Alice was right and so began the beginning of our new life in Spain.

Letter 3
Barney

Neither of us were the kind of would-be 'expats' that seize an opportunity to leave Britain's shores in search of a new life and then to spend the next twenty years or so criticising the country of their birth, only to return back to the UK when the going gets tough or sickness and old age finally gets the better of them.

We love the UK and always will. The wrench from our picturesque cottage in the heart of the Dorset countryside was a hard one to deal with. The loss of our friends and family, despite telling ourselves that they were only a two hour flight away, was even harder to deal with. What were we going to tell our mothers? As it turned out, both mothers were the least of our worries as both seemed happy (on the surface anyway) reassuring us that they would be fine and that we must live our lives in a way that was best for us. As it turned out it was only Aunt Gladys who wailed uncontrollably once she heard the news, even though we only managed to visit her a couple of times each year at best, so nothing would really change for her anyway.

Friends were a very different matter. There was the supportive group of very close friends who understood our reasons, wished us well and did all they could to help us during those last frantic days of packing. They were the ones who smiled politely and thanked us as we passed on items to them that we could not take to Spain, yet could not bear to take to the charity shop or to the tip. However, there was the larger group of 'so-called' friends and acquaintances that caused more difficulties.

"You are so lucky," was how the conversation usually began, together with an endless list of likely pitfalls. I believe that in life we make our own luck depending upon the talents and skills that we have been given. Little did they know of the uncertainties and worries that kept us awake at night.

"What will you do for money?" and, "You will never learn Spanish at your ages," were the most usual openers to a conversation when we were also continually reassured that it was 'for our own good'. We always listened, nodded politely and carried on with our packing.

There were also a small group of 'friends' who, once they heard the news, changed the subject completely and from whom we have never heard again. Oh well, such is life.

What we were going to do for money was a very good question and one which, looking back, we may not have thought about too thoroughly. From the sale of the Dorset home we were left with sufficient funds that we thought would keep us going for about a year. After that we would have to get jobs, but that was an issue for another day. If all else failed I would return to the UK from time to time to carry out the occasional inspection and freelance consultancy work to keep the wolf from the door.

The big day finally arrived, the men from Pickfords Removals descended upon our home and by the end of the day a very full lorry was heading towards the port and we were heading to the airport.

Barney, our much loved and wilful corgi, was duly sent to stay with David's brother for a few weeks whilst we settled into our new Spanish home. The plan was that rather than to fly Barney to Spain, which we did not like the thought of, he would travel overland to France on holiday with David's brother and wife and then on to Spain. Neither of us liked the thought of Barney flying and we knew that he would much prefer the pampering and extra attention that he would no doubt receive from his admirers in Bognor Regis.

It was a warm, dark evening by the time that we finally arrived at the villa. The sounds of the cicadas in the trees finally made us realise that we had moved to another, much warmer country. We dragged our suitcases down the drive, climbed the flight of steps on to the sun terrace and turned the key in the lock of the front door and flicked on the light switch.

This was to be the first of the many issues that faced us in Spain – there was no electricity nor, indeed, was there any water. Both utilities were working when we left the villa after the purchase a few weeks earlier, but neither taps nor light switches would work now. Our villa, although it was finished, was built in a new urbanisation that had not yet been handed over as complete to the local authority. Indeed, some would say at a later time, that the necessary habitation licences were not issued at the time of our purchase and we shouldn't have been living there anyway. We were on 'Builders' Electricity' and 'Builders' Water' and would be for many months to come. This meant that we were not directly connected to the utilities, but via a thin plastic hosepipe to the builders' water supply and by an even thinner cable running down the driveway to the exposed builders' live electricity supply that ran down the middle of the street. So much for health and safety! The good news was that there would be, in theory, no utility bills to pay until a permanent connection was made. The bad news was that the connection would be cut off at a moment's notice if, for example, a neighbour turned on their oven or had a hot bath at the same time.

It was our next door neighbours who quickly became good friends and immediately offered the help that we needed. The couple insisted that we stay with them for a few days until we had sorted out the problems with the builder and Villa Sun. Indeed, there was often a time when we had to make use of their hosepipe thrown over the wall for a water supply because they had one of the few villas already blessed with a mains electricity and water supply. Those first few days in our new home were not entirely as expected,

The Pickford's lorry finally arrived with the contents of our home onboard, complete with a bad tempered, unshaven Englishman who was determined to complete the job as quickly as possible.

"Want them unpacked?" the unshaven one grunted, pointing to the dozens of boxes stacked outside the villa.

"Well, we did pay extra for that service. Yes, please," I replied.

I regretted those words because within minutes, the bad tempered one had unloaded a very large Victorian style reproduction mirror and promptly dropped it on our patio. I said nothing, but he accurately read my thoughts and he became a much better person afterwards. I handed him the dustpan and brush.

A home is not a home without a dog. We have always had at least one scampering about and making a nuisance of themselves. Both David and I have always had corgis in our families. They have occasionally been described in dog books as 'short, irritable little beasts', and to some extent this is true, but they are intelligent, reliable, immensely loyal and busy little dogs. Indeed, with a corgi you get a lot of dog for your money! We missed Barney dreadfully and couldn't wait for the day that he arrived after his extended holiday in France to inspect his new home.

We were blessed with some excellent neighbours. Our next-door neighbour, George, leaned over the wall on our first day and after a very brief few words of welcome, lectured us on the security problems in the area. George was an ex-Metropolitan Police Officer and after having been held up at gunpoint with his wife at their home in central London had decided to move to Spain. Sadly, he had found himself in a new centre of crime.

"You need bars on the windows, change the door locks, a high wall, a locked gate and an alarm system. Whether or not you have a dog, you need to put up a 'Dangerous Dog' sign in Spanish on the outside gate. It helps."

George was quite right. We took his advice and did all that he suggested. Indeed, by the time that we left the Costa Blanca, we were one of only a very few properties in our road that had not been burgled. For this, we thanked George and Barney.

Once Barney was installed in his new home, he patrolled his home and grounds with relentless determination. Indeed, we were often told by neighbours, who were no doubt fed up with Barney's security efforts, that the only reason that we had not been burgled was because of his barking.

"He is a little dog, but he has a bloody big bark," came one angry comment.

Looking back, maybe I regret two things that we should have done, but did not. Firstly, we should have learned Spanish before we left the UK. Thankfully, our new home was very much part of a British enclave in Spain. This was not what we initially wanted, or were looking for, but we met some really kind and helpful people who had the time and the motivation to help each other. We were never in a position where we needed help. Advice and support was on hand at any time and we could not have wished for better and more supportive neighbours. One such couple from Northern Ireland quickly became our closest and dearest friends and we were accepted as very much part of their family as they were part of ours. I look back with fond memories at the many glasses of Carlos I (a fine Spanish brandy) that we enjoyed on our terraces during those balmy summer evenings, with mosquitoes busily tucking into my flesh.

The second thing that we should have looked at more carefully was what we were going to do after the money ran out. As I explained earlier, we had allowed, or so we thought, sufficient money to live quite comfortably for twelve months or so. After all, the price of food and other essential items was far less than in the UK, nor did we need to spend so much on heating. Or did we? Certainly there were some very cold evenings and I well recall hanging clothes on the line with the temperature reading at minus 2 on one bitterly cold January morning. No, we had not come to the Spain for these freezing conditions and unlike the UK, the properties were not built for low temperatures. Solid, concrete walls and tiled floors were no answer to the cold weather and it was interesting to see how many of our neighbours were fitting wall-to-wall carpet and installing central heating in their new homes. Climate change appeared to be already taking its toll and a number of well established people living in the area that I met told me that the winter temperatures had certainly been warmer some ten or twenty years earlier.

Money that was intended to last for about a year ran out after about six months. Yes, we had overspent, but it had been a lot of fun! Now, it was time to get a job. We both realised that we would have to learn Spanish rather quickly and we had enough spare cash to send David on an intensive one-to-one course for two hours a day, five days a week for a month. David used to arrive home looking very pale and numb after all the exertions of intensive learning, but it did the trick, and David seemed to be a natural when it came to learning a new language. Within one month he had learned sufficient Spanish to be able to apply for and get a job as manager of a local English language newspaper office. Now it was my turn.

I had already begun delivering newspapers for the local 'freebie' in our area. It wasn't a particularly pleasant job and involved me getting up at three o'clock one morning a week, which I hated, driving to a central distribution point and then delivering stacks of the newspaper to the paper's main outlets, advertisers and the like. I usually managed to complete the job during the late morning. It was not well paid, but at least it paid for the groceries. This was a salutary lesson and certainly taught me one important thing. It is no use moving to another country, and certainly not the Costa Blanca, with the view that 'I am an architect', 'I am a brain surgeon', or, in my case, 'I am a school inspector', and expecting everyone to fall over in their rush to offer you a job. It will not and does not happen like that. My best advice to all potential 'expats' is be prepared to do anything – even if it appears to be below your expectations. Who knows, you may even enjoy the change of direction!

A few weeks later, the same newspaper was looking for sales staff and so I applied for the job. The interview went well, or so I thought, and I was disappointed to learn that I was not considered suitable for the job.

"Come off it, Barrie, you would be crap at sales," was the delicate feedback that I received. "Why don't you try your hand at writing? Let me have a couple of articles by Monday and we will see."

So began a change in our 'fortunes' as I became a news reporter covering all sorts of events in the Costa Blanca. Most of the time it was great fun and I met some truly wonderful people. It was a community of British, German and Scandinavian 'expats', mostly working together to make a new life for themselves in Spain. There were clubs and associations representing any manner of interests that you could think of. Stamp collectors, walkers, folk dancers, ninety-year-old tap dancers, singers and musicians were all represented in this kaleidoscope of possibilities.

Sadly, there was also a worrying level of crime in the area. Burglaries, stabbings and murders were not uncommon and it was clear that organised crime was taking a hold in parts of the area. Indeed, as a naive new reporter, I stumbled across several stories that when published resulted in unpleasant threats of my imminent knee-capping and worse. It was after checking beneath my car each morning for bombs that I began to wonder if we really had made the right decision to move to Spain.

Barney had settled well into his new home. He always had a superior view of life and we were convinced that he thought everything was beneath him. After all, should he not be roaming the grounds at Windsor Castle or Buckingham Palace? Here he was, dragged out of his native, damp Wales, living in a Romanesque style villa in a very hot Costa Blanca. It must have seemed ridiculous to him, and he showed his feelings whenever he had the opportunity. Often, when we had to leave for work, he sulked and would not look at us. He did not like us both leaving home and leaving him behind.

Letter 4
Out of the Closet

When we lived in the UK, the issues of gay marriage and the recognition of same sex relationships were, at that time, highly controversial and divisive. Few other current issues had raised the public's attention and caused so much long-term media exposure both for and against. There had been enormous media attention on the issue of same sex marriage and the legal recognition of same sex relationships over the years, and some churches were quick to denounce any intended relaxation of the marriage laws as 'evil'.

The tide was turning and there would soon be an unstoppable force working its way through the governments of many nations, thanks partly to the equal rights legislation that had preceded it. In early 2003, two provinces in Canada announced legislation that would legally recognise same sex relationships through gay marriage. A small number of countries, including the Netherlands and Belgium, had allowed same sex marriage for many years. Countries such as France, Germany, Denmark, Argentina and Finland also provided the same legal recognition for same sex relationships as heterosexual relationships.

The UK Government announced plans for same sex couples to be granted many of the same rights as married couples as part of a legally recognised 'civil partnership' scheme, but had not yet decided on the details of the scheme. Many gay couples were already having their relationships blessed, and in London they could also register their relationship – although doing so brought no additional legal rights. In Spain, the possibility of registering same sex relationship already existed – yet another first for Spain, which was emerging as a successful, relatively new democracy that supported and defended equal rights.

David and I first met at teacher training college, and had been in a loving and stable relationship for many years. We were continually frustrated with being treated in the United Kingdom as second-class citizens within a system where gay men and women were expected to apologise for their commitment to each other. In all areas of law, including inheritance, pensions, social security and next-of-kin status (to name but a few) gay men and women were treated unjustly and unfairly. Many of our gay friends had been badly damaged psychologically by this denial of their sexuality, and it was only through mutual care and support that many coped with their day-to-day lives.

As teachers and head teachers, we were painfully aware of the need to hide our sexuality and love for each other. Although many of our closest colleague were, I am sure, fully aware of our situation, we both knew from the experiences of other gay colleagues, that if we had made our sexuality public, school governors, together with pressure from parents and local communities, would find ways, one way or another, of dismissing us.

As it was, we lived our lives in quiet rural areas where very few people knew us. We had a circle of close, like-minded friends and we were well supported by the church that we attended at that time. This was the Metropolitan Community Church in Bournemouth, part of a worldwide, all inclusive church community that did not judge, and valued each and everyone for who they were. It was a truly Christian Church, in the broadest sense, and I shall never forget the warmth and genuine welcome that we received from the pastor and his congregation when we attended our first service, as well as their love and support during the time that we were part of their community. For the first time in our lives we were welcomed and valued for who were we, and not judged solely upon the basis of our sexuality.

The church congregation included many broken people who were trying to piece their lives together. Rejected gay men and women, transsexuals, the transgendered, alcoholics and drug addicts were all welcomed in the warmth of this extraordinary church. 'Ordinary' men and women, families, children, the rich and poor would all come through its ever-open door. It was a community that we were proud to be part of. The pastor, Rev Neil Thomas, a charismatic, amusing and charming man, was the driving force, champion and defender of gay rights within the community. Indeed, not only did the church congregation, but gay men and women, alcoholics, drug addicts and minorities of all faiths, and those with no faith, in the town had much to thank Neil for.

In many ways, the church gave us the confidence to 'come out of the closet' for the first time in our lives, and have the confidence to be ourselves at last. Looking back, I guess that the move to Spain was part of this process, a new beginning where, never again, would we hide our love for each other. However, 'the outing' came rather quicker than we had originally intended!

It was shortly after our move to Spain that we had a meeting with our Spanish lawyer to discuss some of the essential documents that we would need. During the conversation Alberto suddenly blurted out, "You are a couple, aren't you? You are gay? Well, why don't you register a Civil Partnership? It will make things easier for you."

The new law had only very recently been passed in Spain and our lawyer was still very unsure of the process. However, he assured us that it would bring benefits: one example being that as David already had a full-time job together with a contract, health and social security benefits, I did not, yet by registering as a couple, those benefits could also be shared by me in just the same way as for a married couple.

We were well supported by our lawyer, Alberto, although the paperwork was challenging, to say the least! Our visit to the local registrar was confusing and the registrar, although very helpful, was apologetic that he had only three registers on offer – one for births, one for marriages and one for deaths. I suggested that he might like to get a new, pink one! Finally, on the 17 October, and lovingly supported by two of our new neighbours and good friends as witnesses, together with a Spanish schoolgirl who agreed to be our translator, our relationship was finally legally recognised by our newly adopted country at a civil ceremony in Alicante Registry Office.

It was a legal process, with no exchange of rings, ceremony or wedding guests. There were no flowers, new suits or expensive receptions. It was a brief, yet poignant process, in which we declared publicly our commitment and love for each other. We celebrated the event with lunch at the department store, El Corte Ingles, and David was back at work the following day. It was an emotional day and one that we thought would never happen, and one that has made us both very happy.

Letter 5
The Fruit Bat

Bella burst into our lives shortly after the death of my mother. At the time, I thought that it was the last thing that I needed. I really was not in the right frame of mind to deal with a new puppy – the inevitable vomiting, peeing and pooing and all those interminable walks really were the last thing that I needed – or so I thought at the time.

At the time of Bella's arrival I was taking part in a weekly news programme for one of Costa Blanca's English language radio stations. There were a number of such stations in the area and I worked for several of them. They were usually very entertaining and relaxed occasions, and were transmitted from the most unusual and unexpected venues. I usually looked forward to my weekly visits – the radio presenters and station staff were friendly and amusing and were highly committed to their cause. I guess, in some ways, they were pushing boundaries rather like the early days of pirate radio in the UK. Indeed, I now realise that most of these radio stations were illegal because, to the best of my knowledge, the provincial government in Valencia had not issued a new radio licence to any new radio station for many years. However, it was all 'par for the course' in the Costa Blanca, as there were illegal TV and radio stations broadcasting throughout the Costa Blanca and the Costa del Sol. After all, what would the British do without their regular 'fixes' of *Coronation Street* and *Eastenders*?

Radio Costa Blanca operated from the main bedroom of a newly-built villa at the edge of a new development. From the outside of the property it looked to be a perfectly normal villa, but once inside it became clear that this facade was merely the front for what was billed as 'Costa Blanca's foremost English language radio station'. The living room was a waiting room and sales office, surplus sound equipment was stored in the bathroom and the all-important transmitting equipment seemed to be scattered throughout the corridor and the second bedroom. Although Radio Costa Blanca was not operating exactly to BBC standards, it did have a large and loyal audience, anxious to hear programmes in their own language with plenty of reminders of life in the UK. In many ways, Radio Costa Blanca reflected the aims of the newspaper that I was now working for – it acted as a bridge for the newly arrived 'expat' in Spain. It helped them to settle and 'drip fed' essential information in their own language. As a community radio station, it helped to encourage local activities, gave valuable information about local clubs and societies, as well as keeping listeners informed as to what was going on back in Britain.

The arrangement of transmitting from a villa in a residential area had the definite advantage that when the station staff were off duty they could use the sun terrace and swimming pool to relax. Certainly, the staff at BBC Television Centre in London would, no doubt, be very envious of these 'not to be sniffed at' fringe benefits. Of course, the listener at home was totally unaware of these less than traditional standards and would, no doubt, have been very surprised if they could have seen the station's casual presenters in action and even more surprised if they had been aware of the studio's location. To their credit, as a listener at home, I was always amazed at the professionalism of production and the high quality of its programming. Maybe it was just as well that it was not television.

Financial matters at Radio Costa Blanca were not a strong point. Indeed, financial matters never seemed to be taken too seriously. The station was always short of money and it was very much a 'hand to mouth' company. Advertisers were not quick to pay their bills and staff were often left with salaries unpaid for many weeks. Although I would hear the occasional moan from the staff, it was always good-natured and was passed off with a shrug. I always enjoyed my weekly visits to the radio station, and would look forward to the cheeky (and often risqué) banter with the station staff, gratefully accepting a cup of coffee, and sometimes a glass of wine or beer, before taking to the 'air'. My weekly visits would also provide me with plenty of local gossip, news and ideas for my own newspaper articles and so they were always afternoons well spent.

It was during one of the frequent advertising breaks that community announcements were usually aired. These often focused upon information about local meetings, charity events as well as contact details for the many clubs and societies in the area. One of the announcements suddenly took my attention. Apparently, a small black and very frightened puppy had been found in the town near to where the radio station was based. Although a temporary home had been found, the family concerned was due to move back to the UK in a few days' time, and a new permanent home had to be found urgently for this unwanted puppy.

At that time, the Costa Blanca was a very bleak place for abandoned dogs and cats and many perfectly healthy stray cats and dogs were euthanised within days of being found. Indeed, I always maintained that this was the worst side of our new life in the sun. Thankfully, as time went on, matters began to slowly improve due, in no small part, to the tireless efforts of many British 'expats' as well as those from Germany and Scandinavia. A number of animal welfare charities became established and were well supported by local volunteers and imaginative fund-raising events. Although the situation was by no means perfect, I sincerely hoped that these efforts would form the basis for a workable and compassionate animal welfare programme in the future.

Later in the news programme the appeal for a home for the puppy was broadcast again. I began to wonder if the time had come for Barney to have a little friend to play with...?

"Poor little scrap," said the kindly female secretary entering the studio carrying another cup of coffee for me. "The family who are looking after her brought her in for me to see this morning. She is such a pretty, affectionate little thing. I would love to have her myself, but we have no garden."

By the time the announcement was broadcast for the third time, I had made up my mind to go and see the abandoned puppy for myself. Surely David and Barney wouldn't mind an addition to the family?

"We'll just go and have a look at her. We needn't take her on if we don't want to," I announced breezily to David when I got home. Surprisingly, David didn't put up too much resistance, although I did notice Barney giving me a withering look as he wandered off to the kitchen. He knew what was about to happen and he wasn't too keen.

Eventually we found the address that the lady I was speaking to on the telephone had given me. The young woman opened the door of the small villa and smiled.

"You the guy from the paper who's come to look at Pepsi?" she asked.

David and I greeted the woman, a young, harassed-looking woman in her early to mid-thirties. She looked as if she had been crying.

"I'll call the kids. They are playing with Pepsi on the terrace. She is a sweet little dog, but we just cannot keep her. As

I said when you called, we go back to England on Friday. I'm Anne, by the way."

The two children appeared, a small boy and an older girl. The girl was carrying a small bundle of fluff. It was Pepsi.

"Let the man hold her," instructed the mother. Reluctantly, the girl handed me the tiny puppy.

I gathered the small scrap of life in my arms – she was so tiny and nuzzled into my arm. I could feel her heart beating very fast. She licked my finger and I fell immediately in love with her. Yes, Pepsi would certainly be coming home with us.

It was clear that the young family were quickly becoming attached to her. The two children began to remonstrate with their mother. They wanted to keep Pepsi and I could understand why.

"Look, kids, it's simply not possible. We are moving back to England in a couple of days. Even if we had time to sort out the vaccinations and things, we cannot have a new puppy living with Grandma and Grandad as well. It is enough that they are taking us on until we get ourselves sorted back home. Your Dad just won't hear of it. Looking after a dog costs money and we don't have any."

From the brief conversation that we overheard, this was quite clearly a very sad case of a family who had moved to Spain with the usual 'high hopes' and expectations of a new life in the sun, and it hadn't worked out. I had come across a number of such cases where sometimes expectations were far higher than the reality. Often the money simply ran out, or maybe getting the job that was expected hadn't materialised. Whatever the case, it was always a heartbreaking story and particularly when children were involved. Often these situations led to such stress for the family that it led to the break up of a relationship. So many hopes and dreams suddenly gone.

It was rare to hear of circumstances where young children failed to settle quickly and easily to a new life in Spain. Children usually quickly adapted to a new life in the sun and the language barrier was rarely of consequence to young children – they simply invented their own methods of communication and rapidly adjusted to life in a new culture. Older children, those in their late primary years and those of secondary school age, could often be more problematic. Sometimes, older children would find difficulty in settling into a new school; they would often miss their friends and, above all, had trouble learning subjects in a language that they did not understand. I knew of a number of cases where, after a short time, teenagers were sent back to the UK to live with grandparents or aunts and uncles to enable them to return to their previous schools to complete their GCSE examinations.

Anne turned to me. "It's all gone badly wrong over here for us. Our new business failed and we have to get out of here by the end of the week. We are going back to live with my parents in Reading until we get back on our feet. So, if you could take the puppy we would be so grateful. We don't want to hand her over to those municipal kennels, we know what will happen if she goes there."

I looked at Pepsi and then turned to David, who nodded without any hesitation.

"Yes, we would be delighted to give Pepsi a home," I replied. I then turned to the children who, I am sure, were desperately hoping that we wouldn't take their new puppy from them. "Don't worry, we will look after her, I promise," I said quietly.

The children nodded and watched as we drove away with the new member of the family.

Pepsi's initial welcome to our home was not as warm or as smooth as we would have wished. After a short time we decided to introduce her to Barney. We decided that the best place to do this would be in the garden where they could run around and get to know each other.

Barney strode out of the front door, took one look at the little dog who was trembling on the pathway and decided to chase her. Pepsi fled as fast as her long legs would carry her – around the villa, in and out of the plants and towards the swimming pool. Barney was certainly enjoying himself and we certainly hadn't seen him move so fast since he too was a small puppy.

Suddenly there was a splash – Pepsi had fallen into the swimming pool. I plunged in after her and handed a very bedraggled and soaking wet ball of fluff to David. Pepsi was duly dried off, fed and settled down into her new home.

After a day or two, this charming little dog had quickly won us over. She was very little trouble, other than in the toilet department, which took many months to overcome. Barney too, seemed to move quickly from complete indifference to a degree of tolerance, and sometimes even seemed to actually enjoy having her around. However, both David and I agreed that the name Pepsi did not suit her and neither did we care for the product that she was named after. We mentioned this to our neighbours from Northern Ireland, who had quickly become close friends. They had young nephews staying with them and we agreed that we would leave the boys to come up with a number of names, and we would then all vote to find the new name. David and I began to wonder if we had done the right thing as we overheard a number of names being suggested. Names of pop stars and other famous people that would be even more unsuitable for our little girl. No, the name 'Madonna', would in my view, be even worse than Pepsi. We kept our fingers tightly crossed for a conclusion that would please us all.

After much discussion between the boys, a vote was taken and a name was finally chosen. Pepsi would now become Bella. We thoroughly approved of the choice. It was a very pretty name and well suited to such a beautiful little dog. The boys had done their work well.

Very quickly, Bella and I became truly inseparable – this little 'Spanish stray' and I had well and truly bonded. Her pretty, fine, chiselled features and huge ears quickly earned her the name of 'The Fruit Bat'. She followed me everywhere, sat near or on my feet when I was working on stories, and dragged me away for yet another walk when 'the going got tough'. In short, both David and I adored her.

Letter 6
Lost in Cartagena

Readers, who are dog lovers will, I know, understand that stomach retching feeling that you have when you have lost your much loved pet. Whether it is through death or through another cause, dog, cat, rabbit and iguana lovers everywhere know that is like losing a close member of the family.

The Costa Blanca is a wonderful place to live and work and David and I took every opportunity to explore as much of the area as we possibly could. It was rare that we could take a weekend off work and so most of our visits had to be achievable in one day. One Sunday morning we went on another of our 'Exploring Spain' day trips. We always took Barney and Bella with us – although often we wished we hadn't. Bella was always car sick, something that we had never come across with all of our previous dogs. However, after a chat with Rita, our long suffering vet, and a little trial and error, we discovered that by not giving her breakfast, a walk before the journey began and a few stops on the way, we would sometimes arrive at our destination relatively unscathed. Barney always enjoyed a car trip and he knew that at the end of it he would have a decent walk, lots of sniffs and many a pee. It was easy to see the look of contentment on his face as we set off, although travelling with Bella was a very different matter. We lived in hope that she would eventually get used to car travel and the car-sickness would eventually ease.

This particular time our visit was to Cartagena. Even though it was a Sunday morning the town was very busy. We parked a good distance away from the town centre, reasoning that the dogs needed a good walk and that we had plenty of time to spare before our return home. The visit started off well enough until we heard the sound of a marching band in one of the small squares in the centre of the town, 'Parque Para Majores'. We saw a group of men dressed as Roman soldiers marching around the square – accompanied by rhythmic drumming. Suddenly, the drumming got louder, Bella was clearly terrified and, in the panic slipped her collar and fled. All I saw was a flash of black fur disappearing into the distance. We chased after her, but she was too quick for us and, suddenly, she was gone. All I had left was a collar and lead, but no Bella.

We looked everywhere that we could think of and assumed that as the sudden noise had frightened her, Bella would try to get out of the noisy, crowded area and would be cowering in a nearby corner somewhere in the square. She was nowhere to be seen. We searched nearby streets, under cars, disused ground, but there was no trace. We mentioned Bella's disappearance to many local people. They were all very helpful and most concerned about our predicament and said that they would keep a look out for her and telephone us should they spot her.

Four hours later, we began to realise that Bella's disappearance was serious. Bella had fled and showed no sign of returning to the noisy square to find us. Although Bella had been recently 'chipped', she had lost her collar together with our contact telephone number. Either she was lost and was cowering somewhere, or someone had picked her up and was looking after her. We dare not think of alternative scenarios. Reluctantly, we decided to return to Torrevieja to prepare 'Lost Dog' posters with a photo to place around the town. We left Cartagena with heavy hearts.

Back at home we prepared dozens of posters. I was cursing as the ink cartridges in our well-used printer began to run out and had to be replaced. It was upsetting to see Bella's toys strewn around the house, her bed and bowl – would she ever return home again? Eventually the task was completed and we set off on our return journey to Cartagena, this time with torches. We were prepared to spend the evening searching the streets for our Bella and stay overnight if necessary. We tried to park the car where we had parked before, but the area was crowded and we had to drive around the town centre yet again, searching for a place to park. We were held up at a red traffic light. Suddenly, David shouted, "There she is, get out and grab her!" I spotted a black bundle of fluff running round the corner, near to where the car had been parked some seven hours earlier, but about one mile away from where we had last seen her. It was Bella! I leapt out of the car and grabbed her, returning to the car just as the traffic lights turned green.

We returned home in silence, thankful for the happy outcome to our worries, yet mindful to what could have happened. Bella slept contentedly on my lap all the way home and, fortunately for once there was no car sickness. We examined her closely for injury as soon as we got home and there appeared to be no real injuries sustained.

As soon as we went shopping again we bought Bella a harness to wear whenever she went out of the house, and from that day to the present Bella always has walks on a lead, admittedly one of the extending variety. We could never face letting her off her lead again.

I wrote a brief account of our weekend ordeal for our local newspaper and I was amazed, and grateful, for the response that we received from so many readers, empathising with our story, as well as giving some equally amazing accounts of events that had occurred with their cats and dogs and made me realise, once again, the very special relationship that so many people have with their pets.

How did this ten-month-old puppy, of a naturally flighty disposition, manage to find her way back to where the car had originally been parked some seven hours earlier and at least a mile from where she had fled? How had she managed to cross a number of very busy roads without being hurt? How had she managed to be in the exact spot within a busy city at the exact time that we had stopped at a red traffic light? Thankfully, Bella was unharmed and, other than being very hungry and thirsty, appeared to be unscathed after her ordeal. Some may say we were lucky, others will say it was co-incidence. For me, this was more than lucky – it was definitely Angel business.

Letter 7
A Little Piece of Britain

It is a strange, but I guess not unusual, phenomenon that one of the first things that many British 'expats' do when moving overseas is to create a little piece of Britain in their new adopted homeland. The same is true of Germans, and possibly more so, and certainly the Scandinavians become very focused in their Swedish, Norwegian and Danish enclaves that are scattered around the Costas. When David and I moved to the Costa Blanca, we naively thought that we would be living amongst Spanish people. In reality, nothing could have been further from the truth as we found ourselves in the centre of a British enclave. Indeed, learning the Spanish language became less of a priority, because most things could be done in English alone. For an Englishman living in Spain, this was indeed initially a great comfort, but it is very easy to become 'desensitised' as to the real reason for moving to another country in the first place. Most of our neighbours were from the UK, interspersed with the occasional Norwegian, French or Spanish invader, and a delightful group of people they were too. Nothing was ever too much trouble, and the British groups in the area quickly became involved in charity work and fund-raising, particularly for animal rescue charities, orchestras, dance and theatre groups. Interestingly, it was one of the main concerns that seemed to unite the 'expats', particularly from Northern European countries. It was a good life for most, and particularly for the retired, as their pounds 'stretched' a long way in the warm sunshine. There were also the dubious delights of many British supermarkets where all things British could be found. Favourite toothpaste, washing liquid, Cornish pasties, Stilton cheese, 'Mr. Kipling' cakes and pastries could all be enjoyed – often at a hefty mark-up, and without the inconvenience of all those labels written in Spanish too! We also used these shops from time to time, but our main supermarket was the wonderful Spanish Mercadona chain. It used to both amuse and shock that a can of Heinz baked beans could be purchased in the Spanish supermarket for around sixty cents, whereas the price was nearer to one euro thirty cents in the British supermarkets. English language newspapers and magazines were in abundance, as were copies of the UK daily tabloids. A number of English language radio stations beamed across the airwaves, and there were even competing television systems that rebroadcast Sky television programmes, via a system based upon a new technology called 'micromesh'. This basically involved fixing a 'baking tray' kind of fixture to the top of the property, as well as plugging a decoder box into the television. For a princely sum of around twenty-five euros each month, one could watch as much British television as anyone would wish. Of course, if we had stopped to consider why this service was offered so cheaply, we would have realised that it was an illegal, and indeed criminal, service, but everyone had the system, and who were we to argue? The authorities eventually managed to close these TV transmission systems down when it was discovered that these were essentially pirate outfits. A 'blind eye' had been turned to this fringe activity for a number of years, because so many 'expats' had the system and were thoroughly enjoying it. They had TV 'soaps', such as *Eastenders* and *Coronation Street* as well as paella and sunshine! When the big switch off came there would be an outcry but, in many ways, it was helping to promote, support and popularise the idea of moving to, and enjoying life, in Spain. Dealing with the Spanish authorities was not always easy and this is where many 'expats', including ourselves, were often exploited. Many lawyers, as well as non-qualified entrepreneurs, would set themselves up in business to offer services to the newly arrived and bemused British 'expat' trying to deal with the Spanish authorities, particularly as laws and requirements seemed to change frequently. In reality of course they did not, but it was in the interests of these local service providers, as well as the English language newspapers and their advertisers, to promote the idea that they were. Over time, this need for current information about perceived change became a self-fulfilling prophecy. One of the first challenges to face was obtaining a Spanish fiscal number, called an NIE number. This is an essential number that all residents have to obtain in order to receive a supply of electricity, water and telephone service, open a bank account, get a mobile phone or indeed buy a car. It was essential to obtain one and an effective Spanish lawyer would usually ensure that one was obtained for their clients before they moved to Spain. Our Spanish lawyer was supposed to have done this when we bought our villa, but had forgotten to do so. During the first few weeks of our new life in Spain, we became increasingly frustrated by the lack of this essential number. For some purposes a UK passport would suffice, but this number, together with the all-important National Identity Card, were essential pieces of kit in Spain. Our lawyer told us that the process of getting the NIE number would take around six months, and this would mean that buying a car would be out of the question until it was issued. We managed for a few weeks by using public transport and taxis, but this became increasingly expensive and inconvenient, particularly when trying to furnish and equip a new home. Bags of sand, cement and compost did not travel easily in buses and taxis. Buses did not run on time in the urbanisation or ran anywhere near our villa, as the area still had roads that were little more than gravel tracks and were not yet adopted by the Town Hall. It was rare that taxis could even find us and we would have to walk some distance to get to the taxi rank, where a wait of an hour or so would not be unusual. As funds were beginning to run low it became increasingly essential to find work and for this we would just have to have a car. We tried hiring them, but they were often poorly maintained as well as expensive. Our visits to local garages in the major town of Torrevieja were both amusing, yet worrying experiences. It was rare for any of the sales staff to speak English, but most were friendly and helpful and a mixture of 'Spanglish', speaking loudly and waving our arms around usually produced the desired result. It was in a Hyundai garage that we met Carlos, a lively young man, with an appearance that was more Scandinavian than Spanish. He spoke a little English, gave us a good deal on a Hyundai Getz, which was a small, economical car that we both liked. It was certainly going to make a big hole in our savings, but it was an essential purchase and we had already been warned never to buy a second-hand car in the Costa Blanca. However, there was going to be one problem – neither David nor I had an NIE number. We explained this to Carlos as we felt that this would be a hurdle that could not be overcome. "It is an easy problem for me," he beamed. "It will cost you two hundred euros and I get it for you in two days. You give me money and I get you the number. In two days you will have your new car." We duly handed over two hundred euros to someone we had never met before. Carlos beamed and winked, and two days later David had his precious NIE number and we had a new Hyundai Getz. As for me, it took another five months before our lawyer finally produced my NIE number and charged me yet another two hundred euros for the privilege. Of course, I now know that it is a question of only a few hours waiting in an office and a few euros to get that precious NIE number, but hindsight is a wonderful thing.

Getting our own supply of water and electricity was quite another matter. Now that we had our precious NIE numbers, we could apply for our own supply. The builders told us that this would take several months, and that we would just have to manage with the temporary supply until it was possible. When we were finally summoned to the builders' office to complete the paperwork for that wonderful day when we would be connected to our own supply, we were duly charged a thousand euros for the privilege. Even then we knew that it cost much less than that for a connection, and the charge being made by the builders was a great source of discussion and resentment within our urbanisation. Neighbours that had gone before us had angrily complained to the authorities about what they saw as pure exploitation, refused to pay and generally made a fuss. The result was that their applications were put to the bottom of the pile and they were still waiting to be connected. We were advised to 'just pay up and keep your mouths shut'. This we did, and after handing over the thousand euros, plus 'estimated charges' for consumption from the date of the purchase of the villa to the date of connection, we were finally connected to mains electricity and water supply – all within twenty-four hours. At last, we could have a decent hot bath!

For many British 'expats' living in the Costa Blanca, the effort of learning the language and interacting with Spanish people in their own language was often seen as being an impossible burden. As a reporter for a local English language newspaper, I quickly became aware of the demand for English speaking services at the Town Hall, police stations and other government offices in the area. Although I could see the issue from their point of view, a visit to the Town Hall could mean taking an interpreter at a cost of around fifty euros a time. However, we were guests in a country of our own choosing and I had little patience with the endless whinging and moaning from a small section of 'expats' whom I always thought would be far happier returning to the UK anyway. It always amazed me that most Spanish officials were so helpful and patient when faced with the arrogance and general abuse from such people. In my experience, an attempt at speaking Spanish, however faltering and feeble, was always appreciated, and most officials would do their best to understand and help whenever they could. These demands, by a minority of residents, for English speaking services at the Town Hall led to a minor revolution in the area. I well recall meeting an elderly, yet lively man called Tim Simms, who wanted to launch an English speaking political party to challenge a number of seats at the local election the following year. He called me one day and asked me to meet him, as he wanted a story in the newspaper about his new political party. He had been inspired by another Town Hall area where a British resident had been elected as a town councillor. His reasoning was that as it was an area with so many British 'expats', their needs should be served by someone who knew their problems and could push for the services that were needed in the area. I recall making the point that if an 'expat' really wanted to be involved in Spanish politics, it would surely be better to do so through one of the existing Spanish political parties? My comments were brusquely brushed aside, and a few days later Tim Simms duly summoned me to report upon the launch of the new party at a forthcoming meeting in a very large conference centre in the town.

When I left to cover the story of the launch of the new political party, I remember telling David that I wouldn't be very long returning home, and that it would all be over in a few minutes. Why on earth had this man hired such a large conference centre for a handful of people, I mused? How wrong I was! When I drove into the car park, I was amazed that it was difficult to find a place to park. The pathway to the main entrance was full of people talking seriously together. I walked into the entrance hall and was shocked to see that the main conference hall was full, additional chairs had been placed in corridors and entrance and others were standing on stairways, on chairs, indeed anywhere to get a view of the main podium. Tim

Simms sat on the podium in the centre with two men and two women sitting on either side of him. He looked very grand and was looking very pleased with himself. He spotted me crushed at the back of the hall and waved me to go the front. He pointed to a chair in the front row that had a large 'reserved' notice sitting on it. My job as a reporter was badly paid with very few privileges, but a reserved seat was definitely one of the perks. The atmosphere in the hall was electric. It was noisy, with some nervous giggling and laughter, but there was an air of anticipation and expectation. Maybe it is just the same before a bullfight. Eventually, the assembled gathering was silenced and the meeting began. I had been to very few political meetings before and I cannot say that I liked them. Indeed, I thoroughly disliked the very tone of this meeting from the very moment it started. It appeared to belittle the Spanish political system, its society and its values and traditions. Some of the comments made me shudder, and I wondered what the reaction of all these people would be if they were back in the UK and a group of foreigners held a similar meeting. I could just imagine how the UK daily newspapers would headline it the following day. I left the meeting both dejected and depressed. This was not how it should be, or how I imagined life in Spain. Maybe I was just naive, and these 'expats' really did have genuine grievances that needed to be resolved. Maybe I had just missed what was going on right under my nose?

"Good evening, Barrie. I thought you would be here."

The voice came from an elderly lady I recognised immediately. I had interviewed her a few weeks earlier for a story about the animal charity for which she was raising money. This lady, despite her poor health, had both presence and a resolute attitude of determination and resilience that would carry her through the various good works that she supported and believed in.

"Hello, Sheila. It is good to see you. What did you think of the meeting?"

I was anxious to find out if anyone shared my views. Sheila thought for a moment or two, and looked around her. She looked very serious.

"Barrie, I am shocked," she whispered. "I didn't move to Spain thirty years ago for this. I came to live and work in harmony with the Spanish people. I came to appreciate and respect their values and way of life in this beautiful country. Of course, the weather here is wonderful, but we all need to put something back as well."

"It worries me also, Sheila, but maybe this is what these people think they are doing, putting something back. Maybe this is just their way of showing it."

"Mark my words, Barrie," Sheila whispered. "This is dangerous stuff. These people won't be content until the Union Flag is flying over the Town Hall."

Letter 8
Ashamed to be British

Sheila was quite correct and it became only a matter of time before first one and then several British 'expats' became elected as local councillors and took their seats alongside Spanish members of the more traditional and well-established political parties in local councils. Did it make any difference? Well, maybe in the short term it did with a few members of the British 'expat' community strutting around the municipality as if they owned the place. Later, I was told that there were a few changes in the availability of services in languages, other than Spanish. However, contacts with Spanish staff in the Town Hall assured me that these changes had been planned for anyway, and it was a just question of funding them. However, for those promoting the 'expat' cause, it was indeed a major victory. Before long their victory was noticed and taken account of in other municipal elections in the Costas, and it was not long before British and representatives from other nationalities began to take their place in local government. Maybe traditional Spanish tolerance had gone a little too far when, due to a number of local issues, a British man was elected as mayor of one of the municipalities in the Costa Blanca. The mayor is a powerful and usually respected figure in Spain, although the new incumbent of this Town Hall could not even speak the Spanish language.

During our time in the Costa Blanca working as a reporter, I received a letter from residents in a nearby urbanisation who were concerned about the way in which the only Spanish family living there were made to feel unwelcome, and were being victimised by some members of the community – mostly of British origin. This single Spanish family were considered to be 'outsiders', victimised and made to feel unwelcome in their home country. Indeed it appeared to be the aim of some of the local 'expat' community to encourage this family to leave the urbanisation – leaving a totally British community in its place. After the letter was published, it prompted a flood of telephone calls and letters from readers expressing their horror and disgust at the way their countrymen had treated their Spanish hosts.

As a local newspaper reporter, I often received unhelpful and ungracious comments from British 'expats', in particular, about their Spanish hosts. Indeed, I had the misfortune to witness a most unpleasant man, encouraged by his equally unpleasant wife demonstrating his 'Northern manhood' by shouting the odds at a flustered receptionist in a builders' office. "Why the f***** hell don't you all learn to speak English?" was his final retort – following an earlier barrage of bad language. I accepted that the outburst may well have been the result of weeks of pent up frustration with the builders – and many of us have been there, but the very fact that this lout of a man and his wife actually shouted those words at a young Spanish woman who was doing her very best to help them was beyond belief and, thankfully, most of the other people who witnessed this disgraceful event were equally appalled.

"Why don't the Spanish learn to drive around roundabouts?" was a comment that I often heard. Criticisms about the quality of Spanish drivers abounded. However, national statistics showed that many road accidents in the Costa Blanca were caused by British and non-Spanish drivers – most of whom were driving under the influence of alcohol and drugs. Indeed, from what I understood from local Spanish driving school instructors, Spanish requirements for learning to drive and passing the driving test were more rigorous that the UK equivalent. As with all things, it was merely a question of perception. Spain is one of those very sensible countries that insists that new drivers are taught properly by a trained and registered driving instructor, in dual control vehicles, at a registered driving school as opposed to a few unplanned, brief lessons from a well meaning, yet impatient father on near empty roads in the family Ford on a quiet Sunday morning in the UK.

The Spanish healthcare service was another area that was often unfairly singled out for criticism by British 'expats'. Most who had been recipients of its wonderful care would agree that the Spanish healthcare system was probably one of the most generous, well equipped and staffed in Europe. Many British residents in Spain did not understand that healthcare was only free for them to use under the reciprocal arrangements between the two countries, if they were over the UK statutory retirement age. Sadly, for the British 'expat' who had retired early, there were three choices. The first was to purchase private medical insurance and the second was to pay into the Spanish social security system, in order to take advantage of the benefits or to get a job with a contract where the employer paid social security contributions. There were after all, broadly similar requirements in Britain.

Sadly, these choices were not an attractive option to the 'expat' who had retired and moved to Spain early, for example, when in their mid-fifties. Many, when challenged, were fully aware of the issues involved, but preferred not to notice, and to rely on using the old 'E111' arrangements for as long as they possibly could. The 'E111' certificate was only ever intended to cover the holder during a short period of medical emergency when, for example, they were on holiday in another European country, and never as a substitute for comprehensive private or national insurance. I well remember the example of one of my neighbours, who would fly back to the UK every six months to renew his 'E111' certificate. He, his wife and mother-in-law were never blessed with the best of health, and it seemed that one of them would always be 'under the doctor'. The medical staff in our local surgery were very tolerant of this couple for nearly two years, until one fateful day when the doctor refused to treat our neighbour any longer using this emergency facility, and insisted that they became properly registered under the Spanish health and social security system or went to a private clinic. Our neighbour was furious and was convinced that it was 'discrimination'. In reality, nothing could have been further from the truth. He had simply been caught out.

The British view of Europe is often equally disturbing. "What has Europe ever done for us?" was the comment that I witnessed over dinner on one occasion. This piece of unintelligent rhetoric did not merit the effort of a reply. The fact that we now had the freedom and good fortune to own our own homes in a 'foreign' country, and all had the rights of residency, work and travel, went unnoticed. It is also very interesting to see that not only the Spanish national flag and regional flag fly from official buildings, but the European flag flies alongside them too. Public works such as roadways, buildings and major projects are given similar credit and flags and notice boards willingly recognise the European Union's contribution to the project. The Spanish appear to be genuinely very supportive of the EU and freely recognise its role in helping them to move from a fascist dictatorship to a modern, stable democracy within Europe.

Foreigners have the privilege of living in a beautiful and great country. The superb climate is one of the reasons that many left drab, grey, expensive and wet Britain. 'Expats' are usually welcomed with open arms by their Spanish hosts. Yes, British and other Northern Europeans have brought prosperity to Spain, but are also guests in the country. There are cultural differences and traditions that foreigners do not understand, but could learn. Systems often appear outdated, slow and bureaucratic, but do work. Learn Spanish? Surely they all speak English anyway? Arrogance can be breathtaking.

'Expats' have chosen to live and work in Spain. Sadly, they seem to have brought with them a significant number of small-minded people with potentially dangerous, jingoistic attitudes that may well draw anger from tolerant, easy going Spanish hosts, and from time to time there are signs of an, often well deserved, backlash.

One Town Hall ordered that all commercial establishments, including bars and restaurants, must also use Spanish on the display material used to announce their products and services. Of course, the new ruling hit many British bars whose owners could not be bothered to learn Spanish, and they were up in arms over the issue that they saw as 'discriminatory'. However, they failed to realise that many Spanish felt intimidated when entering a business in their own country where all the signs were in English. Again, just imagine the response from the locals in towns and cities if this happened in Britain and the likely comments in the *Daily Mail*!

Surely these 'Little Britain' attitudes that have been the stuff of wars and prejudice in the past no longer have their place within modern day Europe? The 'Rule Britannia' mentality is unnecessary and undermines a modern European community. I love my new country and share the ideals of the European dream that has served us so well since the Second World War. Sometimes, although I still love Britain, I am just so ashamed to have been born British and consider myself to be European. Whatever happened to good manners and tolerance that Britain used to be respected for, or was it just never there in the first place?

Letter 9
Who is Going to Squeeze my Oranges?

Most of us who live and work in Spain, work very hard. Although it is a wonderful life here, wages are not good and hours are long. I am sure that friends in the UK have the misconception that we work for just a few hours each day, interspersed with a siesta or two, many glasses of wine and lounge by a pool with a good book. Sadly, this is not true, not all of the time anyway. It is also true that because of where we live, we receive many visits from friends and others that we may not know so well. Most of our understanding visitors work with us and around our busy lives, so that we get time to enjoy their company as well as giving them their own space.

I well recall one horrendous Christmas in the Costa Blanca when we had just moved into our new home. Our new home was quite a modest affair, a small villa with two bedrooms and a garden that still looked like a building site. A few months earlier we had received a phone call from a good friend, Adam, who had moved to South Africa some years earlier and was now doing rather well working for one of the political parties there. Adam had no close family and had sort of 'adopted' us, as we had him. We had seen each other through some good and bad times and it was always good to hear from him, although he was dreadful at keeping in touch. "Can I come over for Christmas?" was the call early one morning. We were delighted and began making plans of where we should go and what we should do to share our new home and life in Spain with Adam. It was the sort of call that we often had received from him in the past. Usually, it meant a crisis – loss of job, split up with boyfriend etc. We had the feeling that this would be 'one of those visits' where the length of stay was undetermined, and may well mean another change of continent for Adam.

Two weeks before Christmas we received another bubbly call from Adam. "Really looking forward to seeing you again! Can't wait to see the villa! You must take me everywhere and I must see everything!" Adam was nothing if not enthusiastic about everything in life, whatever it threw at him – it was one of his more endearing traits.

"Can I bring a friend?" he suddenly threw into the conversation. This was a relief in some ways, because having Adam around was always a little like training a new puppy, which would be into everything with boundless energy. He could be very tiring, so maybe a friend would help to occupy him?

"Boy, or girl this time, Adam?" I asked. "Is this a friend or a special friend?"

Adam giggled. "No, it is a woman, don't worry, we're just friends!"

Yes, a friend was a good idea, but as we had only one small spare bedroom, we needed a change of plan.

We asked some good friends and neighbours for help. They lived across the road and had an apartment that they would let for holiday periods. If only we could rent their apartment for a couple of weeks. It was a beautiful apartment, on a peaceful location, well furnished and maintained as well as being clean and comfortable. My brother and his wife had stayed there a few months earlier, and they couldn't have been more pleased with it. The apartment would be ideal for Adam and his friend. They could both stay there as it had two bedrooms and they could come and go as they pleased, eat with us, but we would all have our own space – it seemed a perfect arrangement.

It was three days before Christmas and it occurred to me that we knew absolutely nothing about Adam's friend. Not even a name, job, background – nothing. I called Adam to find out – it would be nice to know before we met her. I put the phone down and repeated the conversation to David.

"Well, it seems that Adam's friend is an elderly, left-wing, female, black, South African Member of Parliament, whom he described as 'strident'. Adam met her through the political party that they work for and they are good friends…"

I had flash backs to some of our planning – the nights out 'clubbing' in Benidorm would have to go for a start. No, this called for urgent changes to the schedule. Meanwhile, we placed a black Angel on the Christmas tree to ensure it offered a spot of 'cultural diversity'.

Waiting at Alicante Airport for Adam was an anxious time. The plane from London landed on time and we were waiting for Adam and his friend to appear. The glass doors swung open, and a beaming Adam was hugging me. It was so good to see him after all those years when he left us on an unknown journey to Africa, clutching one small suitcase. He had left us his Paddington Bear to look after, I remembered. He looked good – a little older, hopefully wiser, and his previously scrawny frame had filled out a little. I could see that he was still as impish as ever.

"This is Margaret," he announced proudly, thrusting forward a well-groomed, elderly white woman. Margaret must have been in her late seventies – tall, well groomed with tightly permed white hair. I was about to learn that her description as 'strident' was an understatement. "She is so looking forward to meeting you. I have told her everything about you both!"

Hmm, thanks, Adam, I certainly hoped he hadn't.

"It is a pleasure," she said, taking my hand regally. "Is our car here?"

With that she flounced towards the airport exit with a porter trailing behind with her suitcases.

Adam giggled. "Isn't she just amazing?" he said.

I could already think of a far better description.

Amazing, she certainly was, but likeable? No! I suspect I would rather have dinner with Saddam Hussein than the blessed Margaret. She had a very strong Afrikaans accent, rolled her 'r's' and behaved very much like Margaret Thatcher did during her last days in office (apologies to MT fans, but I have to try to give a flavour, and this is as accurate as it gets!). She treated poor Adam like a toy poodle, who beamed proudly at her every move and outrageous statements. We managed to get her into our car with the luggage, and she rubbed her finger across the seats and looked at the dog hairs with disdain.

"You don't clean it very often, it seems."

I mumbled something about the dogs, but my voiced trailed away.

The journey home was uncomfortable to say the least: mostly silent, apart from Adam who was burbling on about everything and nothing as usual. I decided to stop at one of our favourite bars for a drink and a snack. Perhaps Margaret would relax after a glass of Rioja wine or maybe a very large gin or, failing that, a spot of rat poison maybe?

The conversation was difficult. Margaret had never been to Spain, thought the Costa Blanca 'frightfully common', didn't like small roads, paella, urbanisations, the Spanish language or indeed the 'Brits abroad'. She had no patience with Europe and would have much preferred a few more nights at the Hilton Hotel in London where they had spent the first night between changing planes, but that Adam had 'insisted' that she saw Spain and meet his friends.

"Such a backward country," she added for good measure, "but I guess they try," she sighed.

I thought it inappropriate to mention the problems that South Africa was having at that time and felt very uneasy that this woman, who claimed to be a socialist, was representing black Africans with significant social issues, poverty and violence. I later learned that she lived in a large country estate in one of 'the better parts of Cape Town' with two maids, a chef, a butler and a chauffeur. Life in South Africa was certainly good for some. She waved imperiously to the waiter and asked for 'the account'. Our waiter understood and presented a bill on a plastic tray. It came to less than ten euros. Margaret scrutinised it closely and then placed a Diners Club card on top. The waiter pointed out that they didn't take credit cards.

"So surprising," she said. "They don't take Diners and I never carry cash – can anyone else pay this?"

I placed the cash on the tray.

"Well, if that is the attitude over here, I shall not be paying for anything else," she said as she flounced off. Margaret was true to her word, and she didn't pay for anything else throughout the rest of her stay. We also discovered that Margaret had two grown up and married children whom she didn't get on with. The only time that I felt an ounce of compassion for her was when she admitted that, "They didn't want me to stay with them for Christmas." I could see why.

We drove to the apartment with a heavy heart. What were we doing to our supportive, kind neighbours and friends with this woman's visit? What had happened to our planned first Christmas in Spain? Margaret had spent the journey filing her nails, a habit that I personally find disgusting, and upon our arrival viewed the apartment with disdain. "It's very small, isn't it?" she announced, raising her eyebrows. "Oh, I suppose it will just have to do," she added, crossly. Adam said nothing.

Margaret was greeted warmly by our neighbour and owner of the property, Nicole, who was waiting for us, showed Margaret and Adam around the well-maintained apartment, explained how to use the air conditioning and satellite TV system, and Margaret threw herself onto the sofa, looking very bored and generally displeased with life.

"I must be off now," said Nicole, "Peter and the kids will be back and I must start cooking tea. Have a good holiday and telephone me if anything goes wrong, a new light bulb for example – just call."

Margaret got up from her sofa, paused for a moment, drew a deep breath and strode towards Nicole who was heading for the door as quickly as she could.

"Just wait a moment, young woman," she commanded, "I think I have misunderstood the situation. I thought you were staying here to look after us?"

"Oh no," laughed Nicole. "We have a villa in the next road. I live there with Peter and the kids. We are only a phone call away though, and Peter comes over twice a week to check the pool. You will be fine. You even have a microwave!"

"I am not so sure about that," said Margaret, coldly. "Just who is going to squeeze my oranges in the morning?"

Letter 10
A Visitor from Hell

It didn't get any easier. From that first eventful meeting when we collected Margaret and Adam from the airport to the moment that we finally waved off the taxi, it was a nightmare. We awoke in the morning dreading the day ahead of us, and our close neighbours and friends sensed our distress and expressed their concern.

"What a tiny house!" Margaret had exclaimed as soon as she had climbed the flight of steps to our spacious sun terrace, and stepped inside our beautiful villa. No, it was not huge, but it was the same size as the other twenty or so villas in our road and perfectly suited to our needs.

"Where do you all sleep? Look at this kitchen! Tell me, do you manage to cook in it, or do you go out for most of your meals?"

The comments hurt. We adored our blue and white tiled villa. It was all that I had ever wished for and, once the garden area had been tiled and planted, and a swimming pool and driveway built, it would be perfect. Margaret flung herself into one of the two huge terracotta sofas that dominated our living area and surveyed the scene.

"I am so tired. All this flying around is really getting to me. What a charming Christmas tree, but why, for heaven's sake, do you have a black Holy family? Everyone knows that they were white! I don't subscribe to all this multicultural correctness, you know. When I get home to Cape Town, I am going to send you some proper angels and a proper Holy Family. It will look so nice next to your lovely tree next year." Margaret smiled a benign smile of generosity, and her thin lips, for once, relaxed as she spoke.

These comments made me angry and, looking at David, I could see that he was angry too, but we said nothing. We had bought the black nativity models during our holiday in South Africa two years previously. Local village people made them from recycled materials, and we liked them. Apart from that, we were shaken by the comments made by a woman who made her more than adequate living by representing her black constituents in the national parliament. It was a disgraceful comment, and I could see that Adam was also disturbed by it. For once, he had said very little since we had arrived at the villa. No one made any response and we sat in silence, whilst David busied himself preparing drinks in the open-plan kitchen area.

Barney, our corgi, a friendly and usually well-mannered dog, who was well aware of how to behave in company wandered over to the sofa where Margaret was lounging. Adam was squeezed tightly in the far end of the sofa, his large frame sandwiched by a large cushion between himself and Margaret. Barney briefly sniffed at the visitor's leg that was just touching the floor, cocked his rear leg and with immense pleasure on his face, 'peed' all over Margaret's leg. Margaret screamed and stood up, hopping on the non-saturated leg whilst Barney sat at the other side of the room watching the resulting performance with pleasure. Bella was nowhere to be seen.

"That bloody dog," Margaret screamed. "How dare he! If he were mine, I'd have him shot for doing this."

"I am so sorry," I apologised profusely, grabbing a towel from the kitchen. "I don't know what came over him. He is usually so well behaved."

Adam exploded with laughter. "Come on Margaret. You said you wanted a shower when you got in. Barney just happened to read your thoughts. Surely you see the funny side of it."

"It's not funny, Adam," snarled Margaret, still mopping herself with the towel. "Now I shall stink of dog all afternoon. It really is too bad. Why do you people have to have these creatures in the house anyway? Mine live outdoors. They are guard dogs and they earn their keep!"

"Do use the bathroom, Margaret. I'll get you some more towels and you can dry yourself off. Maybe you would like a shower," I replied, now trying to suppress a hearty laugh. "As for you, Barney. Outside!"

Barney, who was not one to rush at the best of times, looked up at me innocently and, at his own pace, wandered out of the front door, down the flight of steps and onto the sun terrace. He looked extremely pleased with himself. He had made his feelings quite clear about that woman. A job well done, he seemed to be saying.

Over the next few days we tried our very best to be good hosts. David, as usual, cooked some excellent meals, which Margaret appeared to enjoy and ate with relish. Despite making it clear that she did not approve of a vegetarian diet and that she lived on huge steaks at home, we noticed that she cleared her plate each time, and was never backwards in coming forwards when second helpings were offered. We had decided to avoid having too many meals out, as Margaret had made it quite clear that she was not going to contribute to paying for anything, and Adam was always short of ready cash.

We were also concerned about our usually very talkative and excitable Adam. He was always very quiet in her company and it soon became clear that he was very much in awe of this dreadful woman. Maybe it had something to do with him wanting to be a politician himself. Maybe he just had to keep in with her, but why he chose to bring her on holiday, and plague us with someone he should have known we would dislike was still very much a mystery. At least he had now stopped looking at her admiringly and endlessly announcing, "Isn't she just magnificent?" I had already reached the position where a sharp retort was just 'sitting on my lips' waiting for the next bout of adulation from her young protégé.

One day we visited the magnificent city of Murcia, one of our favourite places; an architectural treasure that was only about one hour's drive from our home. Our South African guest dismissed this ancient city as 'irrelevant', and even its magnificent cathedral was described as, 'boring'. "I would much prefer a coffee in that bar opposite." However she did add thoughtfully, "Don't let me stop you from going inside the cathedral with your friends, Adam."

A visit to the sea was dismissed as 'not being as blue as Cape Town', an evening at a wonderful Flamenco show in a nearby village was described as 'amateurish' and an evening at our favourite restaurant was passed off as 'tolerable'. We let Adam pay the restaurant bill this time, much to his obvious surprise and concern. Fortunately I had driven him to the cash dispenser a few hours earlier and, amazingly, I had left my wallet at home! Planned evenings and drinks parties on the terrace with neighbours were cancelled as we felt that these may well destroy any friendships that we had established and, besides, what had they done to us to warrant the intrusion of Margaret into their lives and homes?

It was nearly Christmas Day, and we wanted to do our best for Adam, as well as making Margaret welcome. We had come to feel sorry for her, and began to realise what a truly lonely person she really was. Several evenings earlier, and after rather too many glasses of wine, she told us quite a number of revealing things about her own family. She lived on her own, with a number of servants in a very large house on the outskirts of the city. Although she had two sons, she saw very little of them and, besides, her daughters-in-law did not like her and she, by all accounts, did not like them either.

"They didn't want me to visit for Christmas. They never do. Of course, it doesn't matter to me. I would much rather travel and this year, dear Adam said he would accompany me."

Those comments said it all. We were in the company of a very insecure and sad old woman whose family had all but disowned her. We decided that evening to make a very special Christmas lunch for our visitors, complete with small gifts. We had already bought Adam a number of gifts as it had been several years since we had been able to spoil him. The following day we bought a selection of small, inexpensive gifts for Margaret – soaps, body talcum powder, sweets and the like. All were carefully wrapped up in brightly coloured paper, and placed beside the Christmas tree.

Just before the time planned for lunch on Christmas Day, Margaret and Adam arrived. They settled down to lunch on the sun terrace, which they seemed to enjoy judging from the empty plates at the end of the meal. Even though Margaret regularly protested that our Spanish wine was, "Nowhere near as good as Cape", she always drank every drop that we poured into her glass. We said nothing.

"It is so strange not to have turkey at Christmas," announced Margaret, pouring herself another glass of sparkling wine.

"Well, Margaret you seemed to enjoy David's nut roast," I replied.

"It was delicious," beamed Adam. "I have really missed David's wonderful meals over the last few years. He is such a good cook."

After lunch we exchanged, or should I say, gave our gifts. Adam was thrilled with his presents and there were shouts of delight as he opened the small items that we knew he would have missed in South Africa. Margaret seemed pleased with her gifts too, but said or gave nothing in return. Adam gave us a large box of chocolates, which we were pleased to receive, as they were our favourites. The biblical principle that it is 'far better to give than to receive' was certainly relevant, and had a very special meaning for us on that particular sun-filled Christmas Day.

The two weeks of torment were finally coming to an end, and I made the appropriate arrangements for Margaret and Adam to be collected from the apartment and driven to the airport. Originally, David and I had planned to do this ourselves but, as 'the Blessed Margaret', as we had begun to call her between ourselves, had been so difficult, neither of us could find a good reason to take any time off work to drive her to the airport. Besides, it was finally time to get my own back.

Margaret had spent much of the last two weeks talking about and, obviously longing for, the exquisite delights of the Hilton, and Savoy Hotels in London, which she loved so much. She also enjoyed time at the Ritz from time to time, and was looking forward to returning there for an evening on the planned one night stopover on their flight back to Cape Town. "I am always looked after so well in London, you know," she had announced the day before the flight home. "They always send a limousine to collect me from the airport. Never one of those grubby, black London taxis."

Hmm, so Margaret liked limousines, did she? I decided that I really must not disappoint her and would arrange for a 'special' one to take her to Alicante Airport the following day. I called our friend, Juan, at Tony's Cars to make a booking for this very special lady.

The following morning we went to the apartment to say our farewells to Margaret and Adam. We would miss Adam and wished him well, but we were, to say the least, relieved to see Margaret with suitcases at her side ready to depart. For once our guest was smiling and looked quite happy. I guessed that she had disliked her visit to the Costa Blanca, as much as we had.

"Are you driving us to the airport, Barrie?" she enquired.

"No, Margaret, we couldn't get time off work," I lied. "Never mind, I have arranged something very special for you."

We heard a toot from the car outside. Margaret gathered her handbag, leaving David and I to carry the suitcases to the waiting car outside.

"Is this it?" Margaret enquired, her jaw dropping.

"Yes, that's your limousine, Margaret. Best we could get, I'm afraid. You'll need to pay the driver about forty euros plus a tip when you get to the airport. Have a good flight!"

The unshaven Spanish driver, wearing little more than a grubby white and sweaty vest and shorts, turned around to greet his passengers with a toothless grin. The speechless elderly woman and her young friend fell into the back seat of the ageing, rusting yellow Ford Cortina, whilst the taxi driver unceremoniously dumped the suitcases in the boot behind, which was held closed with a piece of rope. Without further words being exchanged, the ageing yellow taxi sped its way out of the drive, and out of our lives.

Letter 11
Sun Pleasure

Moving to any new country is a great adventure and, if entered into in the right spirit, a great privilege. Part of the excitement, of course, is getting to know a new culture and traditions. Moving abroad just for the sunshine and a better currency exchange rate alone are not good enough reasons on their own to make such a major upheaval in life. As long as the potential 'expat' moves to a new country with an open and receptive mind, there is a fair chance that it will be a success. In my experience, the problems come when 'expats' of any nationality try to recreate a little piece of their homeland in their newly adopted country and take little account of local culture and traditions. In the Costa Blanca, the familiar cry of exasperation, "We didn't do that in Derby, Reading or wherever," became the war cry from many an 'expat's' sun terrace. Legal issues in Spain were a case in point. Although there are some similarities with the UK, laws and procedures, particularly when making wills or buying and selling properties in Spain are very different. Having lived in Spain for several years I can see that, in many ways, the legal process, such as when buying and selling a property, are much more straightforward and speedier than in England and Wales. However, there is no doubt that the newly arrived 'expat' needs someone who knows what they are doing by their side when proceeding with some of these 'once in a lifetime' transactions. We were fortunate because the company that had sold us our new villa also had good connections with local English speaking lawyers and banks. Of course, later we discovered that both the bank and our lawyer would receive substantial 'kick backs' and commissions from our introduction and, in the case of the bank, any transactions that we made for many years to come would produce a nice commission for the building company, with ourselves paying higher bank charges to compensate. We closed our bank account shortly after discovering this and managed to open a new account with another bank, and obtained a new mortgage with the new bank at a much more competitive rate. These were the kind of things that the 'expat' had to be on guard for, particularly with little or no knowledge of the language. The lawyer that the estate agency had found for us was a different matter. He was friendly and helpful, spoke English well and was very familiar with all the issues that a newly arrived 'expat' had to face. The main problem was that because he was always excessively busy, it was never easy to make an appointment to see him. His receptionists guarded him jealously, rather like a doctor's receptionist in the UK, and so it was never possible to speak to him on the telephone. Indeed, he often forgot what he was supposed to be doing for us, as was the case of our nonexistent, yet essential, NIE numbers when we arrived in Spain. His fees were high and in time we moved to another lawyer who was much better value and offered an overall better service. However, the point was that an English-speaking lawyer is essential, and preferably one that has been recommended by others in a similar situation. The property boom in the Costas brought with it a heady boom in associated services anxious to help the newly arrived 'expat', but at a price. Individuals known as 'Asesors' were plentiful, and many 'expats' found that these were often useful when dealing with motoring or taxation queries. However, although many of these were unqualified people, they are able to offer some of the services that a lawyer can offer for a much lower fee, although representation in court was not one of them. There were always people around who could help you to get what you wanted, and David managed to get his all-important 'NIE' number through the salesman at the garage where we were going to buy a car – again, at a price.

Newly established estate agents blossomed everywhere in the Costas, and it was a relatively simple matter for anyone to set up an estate agency, and it was a very profitable business for many. In the UK, for example, the going rate for selling a property was around one to two per cent of the sale price, whereas in the Costas the going rate was at least five per cent and sometimes more. The sale of new properties was hugely profitable, because of the additional charges and 'kick backs' for arranging mortgages, legal fees, water and electricity connections, after sales care and such like. It was, at one time, a licence to print money. As a reporter for an English language newspaper, one of my additional jobs was to write the occasional 'advertorial' for a new advertiser. Most of these were fascinating to do, and I met many interesting and very pleasant people. I particularly enjoyed the restaurant reviews, because they would often include a free meal as a bonus! Since that time, I have come to the conclusion that there are no better Indian restaurants than those in the Costa Blanca! However, I used to dread writing articles about newly opened estate agencies, and, towards the end of my time in the Costa Blanca, did my best to avoid them and tried to pass them on to colleagues. At first they were tolerable, but after the first ten or so articles I could not think of anything new to say about them! Most were uninspiring, a fat profit and little in the way of customer service was more often than not the sole reason for their creation and existence. Indeed, I often felt that the articles that I would have to write were misleading readers, as I would not consider using the majority of them myself. From the blur of many Costa Blanca estate agencies, one does stand out clearly in my mind. I remember visiting this new agency, 'Sun Pleasure' that had just opened in one of the rapidly expanding urbanisations in the area.

neither did he suffer fools, but he was a good and reliable public servant who did his best to help his customers. Throughout the year, the residents of this small 'expat' town relied upon their local Post Office not only to post letters and parcels, but also to collect their mail as many of the urbanisations did not have a local delivery service. To make matters worse, there were no private mailboxes available to rent in the Post Office.

Rented private mailboxes were like gold dust in the town and if you were fortunate enough to have been granted the opportunity to rent one, you were indeed a very lucky person, or some would say that you had bribed your way into obtaining one. The limited numbers of boxes were the prize of the fortunate few who had lived in the town long enough, and queued in the endless queues longer than their fellow 'expats' would ever appreciate. Theirs was indeed a sweet victory when the moment came at the beginning of January, to be allocated this final prize of acceptance. Those members of the British community in the town would often sublet their private mailbox to other less fortunate souls in the community – for a modest fee, of course. Indeed, the wily ones in the community did rather well and often made a handsome profit, once the Correos annual fee had been deducted, in subletting to a number of their neighbours. Correos of course frowned upon such profiteering, but one always had the distinct feeling that this was because they had not thought of the idea first!

We all know that Christmas always places a heavy strain upon any postal service – be it in Spain or the UK. In one particular year, the problems in the town appeared to be far worse than usual. As a newspaper reporter, I received a number of angry telephone calls and emails complaining that there were reports of huge numbers of people queuing to collect their mail, and to post their Christmas cards and gifts to the UK. One angry resident told me that they started queuing at around ten minutes past eight in the morning, and by twenty minutes past eight there were forty-six people in the queue – and it was raining! Other angry residents reported queues that circled the inside of the Post Office three times. Another resident told me that he had waited for one and a half hours, and by the time he got to the counter, it was two o'clock and the shutters were brought firmly down leaving crowds of angry customers in the Post Office – still without having posted or collected their mail. Another caller told me that she had been in the Post Office "every day for five days and had still not been served".

Our local Post Office was a branch of the main Post Office in a nearby larger town, where they appeared to always have plenty of staff available. I called in there to see what was happening. There were four people working in the Post Office and only two customers when I called. Surely it would seem sensible to move staff from the large Post Office to our Post Office during the busy Christmas period?

When I called in to our Post Office there were still queues of people – both inside and outside the building – reaching the parade of shops at the front of the building – at least it wasn't raining! I spoke to the postmaster, José Miguel, and he said that as far as he was concerned things were now getting better. He had just been given another member of staff for the Christmas period, yet there was only one set of scales to weigh the post. He hoped that an additional weighing machine would arrive the following week. Until that time, the additional pair of hands would deal with handing out mail to be collected.

For 'expats' living in, or considering moving to an area where the Correos cannot take the strain, I offered the following very simple advice to our readers:

- Always allow a full day to post and collect your mail. If you normally take tranquillisers, take another, just in case.

- Take a flask of coffee and a pack of sandwiches with you – a nip of brandy may also be helpful. However, don't drink too much liquid as there are no toilet facilities close by and you will lose your place in the queue if you have 'to make a dash for it'. Remember, if you are over 50 your bladder is not as strong as it was...
- Take a good book or magazine to read. Alternatively, it can be quite entertaining watching the antics of your fellow members in the queue. Who knows – you may even make new friends whilst you are waiting.
- Take an iPod or personal stereo with some relaxing music to ease away the stress.
- Take your mail to another local Post Office.

So whatever happened to our postmaster, José Miguel? The last that I heard was that he had had enough, and had packed his bags and fled to a Greek island to study philosophy!

Barney

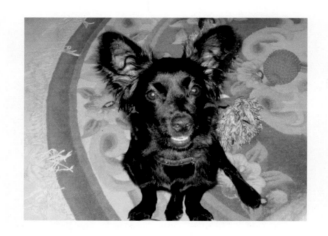

Bella

The Villa

Benidorm

Altea

Our Special Day

Torrevieja Ayuntamiento

Two Men Two Dogs and a Boat

Las Palmas Port

Arinaga

Part 2
The Canary Islands Years

Letter 13
Two men, two dogs and a boat

We had many happy memories of our time in the Costa Blanca, mainly due to the wonderful people that we met. Yes, crime was certainly an issue as were the colder than expected winter months, but we were happy and life seemed settled. Or was it?

It was during a 'boozy' night out with our boss when the subject of how the newspaper should expand that the subject came up.

"Why don't you open a newspaper in the Canary Islands?" I suggested. "We love the islands, and particularly Gran Canaria. We could go over and run it for you if you like?"

It was four weeks later, with our villa placed for sale with local agents, and with replacements found for our jobs, that we found ourselves on a three-day sea voyage to the Canary Islands. Our business plan had been accepted and I had been appointed as Editor and David as Sales Manager of a new English language newspaper in the Canary Islands. That will teach me not to make rash suggestions in future, and particularly after a few drinks!

David and I had made so many good friends with the newspaper family. Readers, advertisers and colleagues alike had all been so supportive to us that it was hard to say our 'goodbyes' during that last week of work in April. All the good friends and neighbours that had become our Costa Blanca 'family' and with whom we had shared the joys and sorrows of settling into a new country had also become very important to us. We would miss them dreadfully. We were asked by many readers for news about what happened to us during the journey, our arrival at our new home and the launch of the new newspaper, and so I continued to write for the Costa Blanca newspaper as well. So this is how the journey to the Canary Islands began...

They all said we shouldn't go by boat. "The food is dreadful," we were told, "take plenty of food with you." "It is dirty and smelly – you don't want to spend three days on that," said another in disgust. "It can get very violent," was one very worrying comment, leaving us with the impression that, at best we would be robbed, if not murdered. It was a big problem, but somehow we had to get to the Canary Islands and we were not happy with Barney and Bella, our two dogs, going by air. As only dog lovers will understand, they were our first priority and so the decision had to be made carefully.

When we first arrived in the Costa Blanca, we were given three very important pieces of advice by our neighbours who subsequently became our close friends. "Never believe what you are told, always check it out for yourselves." The second piece of advice was equally important. "Never pay more than one euro for a bottle of wine..." The first piece of advice we have followed to the letter, whilst the second has not always been fully adhered too – but it too makes a very good point. The third piece of advice was to pick up one of the local newspapers every week, and was of course an excellent way to read about life in the Costa Blanca and Spain.

In my work as a reporter, I had heard a number of stories from readers about problems travelling by air with animals. I hasten to add that I am sure that these are the exceptions and that most flights with animals go according to plan and cause minimal stress for the animals concerned. However, in our case, it would mean flying from Alicante, and a delay in Madrid before an onward flight to Las Palmas. At best it would take four hours, but we had experienced delays lasting up to sixteen hours in Madrid airport on one occasion. A decision had to be made and so the dogs and ourselves would be sailing to our new home in the sun.

Neither of us are good sailors. I have only to fill the bath with too much water and I begin to get that all too familiar 'queasy' feeling! We both remember a most unpleasant sea crossing to the Scilly Isles, just off the coast of Cornwall, a few years ago – we were so ill and will never forget the moment when the life jackets were handed out. Bella, our beautiful Spanish puppy who with her tiny jet black face, chiselled features and gleaming white teeth and who looks very much like a fruit bat, was always very car-sick, even during short journeys, and so flying or sailing would not make a great deal of difference to her, we reasoned. No, Barney, our lazy and loveable, but self-willed corgi was the only one of the four of us who would be able muster up the dignity that corgis, with their royal background, are expected to have when duty calls – that is assuming he is in the mood to oblige.

The fateful day arrived. The removals company, Pickfords, had done their stuff and moved everything out of our home to be transported to Gran Canaria. What a good job they had made of it too – they are not called 'The Careful Movers' for nothing. With good humour, efficiency and politeness the team had managed to wrap and place all our household goods, together with a small car, for the journey to the Canaries the previous evening. "It will take about three weeks to be delivered," their boss had said. They were right; it was exactly three weeks to the day when the furniture and clothes arrived – with much form filling, waiting in the Town Hall and the inevitable 'bonking' of endless pieces of paper with rubber stamps – but that is another story.

Although we had only lived and worked in the Costa Blanca for a little over two years, we had come to love the place. It was the friendliness and helpfulness of our neighbours that had made us feel at home so quickly and the social life had been incredible. During the evenings we had little time to watch television and indulged in the usual 'expat' hobby of 'terrace hopping'. Basically, this meant that we would all sit on our sun terraces in the evening enjoying a drink or two, and then as soon as others were spotted on their terraces we would either be invited to join a party gathering on their terrace, or they would join us on ours. This was indeed the main social activity in our urbanisation and was greatly enjoyed by all. Considerable laughter could be heard coming from one or more of our neighbours' terraces during most late summer evenings and early mornings. Good conversation, jokes and gossip were the order of the evening, washed down with a plentiful supply of good quality wine and beer that no doubt took its toll upon our health and our figures.

The day before we left for the port of Cadiz our next-door neighbour threw a farewell party for us. It was a very kind thought, typical of this warm and friendly community, and a gesture that we gratefully appreciated. We were certainly going to miss our new-found friends and neighbours, and part of us wanted to stay in the Costa Blanca.

Our beautiful villa was now as empty as the day that we had found it – it was now once again bare and unwelcoming as all our possessions had once again been packed and collected for onward transit to the Canary Islands. All we had left was Barney and Bella's baskets, a small suitcase and a laptop computer. I wandered around the patio and terrace for the last time, looking at all the plants that we had so carefully chosen and planted, the watering system installed by our neighbour and the salt-water swimming pool that was only recently completed. Our new life in the Canary Islands was once again going to be a bit of a gamble, but David and I were both of the view that it is better to try something and maybe fail, than not to try at all. Besides, we had been visiting Gran Canaria on holiday for the previous ten years or so and had always adored the island. The climate was superb and we were about to create and launch our own newspaper. It was all very exciting.

Our neighbours had kindly offered to accommodate us for our final night before we set off on the long car journey to the port of Cadiz, the main sea route to the Canary Islands. Neither of us was looking forward to the long car journey. First of all, Bella usually became anxious in the car and was often sick, and Barney tended to get very impatient after a few kilometres and wanted to go for a walk, and so we were expecting a nightmare journey.

Morning finally came and we made our tearful farewells. Barney and Bella were safely installed in the car and the journey began. We had allowed three days for the journey – with two hotel stops on the way. Although we really didn't need quite so much time to get to Cadiz, it did help us to wind down, begin to relax and, more importantly, allow plenty of walks for the dogs that were, surprisingly quiet and well behaved. We didn't need to give Bella one of her pills – all we did was to cut out her breakfast! We stayed in Ibis hotels – which are dog friendly – and we found something remarkably comforting and reassuring about them. When I worked in the UK, I would often stay in one and it didn't matter whether I was in Cardiff, London, or Birmingham – they were all more or less the same.

It was a beautiful journey and one that I would certainly recommend to readers. Three days after we had left the Costa Blanca we entered Cadiz. We heaved a sigh of relief as we eventually found the busy passenger terminal. Panic began to set in. Did we really have all the correct papers for the dogs and the car? The ship looked watertight enough. Indeed, it appeared to be a very nice ship. However, I am ashamed to admit to knowing very little that is nautical, but I was quite impressed as we drove into the 'holding area' in the Cadiz Port. After confirmation that we were expected and that on-board kennels had been reserved for Barney and Bella, we were ushered into a waiting queue. We were relieved, as several non-Spanish registered cars had been sent to another area where the port police were giving them a close examination. We were very early and set about 'killing' two hours in Cadiz – a very pleasant town and I would like to have stayed there longer to explore.

We saw several cars being denied access to the ship and we noticed that police were examining these very closely. Although we were, technically, travelling from one part of Spain to another, we were also aware that the Canary Islands were a bit of an anomaly, because of differences in taxation and customs' requirements. At last we were waved on board – with a strange mixture of sensations that ranged between apprehension and excitement – the journey to our new lives had begun.

Barney and Bella thought it was great fun and tried to chase any other dog in sight. We managed to find the kennels – basic but clean – and put the dogs into two separate kennels with a sort of German Shepherd dog called Joe sandwiched between them. Bella took to Joe and, by the time we left, seemed to be on good barking terms with her new neighbour. Barney surveyed the scene with his usual air of indifference and gave me a look as if to say, "You are not leaving me in this dump, are you?" It was clear that he was fully expecting to be with us in our cabin and not to be left in a kennel. He ate his tea, as if tomorrow would never come, and then sulked all evening. We knew only too well what he is like when in one of those moods. We left the dogs to find our cabin, and some food.

Our cabin had a sea view – I was disappointed that the window would not open, but David pointed out to me the reasons why it would not be such a good idea. Apart from the odd trip on the Isle of Wight ferry and a horrendous journey to the Scilly Isles a few years earlier, I had very little to do with cabins except in the odd caravan maybe. I was amazed at how compact and well fitted out it was and, above all, very clean with crisp, white sheets on the bunk beds. It is always a little worrying to see vomit bags and life jackets, but we were wearing our trusty 'non-sickness' wristbands that our neighbour had told us about. Twenty euros a pair was a little 'over the top', I know, but hopefully they would do the trick. Anyway, I had also packed several packets of 'Quells' seasickness tablets.

The ship was amazing. There were several bars, lounges, a swimming pool, cinema, two restaurants and even a disco, as well as the on-board kennels. We had not yet left port, but already I was feeling 'just a little queasy'. I tried not to think about it and headed for the nearest bar. I am a great believer in the medicinal properties of brandy and felt that a glass of two would help to 'settle the stomach' whilst keeping eyes firmly on the horizon. One of our 'sea-dog' neighbours had reassured me that 'ships nowadays are fine – they don't roll like they used to'. I tried to believe him. Eventually, horns sounded and we were off. Already some of the braver passengers were dashing in and out of the swimming pool. Leaving the mainland, or "peninsular", as I have since learned that the Canarians prefer to call it, was a strange feeling. Although we had only been in the Costa Blanca for two years, it did feel like leaving home once again.

David and I went to see Barney and Bella. Bella was her usual boisterous, happy self and Barney was still sulking and wouldn't look at us. We took them for a short walk on the deck that, I assume, is called the 'poop deck' for obvious reasons. Dogs were only allowed in the kennel area and the 'poop' deck and most definitely not the cabins. I reasoned that a spot of 'sea air' would do us all good. We were feeling hungry – it was time for dinner.

Dinner anywhere in Spain can be a bit of a problem for vegetarians such as ourselves, particularly as most Spanish chefs are convinced that tuna is a plant. We had already been warned about the food on board ship and that we ought to take a supply of food with us. We mentioned the likely problem to one of the stewards in the self-serve restaurant area; he beamed and said "No problem," in his best English. We joined the end of the queue and suddenly were both called to the front where a beaming chef produced two plates of pasta and two enormous plates of mixed vegetables. We were most grateful for the effort and thanked him although it tasted a lot better when doused with tomato sauce! It was very acceptable but, sadly, exactly the same dish was produced for the following two days' meals – lunch and dinner. Once the voyage was over, it would be quite a while before we ate pasta and frozen mixed vegetables again.

As the evening wore on I felt more and more 'queasy'. Eventually I reasoned that more brandy would not be a wise move, and that I should aim for the cabin and the bunk. The cabin seemed to be moving up and down rather vigorously – or was it my stomach? No, David was feeling just the same and was, worryingly I thought, also clutching a sick bag. We aimed for the bunks, sick bag in hand – just in case – and fell asleep.

The next morning the sun was beaming into our cabin when we awoke. We had a good night's sleep and both felt pretty good. The cabin and bunk beds had been really comfortable and we were ready to face another day on our cruise to the Canaries. It was really more of the same and consisted of eating pasta and vegetables, walking Barney and Bella on the 'poop' deck, downing a few brandies, sunning ourselves on the main deck and catching up with reading and sleeping. For the first time in my life, I was totally surrounded by water (other than in a plane, of course) with no land in sight. It was a strange feeling, but served to prepare us for the radical change in our lives that lay ahead. Thankfully, Barney was now speaking to us again and seemed to be enjoying life as a sea dog. Bella – well, Bella just didn't care, as usual. However, we all thought it strange that Joe, the German Shepherd dog, was never in his kennel and was only rarely seen on the 'poop' deck. I can guess where he spent his nights!

The following morning we got up early as we were due to dock at around eight o'clock. We were anxious to stand on the deck and look for sight of land once again. Eventually, we saw the welcome twinkling of thousands of tiny lights, which we reasoned was Las Palmas. By the time the ship docked, we were getting really excited. Dogs and luggage were loaded back into the car and we waited for the final clearance to drive off the ship. Mostly it had been a very good, and memorable, experience. We had arrived in Gran Canaria and another adventure was about to begin.

Letter 14
Islands and Dreams

I have always loved islands. From early childhood, my favourite stories always seemed to have islands and castles somewhere in them. Maybe it was a beautiful maiden trapped in a castle awaiting the arrival of her lusty prince, or the adventures of *The Famous Five* trapped in a lighthouse.

One summer holiday, when I was about six or seven years old, I remember standing on Poole Quay, in Dorset, with my parents and elderly Aunt Gertie. She was a fascinating old lady with white hair tied in a severe bob. As a spinster, she had a crusty demeanour towards children, yet beneath her austere exterior had a heart of gold that I quickly warmed to. She pointed out to me, and I just caught a glimpse of, a magical paradise glistening in the centre of Poole Harbour. It was, Aunt Gertie explained, a forbidden island – one where we could not go and where an old lady lived with her manservant in a magical castle. They lived all alone on this island, apart from the peacocks, red squirrels and giant ants that lived in an enchanted forest, and it was a place where no one was welcome. No doubt the story had been suitably enhanced for the benefit of my vivid imagination, but this was the real stuff of fairy tales. Fairy tale maybe, but as I found out in later years, this was very much a true story. It was a story that had all the ingredients of a good television soap opera. It was a story of adventure, love, greed and betrayal – too long a story to tell in this letter.

Years later, I stood on the quayside of Brownsea Island right next to the castle, which was then leased to the John Lewis partnership as a holiday home for their staff, recalling all that Aunt Gertie had told me all those years ago, and I guess that this was where my island story had really begun. The rich old lady had died and the island had been left in the care of the National Trust. I was free to explore it at last.

At least once a year, either on my own or later with my partner, David, I regularly visited the island and saw the red squirrels, peacocks and giant ants for myself. Later, as a teacher and head teacher, I always found a way of taking at least one class of primary age children on a school visit to the island. I watched their excited faces and listened to their noisy chatter, as they wandered around a place just one and a half miles long and three quarters of a mile wide, with no roads or motor vehicles. They too marvelled at the peacocks and giant ants, just as I had done, although we never did spot a red squirrel during those wonderful summer days. The children were far too noisy and excited for any self-respecting squirrel to appear. I guess that most of my ex-pupils will still remember their first visit to Brownsea Island too.

I also loved the Isle of Wight and David and I, and earlier generations of corgis, had spent many happy holidays there. After one particularly happy holiday on the island, I applied for a post as head teacher of a large primary school in a seaside town. It was only when the reality of having got to the final interview, narrowed down to being one of two remaining candidates that reality set in. The horror that I just might get the job began to hit home. After a sleepless night, I realised that it was a truly dreadful school and that I really didn't want to be there, even if it was on an island. I fled to the port and caught the six o'clock ferry and arrived back at Lymington Pier well before the final interviews were due to begin. I hastily telephoned the school to say that I had decided to withdrawn my application. This unpleasant experience cured me of my obsession with islands for a year or two.

My island obsession surfaced once again after a day trip, and then later a week's holiday, to the Isles of Scilly, off the south west coast of Cornwall. A charming place indeed, which previous UK Prime Minister Harold Wilson had made his holiday home. I still remember seeing his 'long johns' hanging on the washing line outside his none too impressive bungalow on the island of St Marys. The island had a truly continental feel and, apart from the horrific sea journey from Penzance, was indeed a paradise island, despite the weather. The sea journey on the rusty old 'Scilionia' was horrendous – the sea sickness was so bad that I imagined death to be rather more pleasant. David and I cashed in our return ferry tickets, and one week later flew back to Penzance in a helicopter, with our two corgis, Sammy and Ollie, sitting in a large crate strapped to the seat in front of us.

In later years, we enjoyed holidays in most of the Western and Northern Isles off Scotland. The Isles of Mull, Skye, North and South Uist, Benbecula, as well as the Outer Hebrides islands of Harris and Lewis were all explored from 'top to toe'. The Isles of Orkney were delightful too, but far too cold and damp to exist for any length of time, and so a wider search was begun. The isles of Capri, Mallorca, Ibiza, Formentera, Tenerife, Robben Island and many others were explored over the years.

It was after a week's holiday in Gran Canaria that I realised that I had finally discovered an island that would eventually be our home. I didn't know when or how it would happen, but I did know that one day in the future, David and I would be living on our very own paradise island. In this letter, I hope to put Gran Canaria in context and to share with readers some of my excitement about this amazing 'continent in miniature'. It is a fitting title because of the island's uniqueness of having several climatic zones within the one relatively small island. There can be snow on the mountains, whilst you are swimming in the sea or sweltering in the heat of the desert.

In Gran Canaria, there are craters, volcanoes, waterfalls, mountains, pinewoods, palm groves and beautiful sandy beaches making it a naturally stunning and interesting place to visit or to live. With its seemingly endless sandy beaches, dramatic mountains, deep ravines, sweeping sand dunes and lush green vegetation, many have come to regard Gran Canaria as the jewel of the seven Canary Islands. Whilst the north of the island frequently experiences dense, low cloud, often blocking out the sun for hours at a time; the southern coast of the island is perpetually cloud-free and guaranteed rain-free during eight months of the year, making it a popular destination for sun-seeking tourists. Average temperatures on the island are 24°C in summer and 19°C in winter. Unlike some of its neighbours, Gran Canaria has extremely varied landscapes with European, African and even American vegetation.

There is hardly anywhere else in the world where you can find such differing landscapes and climatic zones in such close proximity to each other. What is the reason for this uniqueness of the island's climate? One of the reasons is the unusual shape of the island, which leads to a great variety of microclimates. While the climate is dry and sunny almost all year round in the coastal regions, particularly in the south, as you move up to higher altitudes, the influence of the sea is reduced and the clouds are retained by the mountains. This produces great variations in temperature from the temperate zones of the lower regions or valleys and subtropical forests, to the highest zones where the temperature can fall to zero. It's not too unusual for people to go sunbathing and swimming on the beach and then to find themselves playing around in the snow on the mountain tops just one hour's drive later. The sea is equally as warm with temperatures fluctuating between 18°C in the winter months and 22°C during the rest of the year. This, together with the estimated annual rate of nearly three thousand hours of sunlight in Gran Canaria, allow you to make the most of the day, whether you are on the beach, playing a sport, on a day trip or enjoying an outdoor activity.

People often mistakenly think that if the winter is so warm on the islands then the summer heat must be overwhelming, but this couldn't be further from the truth. Summer in the Canary Islands is softened by the trade winds that refresh the islands and give it mild summers. Indeed, the village of Pozo Izquierdo on the island's east coast is often said to be the 'windiest place on earth' and there is rarely a shortage of a refreshing breeze, and is very popular with windsurfers.

Research from the international scientific community claims that the island's capital, Las Palmas, is one of the cities with the best climate in the world. The journey from the airport to the south of the island and to the modern holiday hotels and complexes can be deceptive. It is hard to believe that none of the hotels, shops, bars, restaurants and, indeed, the resorts themselves, existed just fifty years ago. It was only since the 1950s that the Canary Islands became popular as a tourist destination, and although Gran Canaria had been a popular place for cruise ships to stop and for wealthy holidaymakers to visit for many years, this relatively small tourist industry was mainly focused upon Las Palmas in the north of the island. This lasted until the delights of Las Palmas and Las Canteras beach began to lose their appeal in favour of the all year sunshine and warmer climate of the south of the island. With the death of General Franco in 1975, Gran Canaria's future as an all year tourist destination became assured.

Full integration of Spain within the European Union in 1993 brought with it great improvements in the island's infrastructure, including the many excellent roads and motorways, many driven through rock, particularly in the south of the island. It is hard to believe that just fifty years ago, beyond the large and impressive gates that were sited near to the present day Texaco petrol station at Juan Grande, it would have been a very different picture for the visiting tourist – if, indeed, any braved the poor roads and made it this far south. These gates marked the ownership and beginning of the south of the island. In those days there were no hotels, shops and bars to be seen. Indeed, there was little other than scorched scrubland, occasional farm buildings and small communities of fishermen working and living near the coast. To understand a little more about how this came about, let us briefly put the clock back five hundred years or so…

The King of Spain had decided to reward the Castillo family generously for their loyalty and support during the Spanish conquest of the Canary Islands. Indeed, the Castillo family was given most of the southern part of Gran Canaria from Juan Grande to Arguineguin. Later, it was to be the Castillo family who were responsible for developing much of the south of the island for tourism. This project started in the early 1970s and El Conde (the Count), and his family continue the family's interest in the development of the south of the island to the present day. Gran Canaria is much more than just sea, sand and sunshine; this beautiful island is also blessed with some magnificent scenery, which is very diverse in nature. The arid but spectacular canyons of the south and the greener north combine to create a paradise and fully justify the islands description of 'a continent in miniature'. One interesting feature of the island is the 'caminos reales' or royal roads. These paved tracks or paths, and now roads, were so called because the king built them after the Spanish conquest to connect remote mountain villages with the coast. Walkers, cyclists and motorists now regularly use these roads alike in an attempt to get away from the busy beaches and to explore 'real' Gran Canaria. The south of Gran Canaria is a barren, arid landscape combed with many dramatic ravines and is easily accessible from the main tourist resorts.

Letter 15
Iguanas and Denials

In the early hours of the morning we made our way from the port of Las Palmas to the apartment that we had purchased a few months earlier. It was good to get off the ferry and to be properly reunited with Barney and Bella, as well as with our car that had travelled securely on the car deck. The voyage from Cadiz to Las Palmas had been a surprisingly good experience, and we both felt relaxed yet still apprehensive about what we had done and what we still had to face.

We had been visiting Gran Canaria once or twice a year on holiday for the last ten years or so, and it made sense that we should purchase a small apartment for holiday and investment purposes. We had only ever intended it to be a holiday home and certainly not as a permanent home to live in with our two dogs. We had deliberately chosen a new apartment without an outside terrace, for ease of maintenance during the long periods when we would be away. Also, we decided that, for security purposes, a ground floor apartment was not a good idea and therefore chose one on the fourth floor. These decisions we would come to regret.

The new block of apartments was built on the outskirts of the busy working town of Vecindario. The sprawling town itself could not in any way be described as attractive as it was clear from the chaotic road network that it had grown rapidly and without much in the way of planning. Nor was it any area where tourists from the busy south would venture. No, this was a town where ordinary working Spanish and Canarians lived and was a far cry from our British enclave in the Costa Blanca. We wanted the opportunity to practise and develop our Spanish, which was something that was not really necessary in our previous urbanisation. Vecindario also had the considerable advantage that properties were much cheaper than in the south of the island, as was food and other essential items.

The busy main street through Vecindario, called the Avenida de Canarias, is probably one of the worst streets that I have ever had to drive through by car. Despite dozens of traffic police and parking wardens on duty, it can easily take an hour or longer to drive through. However, on the plus side, it is one of the best streets for shopping on the island. Although it is not particularly visually attractive and often chaotic, if you take the time to look, you can find everything that you need and at very good prices too. I like to wander through the busy streets, sitting at one of the many café bars, people watching. The island itself is home to people of many different faiths, backgrounds and cultures, and it is wonderful and humbling to watch dusky Canarians, white Europeans, black Africans, Chinese, Moslem, Christian and Jew living and working together as a community in this amazing town. Indeed, the island itself benefits tremendously from the richness and variety of this cacophony of cultures, and this is demonstrated to wonderful excess during the many fiestas and carnivals.

Ours was an attractive, bright apartment, on the fourth floor, with particularly outstanding views of the mountains to the left and the sea to the right. In the middle of the view from our window was a branch of the large supermarket chain, Mercadona, of which we are both great fans. Indeed, we had been pleased to see, whilst shopping in the local store, that the prices of grocery items were virtually the same as in the Costa Blanca, something that we were concerned about when moving to an island community.

In view of the trauma that we had suffered in the Costa Blanca relating to both electricity and water supplies, we entered the apartment with some trepidation. We turned on the light switch and to our relief, it worked! I then turned on the tap and a steady stream of water flowed. Maybe, it was not going to be too bad after all. Barney and Bella scampered around the apartment enjoying all the new smells and different surroundings. They were obviously pleased to leave their on-board kennels and car at last, and be able to run around. Sadly, being on the fourth floor, there was no outside space, and sadly not even a terrace for us to use. Anyway, it would be an easy matter to whisk Barney and Bella outside in the lift, or was it?

Sadly, we soon discovered that the lift had not yet been completed. Alarm bells should have rung when we arrived that first morning, because nothing had happened when we pressed the call button. We had trudged up four flights of stairs with the dogs – an easy task for Bella with her long legs, but when one has short stubby legs, as was the case with Barney, it was no easy feat. The truth finally dawned that Barney and Bella, as well as we, would have to negotiate four flights of stairs whenever it was time for the 'call of nature'. No matter, we reasoned, the lift would soon be working. Little did we know then that it was to be a further two years before the lift started working and that it would be erratic at best. The lift never worked all the time that we lived in and owned the apartment.

A few weeks later, I woke one morning feeling quite buoyant and very excited. Not only had we arrived safely on the island, but also it was the day when I had to go to our local Town Hall to get a precious piece of paper that would release our clothes and furniture from the docks. I had been in the same clothes for nearly three weeks – I should stress that they had been washed from time to time, but it would be nice to wear something different once again. The weather was getting hotter and I desperately wanted my selection of shorts.

Clothes and furniture were due to arrive any day now – courtesy of Pickfords Removals back in the Costa Blanca. They had arranged for local agents to deal with the Canarian side of the move. It had been a difficult three weeks – although our goods had arrived at the port two weeks earlier, they were still sitting there because we had failed to provide the appropriate (and 'bonked') piece of paper. We had spent three days trying to get the various members of staff to issue us with something that sounded very much like an 'iguana'. The 'iguana' was something to do with the customs office and it was very, very important. We were passed around the several departments of the Town Hall, met many charming people, forms were filled in and filed, papers were shuffled and there was much shaking of heads. No, I was told firmly by a very cross looking young woman, whom we later called Miss Denial because of several subsequent challenging encounters, I could not be given the 'iguana' until my previous Town Hall in the Costa Blanca had confirmed who I was. Was not my 'residencia' ID card sufficient to prove this? I asked. No, apparently not. "How do I know who you are?" was her curt response. There really was no answer to this. It was beyond belief and my patience, already stretched to the limit, was rapidly evaporating. Fellow members of the various endless queues that I had joined gave me knowing looks and sympathetic smiles, although I found the shaking of some of the older heads somewhat disturbing. I left the building – for the third day, angry and fed up and, once again, empty-handed. This was something that I would gradually come to terms with in the Canary Islands.

The initial excitement that we felt when arriving in Gran Canaria was beginning to evaporate. Neither of us liked living in chaos with only the bare minimum of clothes and personal effects around us. We wondered if everything had arrived safely on the island, and was it all being stored safely in Las Palmas? Then there was the car. We had bought a second hand Daewoo

Matiz, a very small car that was ideal for negotiating the busy streets in the Costa Blanca. Although reluctant to part with it, we knew that we couldn't drive two cars to the Canary Islands and had placed it for sale before we left peninsular Spain. As it turned out, despite many calls, it did not sell and we had decided to leave it with neighbours to sell for us. It was only when one of the removal men was chatting to us over a mug of coffee that he revealed that there would be some space left in the removals container. I laughing suggested that they put the Daewoo Matiz in the container as well, and he agreed! We wondered if this was still sitting at the dockside in Las Palmas in the baking sun.

There was also the question of the newspaper. We were due to launch the first issue in a few weeks' time. All we had was a laptop computer and often no electricity, and certainly not a working telephone line when we arrived. We had been promised stationery and items from the company in the Costa Blanca, but so far nothing had arrived. Indeed, our company mobile telephones had stopped working and we suddenly had a terrible sinking feeling that our company had abandoned us, and it had all been a clever ploy to get rid of us! As it turned out, the company had decided to change mobile telephone companies and, as was often the case, had forgotten to tell anyone else of the change.

The day after we arrived, there had been a buzz on the intercom phone. It was Telefonica, the telephone company, to install our new line! Having had considerable problems with this monstrous and ineffective company in the Costa Blanca, as did many of our readers, these were the last people that we were expecting to arrive. True to their word on this occasion, a new telephone line and ADSL broadband Internet connection were installed within the hour without fuss. Surprisingly, the engineer even brushed up the dust and took away the packaging for the new telephone afterwards! This was high quality service from a company that I did not expect to experience nor, I doubt, will I ever experience again.

It was a telephone call to Naomi, the very wonderful Pickfords Removals local agent that saved the day. Somehow she managed to find someone sensible in the Canarian Town Hall who would listen to reason and asked me to call in again to see a lady called Carmen. When I got to the Town Hall, I asked for Carmen and was immediately sent to the front of the queue. Carmen was one of those very organised and understanding people who would always find a way around a problem – she also seemed to be in charge of something important. Of course, no one in the Town Hall was admitting to speaking English (and why should they?) and so it was up to me, in faltering Spanish, to try to explain what I wanted. Carmen listened very patiently, suddenly looked very cross and then went storming over to 'Miss Denial' who had sent me away the previous day. Sharp words were exchanged and Carmen returned, smiling in triumph. "No problem," she said in her best English. Suddenly she picked up the precious rubber stamp, lifted it to a great height and then very firmly 'bonked' the precious piece of paper with a flourish. This must be a very important piece of paper indeed. I left the building victorious – only 'Miss Denial' was glaring at me angrily from the other side of the counter. I smiled and waved to her – she glared back. On this occasion, we had won.

PS. I should also add that the 'iguana' turned out to be the 'aduana' – meaning customs. Sometimes, it is easy to forget that the Canaries are still part of Spain.

Letter 16
The Last of the Mohicans

It was Moving Day at last! We had been looking forward to this day for many weeks and it had taken considerable skilful pleading with the removals company, Town Hall and customs authority to get to this point. Indeed, the tedious process appeared to speed up as soon as I told them that I worked as a reporter for a local newspaper. We already knew that life in Spain could be very relaxed in its way of dealing with such matters, but sometimes the Canary Islands seemed to operate in an alternative time and space dimension. All we could do was to telephone or visit the relevant offices each day, and be very firm, yet polite. Finally we achieved the relevant 'bonks' on some very important pieces of paper and we were assured that the problems had been resolved. We never did really find out what the problems were, but assumed that it was customs issues. Although the Canary Islands are part of Spain and within the European Union, the islands are regarded as being outside the European Union for tax purposes and, indeed, have their own low rate of value added tax, known as 'I.G.I.C.' as well as a number of other significant differences that I won't go into in this letter.

This was the day when some of the most important items from our home in mainland Spain would be delivered to our new apartment in Gran Canaria. The bulk of our personal effects would be held in storage until we found a new home exactly suited to our needs and, more importantly, those of Barney and Bella. Meanwhile, we had endured a difficult three weeks using only what we could carry across on the boat in a couple of suitcases. Barney and Bella had brought their baskets, toys and rugs with them – a tight fit in a small car. This meant that the same limited sets of clothes for David and I had to be washed and dried quickly and in rotation.

It became an annoying routine, as well as an ongoing joke, that whenever we went into a shop to order tiles, furniture or fabric, the answer would always be the same. Yes, they would be pleased to take our order, but it would take somewhere between six and eight weeks before the goods would arrive from Barcelona. Sometimes even the simplest of items had to be ordered from the Peninsular. This was obviously going to be a major downside of island living. This is not to say that shopping facilities on the island are not excellent in many other ways. With three major department stores, that are very similar to the House of Fraser chain of stores in the UK, four branches of Marks and Spencer, Ikea, as well as a major do-it-yourself outlet, a sister company to B&Q in the UK, we were really very well served. It is just that the long wait when goods are ordered from Barcelona, can be a problem.

I wondered what had possessed us to bring long trousers, long sleeved shirts and, would you believe, a pullover to Gran Canaria? Maybe it was those miserable temperatures that dipped to -2° in the Costa Blanca just after Christmas that were still fresh in my mind! All I really wanted was a decent pair of shorts and some short-sleeved cotton shirts, but they too were in storage. This was the day when some important pieces of furniture, including a powerful tower PC and all the computer equipment that I needed so badly, my grandfather clock, as well as my electric trouser press, would arrive. I felt really excited. The clock was especially precious, as my father had carefully constructed one for each of my two brothers and myself a few years before he died – each one taking months of painstaking work. As for the trouser press, well that had become something of a joke and I had fiercely resisted the suggestion from David, as well as other friends, that I should donate it to one of the charity shops in the UK.

This fabulous piece of kit is a Corby electric trouser press – a rather snazzy deluxe model, which basically means that it has a red light on the top panel to indicate when the trousers are overcooked! I had had it for many years and used it regularly to press all my suit trousers before and after my inspection work in the UK. Yes, I know that it is not regarded as 'cool' to crease one's jeans and I have since, after some negative comments from David, ceased to do that. Nor is it possible to place smart creases in shorts, which I wear much of the time on the island. However, I find it reassuring to look at, and I guess that it reminds of a different time and place.

I now very rarely wear suits. Indeed, one of my last acts in the UK before the move to Spain was a visit to the charity shop bins standing forlornly outside our nearest Tesco store. I had already spent much of my life in one of my many suits, and now it was a time for a lifestyle change. Reasoning that I would never inspect a school again, nor would I ever willingly wear a suit, I dumped the whole collection in the Oxfam charity bin, all my smart black shoes and most of my ties in another, and my well worn pilot-type briefcase in the third. Oxfam was welcome to them. I retained just one suit, which was of the cool summer variety, just in case. I now recall that I attended my mother's funeral in this brilliant white suit, the only one I had left at the time. It looked great in the bars and clubs, but I knew that if she could have seen me, she wouldn't have minded that much. Indeed, she would have been very impressed to see the sharp creases that my faithful Corby had put on the trouser legs!

At eight-thirty prompt there was a ring on the buzzer – it was the removals company. This was a good start; at least they were on time. We could see a huge lorry at the side of the road downstairs – it all looked very promising. I answered the intercom telling the voice that we were on the fourth floor – should I really tell them now that the lift was not working or leave them to find out? Eventually, and it seemed like ages later, there was a brief tap at the front door and there were two men wearing smart overalls adorned with the removal company's logo standing in the doorway. They were not best pleased – one was making strange puffing noises and seemed to be gasping for air – I knew that feeling only too well. The second looked an elderly and rather tubby version of David Beckham – at least he was sporting a carefully coiffured Mohican hairstyle, which looked a little strange for a man of his advanced years and build – but, I gave him full marks for trying to improve his appearance. He had also obviously indulged in a rather violent blond colour wash that didn't match either his moustache or sideburns, but at least it made a statement! They nodded a greeting and strode disapprovingly into the apartment and immediately made for the window overlooking the narrow road below. There was much discussion, shaking of heads and the sharp sucking in of breath – sounds that I knew only too well and have learned to dread, and was convinced would eventually translate into, "There is a problem, we cannot deliver your goods today and we shall return 'manaña'." I really didn't think I could cope with yet more delays. Anyway, we had a newspaper to launch very shortly.

I glanced anxiously out of the window. Two more removals men were sitting outside on the road enjoying a picnic – they obviously had no intention of doing anything for a while. These two looked relatively young and I wondered why they had not been sent to climb the four flights of stairs instead of 'The Mohican'. 'The Mohican' was obviously in charge and started measuring the window. The windows were flung open and the full force of the Atlantic wind hurled itself into the apartment. Doors blew open, 'Welcome to your new home' cards flew around the room, a cheap vase smashed to the ground and

141

Barney and Bella fled into the bedroom. There was a strong verbal interchange between the picnickers at the side of the road and 'The Mohican'. The picnic was promptly put away and the two men propped sullenly against the lorry waiting for further instructions. 'The Mohican' then tied a hefty rope to a pillar in the apartment and this was flung down to the road below. I couldn't believe what was happening. Were these men really going to lift everything from the lorry on a rope to the apartment through a relatively small window and in a gale force wind? By now Bella was whimpering – I knew exactly how she felt as I imagined my grandfather clock smashing against the side of the apartment and breaking to smithereens. I could look no more, and knew that David would be better dealing with it as he was always so much calmer and politer in a crisis than I. I grabbed the whimpering Bella and left them to it. Barney had taken refuge underneath the bed and from 'that look' he gave me, he had no intention of coming out for the rest of the day.

Later, much later, I returned to the apartment with Bella, expecting to see the worst, but received a pleasant surprise. At the end of the rope was now an electric conveyor belt installed between the lorry and my fourth floor apartment. Boxes of clothes, pans and crockery, so carefully packed by Pickfords in the Costa Blanca, were all making their journey smoothly to the window with 'The Mohican' and colleague carefully guiding the boxes through the aperture. I hadn't seen anything quite like it before and I was very impressed. When I reached the apartment I saw dozens of boxes all carefully placed in different rooms with the 'would-be' picnickers carefully unpacking and unwrapping pictures, glasses, cups and saucers. My grandfather clock was carefully put in the place of honour that had been reserved for it, and was already ticking away comfortably.

My first impressions had, once again, been wrong. The team that were working for us were experienced and careful in their work – not at all what we had expected. I learned, once again, the valuable lesson that many 'expats' forget, and that is not to impose UK routines, standards and processes upon the Canarians. They will do it in their own way, at their own pace and at a time to suit them. However, fiestas and siestas willing, they usually get there in the end.

Exactly two hours from the time the removals men had arrived, they were collecting boxes and packing materials and were ready to leave. 'The Last of the Mohicans' smiled gratefully as I gave them all a well-deserved and generous tip, shook hands and said, "Adios." He only had four flights of steps to go down.

Letter 17
Builders' Electric Syndrome

Those readers who are yet to experience the joy and satisfaction of purchasing a property abroad and, in particular Spain, will be totally unaware of a nightmare disease commonly referred to as 'Builders' Electric Syndrome'. If you have already experienced just a hint of this evil 'disease', you may even have been temporarily lulled into a false sense of security by your estate agent that it is just 'one of those things' that happens when you buy a new property in Spain. In any case, it will all soon be sorted and, with luck, you will manage to get free electricity and water for a few months or even years. Wrong, how very wrong. For those of us who have been through or are going through 'the process', the words 'Builders' Electric' strikes terror to the very heart of our being. It is the stuff of sleepless nights that has the potential to destroy relationships and makes you question your sanity, as well as your purpose on the planet. You will forever be plunged into a world where you watch and listen to see if the freezer is still working and plan television and meal times around the next switch off that completely takes over your lives. Indeed, many a stout-hearted soul has been defeated, packed their bags and fled back to the UK.

As a reporter for a local newspaper in the Costa Blanca, I usually had at least one call each day from a desperate reader newly afflicted with 'Builders' Electric Syndrome'. For 'Builders' Electric Syndrome' virgins, I should explain that most people who purchase a new property in Spain, and certainly in the Costa Blanca, Costa del Sol and the Canary Islands catch this 'illness'. Before the 'certificate of habitation' (or Cedula – to give it the Spanish name) is issued by the Town Hall, certain safety assurances have to be given by the water and electricity companies – and quite right too. Once this important document has been 'bonked' and returned to the building contractor, property purchasers are then free to approach the electricity and water companies direct and then have a reliable supply in their own name. For many, this dream remains a mirage for months, or even years. For some unfortunate souls, this dream is never fulfilled.

Until that time, builders are obliged to supply the new owner of the property with electricity and water through a 'builders' supply', which they are supposed to pay for. At best the supply is usually unreliable – damaging appliances through its many surges, and forcing room lights to perform like disco lights. At worst, the supply is nonexistent. I well recall the 'builders' supply' when I lived in the Costa Blanca, when I was charged a thousand euros by the building company for the 'joy' of being connected to the mains supplies and then, adding insult to injury, being forced to pay for the 'builders' electricity and water' that we had used. Being hugely grateful and relieved to go onto mains power, I paid up. If only I knew then what I know now.

It is strange how history repeats itself. We were living in a new apartment in Gran Canaria. It really was a very pleasant place with wonderful views over the Atlantic on one side, mountains on the other and Mercadona supermarket in the middle. It was almost perfect – except for 'Builders' Electric'. My heart sank when I realised that, because a formally constituted community was not yet established to run the apartment block, there was no 'Cedula'. We were, once again, subject to the whim of 'Builders' Electric'. I reasoned that we would have nowhere near the same problems as in the Costa Blanca, but I was wrong. At best, we had electricity from around seven in the morning until late morning, and then we could forget about it as our Spanish neighbours started preparing lunch. Power then resumed in the afternoon if we were lucky, and disappeared again somewhere between seven-thirty and ten o'clock in the evening. Often we heard the angry scream of a busy mother trying to cope with the family meal, or the slamming of a door as dad decided to go to the local bar for the evening instead.

The only way to cope with such a state of affairs is to carefully plan around the likely cut-off times. Cooking was usually best done in the early hours of the morning, a timer to switch on the washing machine at about four o'clock in the morning were all ploys that we tried, and that often failed. It only took one thoughtless and heartless person in our block of twenty-seven apartments to switch on their oven at the same time as our washing machine was on, and the whole block was plunged into darkness.

After one week in the new apartment, our smart new fridge freezer could cope no more with the power surges, and blew up. Eventually, a new fridge freezer arrived from Barcelona (a six week wait), and we were desperately hoping that it would not go the same way as its predecessor. Sometimes the power was so low that it seemed to take an eternity to heat an electric ring on the hob or warm the oven, but at least we had some electricity.

Often when the electricity supply failed, we headed for the nearest bar for the evening or, if we had not eaten, to a local restaurant for a meal. This was costing us a fortune, but was the only way to survive. Sometimes we would eat filled rolls by candlelight in the living room, whilst listening to our CD player or the radio. No, it was not quite what we had thought life in the Canaries would be like.

Although there was no legally appointed community to run the block of the apartments when we moved in, as is required under Spanish law, there was a self-appointed President. Anna was a blunt, strong willed woman of German descent who most certainly never took no for an answer. How grateful we were to her for doing 'battle' on our behalf, as well as for others. However, even she seemed at times to be beaten by the system, and sometimes appeared deflated and fed up.

Anna had a secret. It was a secret that we discovered only by accident when Anna was at one of her low points in the daily battles with the authorities. Once, when the power supplied failed, we trudged down the stairway by torch light and then down a further flight of stairs to the underground floor where the cars were kept. We intended driving out in the car to a restaurant in another town for the evening, as we had become tired of our usual venue. We spotted Anna peering into a large white box that was fixed to the wall at the far end of the garage. She was peering inside with her torch and suddenly all of the lights in the garage came on. She had magically restored the power. We walked over to her to offer our congratulations. Maybe we could now finish the meal that David has started cooking and not have to go out after all?

"I am not supposed to do this," she hissed. "I watched them and found out. They left the box open with a key in the last time they came and I had a key made – look!"

Anna thrust forward a shiny new key for us to inspect. She grinned, wickedly. "You open this box and reset the switch when the power goes off. The builders have set the supply too low to force us to complain when it goes off. They know that this will force us to get our own supply and that will save them money. Here, you can borrow my spare key. Have a duplicate one made tomorrow and then you can do it yourselves when it goes off. It will save my legs."

The following day we had a spare key made and gave Anna back her key. From then on, although it meant a walk down five flights of stairs by torch-light into a dark and unwelcoming garage each time the electricity failed, we did at least now have a way of switching the supply back on, albeit usually only temporarily. More often than not, the supply would fail yet again, sometimes before we reached the door of our apartment.

The following day I spotted a man from the electricity company peering into a hole that had 'electricity' emblazoned on the front. I thought this was a very good omen and that we would soon be connected to our own reliable mains supply. How wrong I was – this wretched man had returned to take away the very box that connected our miserable and unreliable power source to the island's power grid. By mid afternoon, a crowd of angry young Spanish women had gathered outside the building to discuss the wrong doing, and to complain that they could not prepare the family meal or get their babies washed. It seems that the building company were in dispute with the electricity company and that, in a heady mixture of bravado and brinkmanship, had decided to 'pull the plug', so to speak. There was much angry chattering and hand waving, but little in the way of action.

As afternoon led into early evening, the crowd had grown larger, the women were now joined by their husbands and boyfriends, parents, friends and neighbours. Eventually phone calls were made. The builders expressed their 'surprise' that this had happened, and said that something would be done 'mañana'. The electricity company did not work after two o'clock in the afternoon and therefore could not be contacted. Those that called lawyers 'huffed and puffed' and muttered something about it being 'illegal' and that we could apply to the court for reconnection. The national police were called in an effort to issue one of those lovely 'denuncias' (or police reports), but we were politely yet firmly told that it was 'a civil matter' and that a crime had not been committed. Twenty-seven apartments had no power, there were no working lifts and the staircases remained unlit – so much for health and safety. The local police were also called and they were more sympathetic to our plight. The kind lady at the end of the phone said that she would have a word with the builders.

Three hours later, our would-be saviour arrived in the form of Pedro. Pedro was a man of few words, but came with a huge generator attached to the back of his vehicle. There were cheers from the assembled crowd as Pedro began his task. This huge beast of a machine was found a position outside, and just below our main bedroom at the rear of the building. Cables were slung across the basement garage into the huge fuse box – with the gaping hole where 'the wretched one' had removed the vital component and with a large roll of black tape fixed into place. The generator spluttered into life, lights in the basement garage flickered, the crowd applauded, Pedro bowed with embarrassment as the lights went on, but the generator gave a final cough – and then the lights went out.

Four hours later – just before midnight, the crowd had by now given up all hope and disappeared to their beds. Pedro determinedly battled on, sweat pouring off his brow, working from the lights of a resident's car. There was still no light to be seen and no sound from the generator. I stumbled up the stairs with a torch and went to bed, knowing full well that the next few days would mean endless and continuing battles with the electricity company, Town Hall, builders and anyone else who had the authority to magically 'bonk' the appropriate pieces of paper. The beast finally roared into life, but I was already entering a deep sleep filled with the stuff of nightmares. Ugly, noisy, fuel eating generators, thousands of faceless bureaucrats waving rubber stamps, dozens of unfed and unwashed children with their angry mothers and a man called Pedro who would not return home until his mission was completed. This is the stuff of 'Builders' Electric Syndrome' and the cause of many nightmares.

Letter 18
Fiestas, Siestas and Bridging Days

Most people are well aware of the Spanish love of siesta. If on holiday in Spain, it is that annoying part of the day, usually between the hours of one o'clock and five o'clock, and just when you are in the mood for a spot of shopping, you discover that everything remotely interesting is closed. It was certainly a tradition that we found very hard to adapt to during our first few months of living in Spain, and I doubt that I will ever really get used to the necessary 'body clock' adjustment of being able to shop late into the evening. One problem is that the true British 'expat' is pre-programmed to think that shops and businesses close at around six o'clock in the afternoon and do not reopen until the following day, as is mostly the case in the UK. We are also programmed to think that the day is over then, and tend to retreat to our homes for a meal and to relax by the TV and maybe a nice warm fire for the evening. Old habits die hard and it took a few months to adjust to the fact that even after the shops close, it is still warm outside and time to party well into the night. True, the Canarian working day usually starts at around eight in the morning, but this was a time when few 'expats' would be up and about. Even though most shops and businesses still close for the siesta, this tradition does not apply to modern commercial centres, and so this was always the best place to shop during these 'bewitching hours'. Most other shops and businesses would reopen their doors at five o'clock and stay open until around seven-thirty, or maybe later during the summer months. With commercial centres closing at ten o'clock in the evening, there were few excuses not to find somewhere open late into the evening. So why the siesta? I had always assumed that it was a very sensible thing to do, because this was the time when the heat was at its strongest, particularly during those unbearably hot summer weeks in peninsular Spain. To eat, relax and sleep during this hot part of the day seemed a good idea. However, in the Canary Islands without the excesses of the summer heat in the mainland, the main reason for the siesta was that there were many part-time, low-paid jobs servicing the holiday industry in particular. 'Black money' cash-in-hand deals were very common, helping employers to avoid paying national insurance and other taxes that meant that workers often started work early in the morning and then had a break during the afternoon, before starting a second job after their main meal of the day and their siesta. Life on the islands was often hard with locals working long hours for little in the way of decent pay or legal employment protection, despite government efforts to bring this in line with European minimum wage and working hours legislation. In any case, old habits and traditions remain and I remember arranging to view our new property a few weeks before completion in order to measure for curtains and fittings. The builders had let us borrow a key, and when we called to view the apartment one afternoon, we were surprised to find that the door was unlocked. As we went in, it was clear that plasterers and plumbers were still working on the kitchen and bathroom. Maybe they had gone off somewhere for siesta, and forgotten to lock the door? We wandered into the main bedroom and very nearly fell over a group of plumbers and plasterers all fast asleep on flattened cardboard boxes on the bedroom floor. They all looked so peaceful and we didn't have the heart to disturb them, so we quietly left the apartment intending to visit again another day. Nowadays, I too enjoy a siesta, if there is time. Forget the term, 'power nap', that hackneyed over-used phrase used in management theory and stress management

151

literature to excuse the practice in the UK and USA, but to enjoy a leisurely nap after a pleasant lunch with a glass of wine, does work wonders for both the soul and the digestion!

Fiestas are a much more complicated issue. Statistics show that Spain unashamedly has more national holidays than any other country in the European Union, and the Spanish and Canarians certainly love their fiestas. Family life is important to the Spanish and I often think that they have the right attitude to both work and play. As a nation they tend to work to live, whereas in the UK, Germany and other Northern European countries there is a tendency to follow the cultural 'norms' promoted by America, and live to work. No, the Spanish value their days off to celebrate and, most importantly, to spend time with their family and close friends. Be it a national, local or religious celebration, the Spanish are up for it – often regardless of what the event actually is. There were endless fiesta days in our town, but few locals were able to tell me why they were off work for the day. Indeed, it was not always easy to get a list of all the fiesta dates at the beginning of the year. I suspected no one really knew until a few days before the actual event.

Church attendance in Spain had fallen over the years, but there was usually a very high turnout for any of the Saints days on the calendar – not necessarily to the Church, but for the party! In the Canary Islands, I strongly suspect that even more than the usual Spanish fiesta days are taken in deference to the cultural and ethnic mix of people within these islands. As well as Canarian and Spanish residents, the island population now contains a heady mix of people of African and Asian descent, as well as from other European countries and South America, and the Canarians are inclined to celebrate along with the newcomers to these islands. After all, it would be bad manners not to, wouldn't it? Examples of this are Christmas Eve and New Year's Eve, which are not Spanish fiestas or national holidays, yet it is rare to find many shops or businesses open on these days! You can certainly forget all about going to the Post Office and bank. Fiesta days are also very much a local thing. Each village and town has its own patron saint and accordingly, individual towns, villages and, indeed, whole municipalities are closed on different days, although neighbouring towns, villages and municipalities are not. This has now become very confusing, because of increased mobility of the workforce, workers often find that it is a Saint's day in the town or village where they live, but it is not in the town where their child goes to school or where they work. In such cases, there is only one thing to do and that is to take the whole lot off as a fiesta, regardless! It took me quite a while to realise that the reason why many shops and business close early on the day before the actual fiesta day itself, is in order to prepare properly for the forthcoming party that evening, and particularly if it is Carnival! Just imagine telling that story to your boss in the UK.

The fiesta day itself is often very quiet and I realise now that it is intended to be a day to recover from the rigorous partying from the night before! Some of the parades and celebrations are highly colourful affairs with my own personal favourite being the Las Palmas Carnival which, although it lasts for nearly a month, peaks in the final week with hugely colourful, noisy and joyous parades, concerts and events that would put the Rio and Buenos Aires Carnivals to shame. Indeed, it is the South American influence in the Canary Islands that we have to thank for Carnival as we know it – similar events in peninsular Spain being much more sombre affairs. During Carnival nearly a quarter of a million residents and holidaymakers throng the streets of Las Palmas during its last weekend. Nine kilometres of Las Palmas streets are filled for a six-hour procession of floats, and Carnival revellers determined to play their part in the biggest party of the year. Amazing and imaginative floats, colourful costumes, determined 'party-people' of all ages and nationalities fill the streets with singing, dancing and merrymaking until the early hours. After the party, the huge free open-air concert keeps everyone partying until mid Sunday morning! From toddlers to great grandparents – everyone joins in! Cardinals, nurses, demons, nuns, weird creatures, cartoon characters, pirates and cowboys – to name just a few – fill the streets and make Carnival a party to remember! By the end of the evening, or should I say by six o'clock on Sunday morning, the party shows no sign of coming to an end. By now, if this had been certain parts of the UK, I suspect there would have been drunken and drugged louts everywhere, violence and a considerable number of arrests – and we would be ankle deep in rubbish, urine and vomit. Not so in Las Palmas. Although there is a large police presence, they too enjoy the party as much as anyone else and it is a credit to the revellers and policing alike that it is so good natured and good-humoured. Yes, there was a lot of litter around, but remarkably, it had all disappeared by the time I made an appearance late on Sunday morning. The Las Palmas Carnival is sometimes referred to as, 'Second only to Rio' and I know exactly what they mean! I remember driving away from Las Palmas on Monday morning with a feeling of sadness as the party was still continuing with a vengeance! Carnival then moves to the south of the island to Playa del Ingles where it begins all over again a few weeks later. In the south, it is a more 'down-market' and smaller affair, but even so is always great fun and the tourists thoroughly enjoy it, as do the Canarians who travel from Las Palmas to enjoy Carnival all over again.

'Puente' or 'bridging' days are also an interesting phenomenon on the island and are a common and accepted practice. One example of this is the 6th and 8th of December each year. One is a national holiday and the other is a Saint's day. So if, for example, the 6th falls on a Tuesday with the 8th on the Thursday, it is not considered worth going into work on either the Wednesday or Friday. With a bit of luck, with preparation time on the Monday and time off on the Saturday, which are usually half days anyway, clear thinking Canarians could swing a whole week off work. It is logical really! The islanders work very hard: the hours are long and the pay is low. A combination of Canarian pride in their rich culture and heritage as well as the traditional view that 'family comes first' means that fiestas are valued as a time to be together and enjoy life in these beautiful islands.

Letter 19
A Passion for 'Bonking'

I have always loved Spain, and the Canary Islands in particular. It is sometimes hard to remember that it is only in relatively recent history that Spain recovered from being in the grips of the brutal dictator, General Franco, to re-establishing the monarchy, under the careful guidance of King Juan Carlos, and taking its place as one of the modern democratic states in Europe. Unlike the attitudes often very prevalent in Britain, most Spanish men and women are firm supporters of the European 'ideal' and the European Union. They may not like all the rules and regulations and often 'bend them' to meet local need, yet they are only too well aware that the European Union has been an essential mechanism to assist the country to establish itself as a modern democracy within Europe. Just as in the case of the Irish Republic, the country has benefited from generous European Union funding from the very beginning of the establishment of the Union. One example of the way that this money has been used in Gran Canaria is the excellent road network, successfully linking the north and south of the island, and making present day tourism possible.

As a result of huge investment in the islands, the European Union flag flies proudly alongside the Canarian and Spanish flags on all public buildings, joint building projects and indeed from the offices of a large number of private companies on the island. This is not to say that the Canarians wish to have their own identity submerged within the great European 'ideal'. Like the inhabitants of many islands the world over, the Canarians are fiercely proud of their heritage, and accept their position as a self-governing province within Spain as a necessary evil to survive. This is reflected in the popularity of the separatist and independent political parties during local and provincial elections, yet there is widespread support for one of the two main Spanish political parties during national elections.

This is not to say that the Canarians blindly accept and agree with all European policy. I still hear heated debates about how Spain should have maintained their previous currency, the peseta, and blame the introduction of the euro for the rapid increase in the cost of living. There is concern too about the number of illegal immigrants from Africa landing on our islands after a dangerous journey through treacherous waters. Concern is often shown that the national Spanish government, as well as the European Union, are not doing enough to patrol the coastline and thus prevent this growing human tragedy.

Although friendly and outgoing by nature, the Canarians also have a very private side that is often hard for the newcomer to penetrate. They are family people and their world revolves around their immediate and extended families to which outsiders are often unintentionally excluded. I talked to one wise old Canarian gentleman about this observation some time ago. He thought about the question for a while and quietly explained.

"You must remember that in Franco's time, it was only your family that you could trust. Even your neighbours and friends would often betray you to the authorities. This is why, unlike in Britain, the police in Spain are never our friends. We respect them, but we know them only from arm's length."

Yes, this did make sense, given the country's history and remembering that, during the Franco years, starvation on these forgotten islands had been a reality.

Some things never change and it is with some amusement that I reflect on a long-standing tradition carried out by Spanish officials, which is common both in Spain as well as the Canary islands. This is the Spanish 'love affair' with the rubber stamp and black or purple ink pad. Even if you have only been living in Spain for just a short time you cannot fail to have escaped someone wielding one of these dangerous weapons from a great height. We all know that rubber stamps cost little to produce and that they are, I am told, one of the easiest things to forge. In reality, for security and identification purposes, it is a meaningless activity. However, we all go along with it. It is merely one of the many games that we all have to play.

It is a truism in Gran Canaria that the more important you are, the more rubber stamps you have at your disposal. Be it at the bank, Post Office, government office or Town Hall – the clerks have a wide and heady range of rubber stamps to turn that ordinary piece of paper into something very special. Even the lowliest clerk has at least one at their disposal – often a simple round one, but as they grow in importance and stature they move on to a whole arsenal of weapons that may even include the cherished rectangular and even diamond shaped versions. Notice too that the manner in which it is applied is a sign of how well you have done as a foreigner living in Spain. The 'just satisfactory bonk' is a very quick affair – usually applied with just the right pressure to get a decent image on that 'very ordinary' piece of paper – but it is not very special and you leave the presence of the clerk feeling somewhat unfulfilled.

The more important the piece of paper, the higher the stamp is raised and dropped with a loud and meaningful 'bonk'. If you hand over or withdraw a large amount of money or maybe purchase a property then 'the bonk' applied reverberates throughout the whole building. You and anyone happening to be within earshot will be well aware that something important has happened and that you, for a brief while, are a 'Very Important Person'. The action that I dread is the 'reluctant bonk' or, horror upon horrors, being sent away with no 'bonk' at all! This has happened to me several times in my dealings with one of the

Canarian Town Halls leaving me feeling miserable and dejected – in short, a non-person.

In my local bank I joined a very long queue. For a while I accepted that it was 'just one of those things', but gradually I became more and more interested in the activities of an elderly gentleman customer in front of me and a bank clerk who was becoming more and more agitated. My Spanish was not good enough to tune in to all the conversation at first, but as time went by and additional staff were called in to deal with the situation it became clear that the man was not at all happy, because he had been denied a rubber stamp on his water bill. By now the queue was approaching around fifteen impatient customers. We were all watching and listening in anticipation of an inevitable bank victory, but the tenacious old gentleman stuck firmly to his guns and continued to create a fuss. He had paid the water bill through the bank, but now wanted the clerk to 'bonk' the water bill to prove he had paid it.

"It is not necessary," said the clerk.

"I want it stamped – it is not legal otherwise," replied the elderly gentleman.

The manager was duly called to the scene – not a particularly warm or friendly lady, and she made it very clear that she was in charge and would stand no nonsense from anyone as lowly as a mere customer. A battle of words and wills continued for around twenty minutes. Eventually, the manager became totally exhausted – she was very red in the face and too hot and bothered to fight any more. She grabbed the nearest rubber stamp and gave the piece of paper the heaviest and loudest 'bonk' that I have ever witnessed. The old gentleman left with a wry smile and I left the bank with the noise still reverberating in my ears. The lady manager fled to a nearby desk and grabbed a bottle water before collapsing into her chair.

When I had to renew the document confirming my residency in Spain, it was plain sailing. I had completed all the forms correctly. I had the required paperwork supporting my application. The harassed clerk spent a few minutes scrutinising the paper, whilst I sat wondering what I could have forgotten. Finally she sat back in her chair, gave me a broad smile, picked up her large round rubber stamp, and gave this important document the loudest 'bonk'.

If you already live, or intend to live and settle happily in Spain or the Canary Islands, never, ever underestimate the importance of 'the bonk'!

Letter 20
Bella Finds a Body

One of the major disadvantages of living in a fourth floor apartment with two dogs was that there were four flights of stairs to negotiate each time we needed to get out for a 'convenience' stretch, which we did around four times a day. We were still on 'Builders' Electricity' and so the lift was still not working. Sometimes the tell-tale sign of a green light flashing at the side of the door raised our expectations that somehow, someone had switched it on, but this was always false hope and led to bitter disappointment.

The apartments were still not technically 'legal' to live in. This was made very clear to us during one of our endless visits to the Town Hall. Why then, was the property sold to us as 'finished' in the first place, and with twenty-six other apartments that were already inhabited? It was all completed in front of the Notary, appropriate documents had been 'bonked', money had been exchanged and part of it involved a mortgage from a local bank. I found it hard to understand why we should not be living in it.

As time went on it became clear that neither the Town Hall nor the builder had a very high regard for each other. Each blamed the other, shrugged and snarled when the other party was mentioned, leading to a period of 'non co-operation' between the Town Hall and the builders. The bottom line was that before we could get our electricity and water supply connected, the 'community' had to receive the appropriate documentation from the Town Hall, and this was not forthcoming. Indeed, this was another major problem, there was no 'community' legally established to oversee the running of the apartments and services, such as the lift had not been commissioned. Indeed, a number of our neighbours seemed more concerned about getting a community satellite TV dish than they were about electricity and water. Television was very popular in the apartment block, and a number of families were already installing their own satellite dishes to the rear of the building. Television was the very last thing that we were concerned about, as we were far too busy trying to maintain a supply of power to run our freezer and the computer.

The idea of a community, legally established, seemed a very sensible idea in principle, but not if no one, other than our self-appointed President, was willing to stand for office. During the early hours of one morning, it occurred to me that either David, myself or, indeed, both of us should stand for office to get things moving, but I quickly dismissed the thought as my Spanish, as well as my understanding of legal processes in Spain was limited at that time. I could just imagine the response from the Town Hall! So the lift was still not working and it was likely to be some time before it did. Meanwhile, we would just have to turn a misfortune into an advantage and get on with our lives.

Fortunately, because we lived in a windy town, the high temperatures of the south of the island rarely troubled us. Thankfully, we did not need air conditioning, and our ceiling fans were sufficient for our needs, when the electricity supply worked. If the temperatures rose too much, as happens for a few days each summer when holidaymakers and residents alike in coastal resorts such as Puerto Rico and Puerto Mogan roast gently, we simply would open the huge apartment windows and the temperature would quickly fall, even though the force of the wind usually forced Barney and Bella to flee to the kitchen for safety. Indeed, for much of the year, the temperatures remained steady. However, a few times each year, when the wind turbines turned in the opposite direction we suffered from a 'calima' when the hot winds from the Sahara blew across the islands, bringing not only intense heat, but a considerable amount of dust and sand. This is when it paid not to have an outside terrace or balcony because, as residents knew only too well, when the 'calima' passed there would be much work in hosing down and scrubbing patios, walls and outside furniture.

Dogs and humans were getting fitter by the day with all the additional exercise. Indeed, Barney's vet in the UK would have been hugely impressed with this newly reformed 'fine figure of a dog'. When Barney had to step on the weighing machine in the waiting room of our vets in the UK there was always great embarrassment for both ourselves, as well as for Barney. There were invariably gasps of astonishment, sharp sucking in of breath and much shaking of heads, whilst poor Barney wandered off the scales wondering what all the fuss was about, and was promptly put on yet another diet. I had tried the usual plea, on Barney's behalf of, "He is big boned for his breed," but this piece of information was always ignored.

Bella, our eighteen-month-old 'fruit bat', couldn't really care less – she thought walks were a huge game as we dragged her big brother behind us. Although Barney loved the beach and long interesting walks, he preferred to avoid those of 'a convenience nature' if he could, being clever enough to work out a number of avoidance strategies, such as hiding under the bed, in the wardrobe or, if all else failed, laying on his back with paws in the air and then being carried out in a very undignified manner. Not an easy task when dealing with four flights of stairs and a 'slightly overweight' dog.

We walked out of the main door of the block of apartments only to trip over a hose pipe running from the water delivery lorry to one of the houses at the side of the apartment block. Although, on the island, water is quite safe to drink from the tap, few people rarely do. It is full of minerals, mostly smells unpleasant and I personally wouldn't drink it! Besides, although much of it is from the mountains, some is recycled and the remainder is a product of the desalination plant. No, bottled mineral water, or water delivered weekly in a huge tanker is a much pleasanter and safer option.

It always amazed me to see the number of people to come out of that seemingly small house. Elderly men and women, young men and teenage girls, as well as children and babies all seemed to live there. However, as is the case of many traditional Canarian properties, they may well look quite small on the outside, but are usually deceptively spacious inside. Indeed, I suspect that most of the people that we saw coming and going belonged to one extended family. Such is family life in the Canaries, family is everything and it is the tradition for the younger members of the family to look after the older members of the family. Until recent times, there has been little need or use of care homes for the elderly. It is not the Canarian way of doing things.

As Bella and I walked along the pavement in the late afternoon sunshine, the streets were unusually quiet. Usually, by around five o'clock the streets were coming to life again after the siesta period. One of the many things that I love about Spain is the siesta – such a sensible idea and one that I have willingly and easily subscribed to. Everything grinds to a halt at around two o'clock as the shops close and workers go home for their midday break. It is, after all, far too hot to work. At this time of the day, Barney would drag behind – looking for the odd scrap of food that may have carelessly been tossed aside, whilst Bella would be dashing ahead trying to chase cats, find lizards, cockroaches and anything else that she can worry and shake to death – after all, she is a terrier by nature.

Suddenly, Bella stopped in her tracks and pulled me towards two parked cars. I could see nothing unusual. Bella started whining and pulled forward to the middle of the two cars.

Between the two car bumpers was a man curled up in a foetus position. He was a scruffy, unshaven middle-aged man, wearing a dirty coat and he had soiled his trousers. My heart sank; the poor man must be dead, there was not a flicker of movement. I bent down and shook him gently and, thankfully, he stirred slightly and mumbled something in Spanish before he fell into unconsciousness once again. I was relieved that he had said something, which obviously meant he was still alive. Hopefully it would also mean that I would not have to undertake the dreaded 'mouth to mouth resuscitation'. I have always feared finding someone in this condition ever since I took my St John's Ambulance First Aid course in college, not because I doubted the effectiveness of it as an emergency strategy, but because I remember breaking the 'Resusci Anne' doll that we were practising on in my exuberance to breathe life back into the poor creature. I also remember the instructor being less than happy with my performance, and the merciless teasing that followed from my fellow students. However, I did remember the golden rule of not trying to move the patient.

For once, Barney and Bella waited patiently whilst I nervously dialled '112'. It was the first time that I had dialled the emergency services in Spain, and I was not sure if my Spanish was up to the job. Within seconds the call was answered and I asked to speak to someone in English. This again was promptly answered and a very pleasant and efficient lady dealt with my request – in perfect English. I was not sure which service to ask for. I knew three friends in the UK whom I have seen display similar symptoms from time to time. One is a diabetic, the other an epileptic and the third is a part-time alcoholic. I reasoned that the ambulance would be the best bet.

By now a group of Canarian woman had gathered on the other side of the road, and were shouting and pointing at me. I told them that I had called the ambulance. They laughed and shook their heads before shouting back to me in a babble of

Spanish. I gathered that they thought that the police would be more appropriate than the ambulance to deal with the man. They also offered to throw a bucket of water over the poor soul in an effort to revive him. I was taken aback by their heartless attitude and declined the offer, and reasoned that as he was 'Bella's patient' we would just have to wait with the man until the ambulance arrived.

Within minutes the reassuring sound of the ambulance siren could be heard. Our patient was still 'out for the count'. The ambulance swept up and two young men in matching tracksuits got out and walked over to 'the body'. One lit up a cigarette whilst the other started talking gently to him. Giving the man a cigarette seemed a strange form of treatment, but then I realised that the cigarette was for the ambulance driver and not the patient! Eventually one of the men walked over to me and shook his head. "He will not come with us to the hospital," he said. "We have called the police and they will deal with it. You can leave him." With that the two men got into the ambulance and drove away, sirens still blaring loudly. The man was now conscious, but saying nothing – a small pool of vomit lay on the road beside his mouth.

After a few more minutes, a police car arrived. A brief word from one of the policemen and 'our patient' was bundled into the back of a police car. One of the policemen shrugged and gave me a cheeky grin before driving off. The group of woman looked on and said the equivalent of "we told you so". Obviously our patient was quite well known for his alcoholism, and had chosen to spend the night in a police cell rather than a hospital bed. Barney, Bella and I continued with the rest of our walk.

Letter 21
The Notorious Notary

Alongside the priest and the doctor, the Notary is regarded as a very important person in Spain. Although they are public figures they obtain their fees from individuals and companies. They play an independent role in drafting and witnessing many types of legal contracts in Spain. Essentially, their job is to ensure that both parties to an agreement understand the terms of the contract and that the terms of the contract do not contravene any laws. Notaries also ensure that the appropriate taxes generated by the transaction are paid. Property sales and purchase are generally very efficient in Spain and, unlike England and Wales, where long chains of purchasers can lead to many failed transactions, a commitment to purchase in Spain is taken very seriously, and can be completed well within one month, and often much quicker if it is a cash transaction.

If a purchaser is interested in buying a property the normal procedure is to place a ten per cent deposit with the agent to show commitment to purchase. A contract between the vendor and purchaser is then drawn up with a date of completion agreed by both parties to take place in the office of the Notary. In theory, this system works very well because, unless the property is seriously misrepresented, there are few opportunities to pull out of the deal. There are no chains of purchasers to worry about or concerns that the sale may fall through. However, it is essential to have the remainder of the funds readily available to complete the transaction otherwise there is a real risk that the intended purchaser will forfeit the deposit to the vendor. At ten per cent of the deal, failure to complete represents a substantial penalty and one that rarely occurs. However, I did come across one case in the Costa Blanca where a purchaser, for a number of reasons, was unable to gather together sufficient funding to complete the purchase. The vendor felt that he had been slighted and insisted upon claiming his legal right to the full deposit, which in this case, was seventy-five thousand euros – being ten per cent of a seven hundred and fifty thousand euros property. Ouch, that was a very painful lesson learned!

When a property is purchased in the UK, contracts are exchanged, the vendor is paid, and eventually you get the keys and the property is yours, after which you are free to register your title in the land register. The process is different in Spain in that you cannot inscribe your title in the property register – Spain's version of the land register – unless a Spanish Notary witnesses the deeds of sale. Under Spanish law, a Notary's signature is required to enter a private contract into public deeds that can be inscribed in the land register. Some Spanish, especially in rural areas, own property that is not inscribed in the register, thus saving on the hassle and expense (Notary fees, registry fees and taxes) of inscription although this can lead to difficulties when it comes to selling the property again in the future. As a reporter in the Costa Blanca I often came across heartbreaking stories of where property purchased by British 'expats' had seriously backfired. Sometimes these properties would be advertised at an alarmingly low price – and for a good reason. The usual reason was that the land was not registered or maybe the property itself had been built on agricultural land and not land designated for residential building. It was only when the water and electricity authorities refused to connect these properties to mains services that their new owners became aware that they were living in an illegal building. At best, all the new owners could expect would be for the local Town Hall to eventually recognise and register the property, turn a 'blind' eye or in the worst case scenarios, the property would be designated for demolition with the new owners receiving little, if any, compensation. In these cases, the 'bargain' that was advertised so temptingly on the Internet would turn into a nightmare scenario, sometimes crippling the new owners and destroying the dreams of so many for a new life in the sun. There were also very sad cases of many illegal beach and seashore properties being demolished by municipal authorities upon the instruction of central government, anxious to ensure that building policies were enforced. Much damage had been done by previous administrations at both national and local level in 'turning a blind eye' to some of the horrific developments in protected coastal areas. As modern Spain grapples with fast moving and far reaching European legislation, a fair amount of corruption has been discovered leading to the prosecution, and in some cases imprisonment, of a number of municipal representatives, including a number mayors and local councillors. Indeed, we have had a number of cases of mayors and other local officials imprisoned in the Canary Islands for corruption.

Tragic stories of corruption ruining the lives of newly arrived 'expats' to Spain were not uncommon and although most had employed lawyers to check and verify their new properties, somehow many had slipped through the net. For foreign buyers, in particular, it is essential to inscribe their title in the property register, as it is the only secure form of property ownership in Spain. The first person to inscribe title to a property gets to keep it, which is all the reason you need. There are other advantages too: for instance, protection from the vendor's creditors and the ability to take out a mortgage against the property. All buyers need to complete their purchase in the presence of a Notary if they are to enjoy the benefits of inscription in the property register.

Visiting the office of a Notary in either the Costa Blanca or the Canary Islands is always an entertaining experience. Far from being the sober place that it could potentially be, it is usually, in my experience, a place of much excited chatter and laughter. Sales and purchase of property are just a few things that the Notary has to deal with, including the registration of wills and verifying documents in all of the many legal and necessary transactions of life and death passed across their desks. It is usual for everyone involved in the transaction – the vendors, buyers, and mortgage lenders – to be present in person or to be represented by powers of attorney at the signing of the 'escritura' or legal document. When you arrive at the Notary's office, you have to wait until all the parties arrive, and then the Notary starts the proceedings. The Notary confirms the identity and other personal details of the buyers and sellers present, and then reads the property deeds aloud. Some Notaries like to use their English by giving a partial translation, although most will just read in Spanish. Whatever the case, the purchaser needs to be sure that the deeds are correct before signing them, which means having a translator present or relying upon your English speaking lawyer. Some Notaries will refuse to sign the deeds unless a foreign buyer has a lawyer or translator present.

I recall that on one occasion I had a frantic telephone call from a lawyer friend who had just been let down by his usual translator. Would I step into the breach? At that stage I knew very little Spanish, other than basic greetings and the ability to order a glass or two of wine, but I reluctantly agreed. I did not have a job at the time and so had plenty of time on my hands to help out a friend in distress, and ready cash was in short supply. I was well briefed by our friend beforehand. Although I was the official translator, the client's lawyer (an excellent linguist himself) would read out the English translation for me during the meeting. Most of the meeting went well, apart from a very embarrassing discussion with the purchaser of the property whilst waiting for the Notary to become available. He was a very friendly Irishman, complete with a strong smell of alcohol on his breath. When Pat Murphy realised that I too had an Irish background he accepted me as part of the clan and entered into deep discussions, although most were monologues, about life in Ireland and Spain and, indeed, life in general. Pat's questions about my life as a professional translator and interpreter were a little difficult to answer given the circumstances, but I seemed to 'wing it' to his complete satisfaction. In any case, the alcohol was still having its influence upon Pat, and I doubt that he really cared about my professional skills anyway. My lawyer friend had made it very clear that all I had to do was to sit with him and his client around the table with the Notary and when the time came, I had to nod wisely and say, "Si," with as much 'gravitas' as I could muster. Heart in mouth, I sat at the Notary's table, seated importantly alongside Pat and his wife, the vendor, bank representatives and my lawyer friend and his assistant. Finally, my moment came and I was asked that all-important question by the Notary.

"Si," I answered in my most professional manner.

It was exhausting work and I remember being paid fifty euros for my professional contribution. We were all happy and I had suddenly become a professional translator and interpreter, although I decided to retire shortly afterwards! Pat Murphy too was delighted and he shook my hand vigorously at the end of the meeting, promising to keep in touch.

The Notary makes certain legal checks, though these vary between autonomous regions. This leads some estate agents to claim that buyers are perfectly well protected by the Notary and do not need a lawyer. However, in reality, the Notary gives clients little protection, so prospective purchasers do need to be accompanied by an experienced and qualified professional when signing the deeds. If no one objects to the content of the deeds, the Notary will pass them around for signing by all parties, and confirm the payment of any outstanding amounts by the buyer before the keys are handed over.

On the few occasions when I have visited the Notary's office to complete a transaction, it was not uncommon for all the participants to sit around a table and physically hand over cash from one person to another. In the past, it was common for 'black money' to change hands and this did not officially appear on the legal documentation. I gather that this was, in the past, a ruse to avoid paying certain taxes to local and central government. It is a practice that is not to be recommended nowadays as it is an issue dealt with seriously by the authorities, and can have legal consequences when the time comes to resell the property. Overall, Notaries in Spain seem to do a good job although there have been instances in the Costa del Sol of several Notaries and local lawyers being recruited by the criminal element who paid them bribes to 'turn a blind eye' to certain illegal or 'fringe' transactions. Hopefully, this behaviour is not widespread and well qualified Notaries can continue to do their work with their usual impartiality.

Letter 22
Growing up in the Canaries

Taking our two dogs, Barney and Bella, for their last walk of the day took me past the children's playground at the edge of the town where we lived. It is not a particularly pretty town or a tourist trap. It is just an ordinary Canarian town with beautiful views over the Atlantic Ocean and the panorama of magnificent mountains as a backdrop, and where ordinary people live and work. Even though it was nearly midnight, I could see a large group of children and several teenagers still playing football in the netted area of the playground. I stood and watched for a while – it was a good-natured game with the youngest children aged about five or six, and the oldest must have been in their late teens. It was just an ordinary concrete playground, no special architectural features or safety matting in sight. However, from the cheers and whoops of joy, I could see that they were all having a great time.

These islands are blessed with the kindest of weather. There are basically two seasons, representing 'warm' and 'hot' weather. Maybe some evenings are chillier than others during the 'winter months', but we do have the most incredible climate. Excesses in temperature are unusual, and it is only a few times of the year when the 'calima' from the Sahara brings hot winds, as well as sand and dust, when caution is advisable. Most evenings throughout the year are warm enough to sit outside and enjoy a drink or two with neighbours and friends. Indeed, it is often the late evening that is the best time to go out for a walk with the dogs. It is cooler and often more pleasant for both people and dogs.

It was nearly midnight, the playground was lit by floodlights, the temperature was around 23°C, and children and teenagers were still happily playing in the open air. This was not an unusual occurrence, because I saw it most evenings when I walked the dogs – the composition of the group varied each day, sometimes a father would be playing with a group of children, sometimes it was a group of older teenagers. Often the family dog was out as well, helping to chase the ball and generally being a nuisance. Sometimes a child ran over and talked to Barney and Bella, and a group often gathered to look at Barney – a Welsh Pembroke corgi – in amazement.

Canarian children had never seen anything like Barney before, and they were convinced that 'he was a police dog with short legs'. He had made many friends locally, and when he was meeting strangers, and particularly children, he was at his happiest and was always charming. Bella tended to cause less of a sensation, because the children would no doubt have seen many 'look-alikes' in the past. This was probably just as well, as Bella has a very short fuse and doesn't 'take prisoners'. I often think that Bella is typical of many Spanish señoritas – mostly warm and friendly, but if the wind changes or they are crossed in some way, they can do battle with the best of men! In short, Bella either likes you, or she does not. If she does not, and much will depend upon the mood that she is in at the time, she will give a short warning and then you will know for certain. Having said this, Bella seems to accept that children cannot always control themselves and will make some allowances, but she makes no excuses for the noisy adult who should know better, or someone who is too overwhelming or gushing. No, Barney is the far more accommodating of the pair, despite his occasional grumpiness.

Looking at the youngsters playing so heartily together, I wondered why, with all this exercise each day, many of them looked so tubby. I recalled reading a health report that was published in the local Spanish newspaper earlier in the year, quoting a report from the Spanish health authorities that identified the Canary Islands as having one of the highest proportions of obese children in the whole of Spain. Certainly we had seen and commented about this ourselves, as the evidence was all around us in playgrounds, schools, shopping centres and streets. However, cheap and accessible gymnasium and swimming pool facilities abounded on the island, as well as playgrounds such as the one that I was standing by. Indeed, with the sea all around and swimming and surfing possible, and open areas for walking and cycling, the opportunities for exercise were plentiful.

With fresh fish, fruit and vegetables readily and cheaply available on the islands, I reflected on what may be the cause of the 'wobbling flesh' in front of me. Maybe it was the usual reasons that have become so pronounced in the UK and the USA, with too much television and video games, and too many snacks and fast foods. Certainly, McDonalds, Burger King, KFC and other American fast food outlets are very popular on the island. Maybe those rich creamy cakes, wonderful Spanish omelettes and Canarian potatoes with the rich Canarian sauces have something to do with it?

Interestingly, there is usually a father or an older teenager who seems to take charge of the activities and who is nominally responsible for sorting out any of the rare disagreements that occur in the playground. The arrangement is very informal with often an older brother enjoying spending some time with his siblings. Girls as well as boys happily take part in the activities, which are sometimes rough and always noisy. I am convinced that Canarian children are born with a volume control that is permanently fixed to 'very loud' – there is no halfway position!

This is continued right the way through adult life, and only reduces in their twilight years, when many years of non-stop cigarette smoking finally take their toll upon the voice, resulting in 'tell-tale' gruffness of sound.

Residents in the community have a sharing attitude towards the children, a feeling of joint responsibility that I had never experienced in the UK. I often noticed that local youngsters were happy to chat to and mix with the elderly, and the elderly, in turn, were never backward in reprimanding the youngsters regardless of which family they came from. Yes, there is the occasional vandalism and graffiti on some of the blank white walls, but in general, the community is safe and well protected by its residents.

I looked towards a tiled pathway area set some way away from the road and the busy playground. This was where older teenagers gathered at the end of the day and, sadly, with increasing unemployment on the island, often during the day. Certainly the teenagers were noisy, shouting, laughing and playing loud music, but they were teenagers. One thing that sets these youngsters apart from many of their contemporaries in some of the UK's more challenging cities, is that these youngsters are there to meet up, chat, have a laugh and a smoke. There are no youth clubs or billiard halls or planned activities for teenagers, but there is a warm climate, a safe beach and a swimming pool close by. During my time in the village I had not been aware of any trouble, and noticed that the youngsters had moved plastic picnic chairs and tables to the area where they now played cards and, that much loved Canarian activity of old men, dominoes. They were getting plenty of practice in early. The other amazing thing is that their collection of old table and chairs were left out day and night, not vandalised, stolen or destroyed by other teenagers, nor removed by some 'jobsworth' from the local council, as would no doubt have occurred in the

UK, claiming the usual 'Health and Safety' or 'Lack of insurance' excuse.

I couldn't help but contrast all this to our life in a UK south coast town where we lived before moving to Spain. It was quite a 'nice part of town', but vandalism, graffiti, drugs and drunken behaviour were rife – particularly amongst young people in their mid to late teens. Of course, the 'blue rinse' brigade thought this shocking, commenting, "It's not a bit like the old days." It was not until after a local election that newly appointed local councillors to the Town Hall began to change provision for young people – often for the better. Magically, additional funds had been discovered in some recently discovered pot or other, and I recalled receiving a questionnaire asking what local people would like to see improved in the area – one of the choices given was improved playground facilities for children, and football and netball facilities for teenagers. Given the high degree of vandalism that the area was experiencing, it was hardly surprising that improved facilities for the young won the day. The youngsters in the area were asked what they would like to see done, and there was much discussion and changing of plans. I am sure some architect somewhere made a small fortune in fees from the planning and changes of plans that occurred during the three-year 'discussion period'.

Eventually contractors moved in, the existing hard tarmac area was dug up and new coloured tarmac was put in its place. Smart new large 'playground equipment' complete with soft landing areas were installed, new fencing appeared and, best of all, floodlights were installed over the football and net ball areas. This was going to keep local youngsters amused and entertained for many years and would, hopefully, encourage them to move away from their televisions and computer games. The first weekend it was opened was a huge success. A representative of the Town Hall appeared to give it a formal opening, ribbons were cut and speeches were made outlining the high priority and commitment that the council gave 'to the young people in the area'. There was much self-congratulation, and the local evening newspaper gave it a splendid write up the following day. The kids loved it and every evening and weekend the playground was full of happy, shouting and cheering children – if the weather was fine, that is. No longer were children to be seen playing on busy roads, the cases of vandalism and graffiti dropped and even the local police described the scheme as "an outstanding success."

Winter came and suddenly the playground was locked at five o'clock in the afternoon. "It is too dark to use," they said, despite the fact that floodlighting had been installed. Suddenly, the playground was closed on Sundays as well, "It is too cold to use now," they said. In my experience as a teacher, children do not really feel the cold – assuming they are well wrapped up; it is only heavy rain that is likely to put them off from playing outside. Spring came and then summer. The days grew longer and the clocks moved forward. The playground remained locked at five o'clock, the floodlights were never switched on again and the entire playground remained locked on Sundays. "It is too expensive to maintain," they said.

I contrast this with the children who played happily in this Gran Canarian children's playground, with informal adult presence at well past midnight. The playground was floodlit and eventually the group diminished as they decided to 'call it a day'. A goal has been scored, and there was much cheering. Dogs started barking and an adult shouted angrily from an upstairs window in a nearby apartment block for the children to be quiet. The game resumed with gusto. If I were a child again, I know where I would rather grow up!

Letter 23
'Jobsworth' in the Canaries

Many 'expats' will no doubt be familiar with the 'Builders' Electricity' problem that I have already written about, and will possibly empathise with the helplessness, frustration and anger that this particular hurdle causes those of us who are trying to lead a 'normal' life in our new adopted country. Over the last few years, I have learned one valuable lesson. Never, never again will I move into a property until we have the cedula (certificate of habitation) from the Town Hall, and a properly installed mains water and electricity supply. My sanity just would not cope with going through this process yet again.

This was the day when we were finally going to be connected to our own mains electricity and water supply. Many documents had been handed in, forms completed and papers 'bonked'. Anna, the self-appointed president of our community of owners warned everyone to be in their apartments at eight o'clock that morning to allow the electricity company to have access to the individual meters. Woe betide anyone who had not received Anna's message or maybe were away on holiday. During the previous week, whenever we met one of our neighbours on the stairs, we were greeted with beaming smiles and comments such as, "We will have lights next Wednesday," and, "Our problems are nearly over." I had reported upon enough building horror stories for one of the Costa Blanca newspapers, and had learned not to take anything for granted when it came to building, electricity, water and telephone issues.

179

Nothing is ever quite what it seems, and Alice was not the only one to visit Wonderland!

The morning was, as usual, bright, warm and sunny. Long gone were the days when the first topic of conversation each morning was invariably, "What's the weather like today?" No, apart from a few days in February when the rainfall can be particularly heavy, and in some cases alarming, the climate is kind and offers few surprises.

The last two weeks had been particularly horrendous in terms of electricity supply. As more owners of the empty apartments moved into their new properties, the overall electricity supply had deteriorated to such a point that we seriously considered moving into rented property until the problems were resolved. Although we had learned at an early stage not to keep much in the way of supplies in the freezer, because it would surely have to be thrown away as unusable once the power supply failed, we were now entering a new phase where we could be without power for much of the day, and by the time that we returned home, the power would have been off all day, and any dairy produce remaining in the refrigerator was unusable and had to be thrown away. Indeed, there were times when I am sure that the temperature inside the fridge was warmer than in the apartment itself!

We were more fortunate than many of our neighbours. At least, if the power failed we had the resources to drive away from the apartment and get a bar snack in town. Other families were often not as fortunate. Young mothers with babies and young children, some without cars, were trapped inside the apartment for most days with no electricity for hot water, washing and cooking. Often the water supply failed as well, and I can only imagine the distress that this caused the young family in the apartment on floor above our apartment. The father, a handsome Canarian boy in his late teens, often arrived home after a hard day as a mechanic in a local garage, to no cooked meal, a distraught partner and an equally unhappy baby. This was certainly not the way to establish a loving, long term and happy relationship. Nito's partner, Maria, a very pretty dark-haired girl in her teens, was obviously not coping well with either life in the apartment, or the new baby. Sometimes, Maria's parents arrived to give her some much needed company, as well as support. However, after having negotiated five flights of stairs, often laden with bags of groceries, they were not always too anxious to leave the apartment again quite so soon to take poor Maria and the baby out for the afternoon.

At ten-thirty the men from the electricity company arrived. By then, some of our neighbours were already waiting anxiously in the street below. One of the workmen went about his business by going into each apartment and fitting an electricity company seal to each meter. The more important of the two, whom I have since renamed 'Jobsworth', strode into our huge underground communal garage, walked to where our miserable temporary supply entered the property, looked very serious, puffed himself up to his maximum height and made that sharp sucking intake of air noise that I dread. It always meant trouble. This was accompanied by a babble of Spanish directed towards the community president. From the conversation, I gleaned that 'Jobsworth', in his wisdom, had decided that the electricity could not be connected because the garage was dusty and that one of the walls needed painting in order to fulfil the conditions for the connection. What this had to do with installing an electricity supply, I could not find out. Indeed, the floors were dusty, because the electric garage doors were always open because we had no electricity…

There was then a pause as 'Jobsworth' fetched a large pair of cable cutters from the back of his van, walked over to the temporary supply cable and cut the precious cable neatly in half. With a shrug of the shoulders and a glare at the assembled, open-mouthed residents, 'Jobsworth' got into his van with his well-behaved and very quiet colleague and drove off. Everyone appeared to be stunned at what they had just witnessed and, for once, silence fell upon the gathering of neighbours. This in itself was unusual. The community president, a German lady, who was not easily thwarted by such people turned a ghostly shade of white which, after a few seconds, became a nasty shade of pink – I thought she was about to explode. She leapt into her car and chased 'Jobsworth' down the road in her ageing Seat car at breathtaking speed. For a brief second, I actually began to feel sorry for 'Jobsworth' – but that feeling quickly disappeared. Realising that I could do no more I headed, and not for the first time, for the brandy bottle.

Eventually we did obtain connection to mains electricity. Lights blazed in each window of the apartment block, and the heady mix of cooking smells permeated from the apartments below. We could at last cook our own meals, wash our clothes and leave the refrigerator on, being quietly confident that the milk would still be cold when we opened the door later in the day. We met Maria, Nito and the baby heading downstairs and it was a delight to see their happy, smiling faces. Nito beamed as he announced proudly, "We are all going to the bar to celebrate! This is a wonderful day for all of us!"

It had certainly been an unusual day, and one that had stirred the full range of human emotions. We had experienced uncertainty, anger, disappointment, joy and elation, and it had been exhausting. How we finally achieved such a positive result, I have yet to discover. All I can say is that when I saw Anna, our self-appointed community president, earlier that evening, she looked extremely pleased with herself, rubbing her hands and said in a very determined way, "Now for the water company!" I couldn't help wondering what sort of day 'Jobsworth' had experienced. I would love to have been a 'fly on the wall' during that final encounter!

The encounter with 'Jobsworth' did Anna no harm at all. Suddenly, within our community, she became a kind of saint – to be respected, listened to and, in some cases, revered. Anna was now the person whom everyone would turn to if they had a problem, dispute with a thoughtless neighbour, or just did not understand the letter that arrived from the Town Hall. Indeed, David and I occasionally asked Anna for advice and intervention, when all other avenues had failed. Anna was the kind of woman who gave the appearance of being a woman of blunt, ruthless determination with little consideration for the feelings of others, but beneath this challenging exterior, was a well-meaning person with a heart of gold. It was clear from the number of stray dogs and an assortment of other small animals and birds that she gave a home to, that there was a caring and considerate side to this complex character.

Anna was pleasant with all the residents as long as we obeyed the rules. These were clearly displayed upon the notice board in the entrance hall. This was basically a statement in Spanish and German, that Anna was a busy woman, had a full time job and had little time to spare to deal with the many problems of the other members of the community. However, she would see residents in the hallway outside her apartment, but only between the hours of seven and eight on Monday, Wednesday and Friday evenings. As long as we obeyed the rules, Anna was more than helpful.

Two weeks later, another notice appeared on the notice board in the entrance hall. It was a notice convening a meeting of owners the following week. The meeting was to be held in the dusty, noisy and dark bowels beneath the apartment block – the garage. I am not sure whether the meeting had been convened by the Town Hall or by Anna, but we were all instructed to attend.

It was a meeting that I shall never forget. At nine o'clock on Friday evening a few residents had gathered in the garage. Some had brought with them picnic chairs and stools. David and

I joined the small gathering, but there was no sign of Anna or indeed anyone from the Town Hall. By nine-thirty more of our neighbours began to appear – mothers, fathers, young children and babies. Just before ten o'clock, Anna arrived accompanied by an anxious-looking man from the Town Hall. By now the gathering was large and I would guess that most of the apartments were represented by at least one person, and in many cases, whole families. We were slowly getting used to the fact that when Canarians make an appointment time, it is only an approximation. In reality, it is wiser to add a further thirty minutes to the appointment time although, even by Canarian standards, nearly one hour late would be considered as surprising by even the most flexible minded people.

The worried young man from the Town Hall made a feeble attempt to open the meeting. Sadly, he lacked presence and his light voice was drowned by the loud babble from the assembled gathering. Anna, looked increasingly angry and impatient as her colleague tried to establish some kind of order. Eventually, Anna could contain herself no more, and I once again saw the dangerous shade of pink appearing over her round face – exactly the same shade as when she had leapt into her car and chased after 'Jobsworth' a few weeks earlier.

Anna's voice boomed above the babble of sound, and silence fell upon the assembled gathering. The anxious young man began his speech very quietly and after a few moments, Anna instructed him to speak louder. He was difficult to hear and understand, but we could just make out that he was telling us that the meeting had been convened to legally establish a community for the property. We would need to elect officers, as well as making arrangements for insurance and establishing a community fund to pay for repairs and the essential community work such as cleaning the hallways and stairs. It was all very complicated, and much of it went over our heads.

The meeting went on for nearly three hours, and it was just past one o'clock the following morning when we all staggered back to our beds. I promised myself then that I would use any excuse not to attend another marathon meeting, such as the one that we had just endured. I came from a culture in the education services when it was promoted in management courses that any meeting lasting longer than one hour would not be effective, and should be avoided at all costs. I wondered what the management course theorists would have said to this travesty of modern management theory and practice?

Anna was duly elected as the first president of our new community. Her appointment had been unopposed, although there was a potentially difficult moment when it appeared that there could be a challenger within our ranks. There was complete silence as awkwardness fell amongst the community members. One disdainful glare from Anna, and all doubts were swept aside. The potential usurper had backed down, and was now trying to lose himself in the crowd.

Letter 24
So You Think You Have Sold Your House?

I have never known a property sale or purchase to go smoothly. I reflected upon this thought as we flew from Gran Canaria back to the Costa Blanca to complete the sale of our villa. Having an empty property on the market for several months had been a great worry, and although we had kind neighbours keeping a general eye on it, we knew only too well how quickly fabric deteriorates and the ongoing need for maintenance, particularly in the garden. We kept our fingers crossed that the dreaded 'red rain' had kept away and that our white walls, blue and white tiles as well as the sparkling saltwater pool were not covered in a layer of unpleasant red sand and dust from the Sahara that usually follows a heavy rain. It was always an occurrence that provoked much activity, as well as a fair amount of cursing from our 'expat' neighbours whenever this happened. A property covered in red dust was not really going to attract a prospective purchaser.

Sales of properties in the Costa Blanca were already slowing down. From the heady boom days of the eighties and nineties when Spain benefited greatly from the explosion of new building on the Costas, sales of both new and second-hand properties were reducing. Maybe the number of British and other Europeans wishing to settle in Spain had reached saturation point but, as a local reporter, I was also well aware of a number of issues that were of concern to many residents. Many long-term residents made the point to me that the climate in Spain was no longer what it was twenty years earlier. The endless sunshine was the main reason that so many British, Irish and Germans had relocated to Spain, and this, together with a good exchange rate that meant that those 'expats' living on a pension would get far more for their money than they would at home. Spain's loss of the peseta in favour of the newly established euro had meant a less favourable exchange rate and prices were certainly increasing. However, there was another problem that was troubling many 'expats' both in the Costa del Sol and the Costa Blanca and that was the rapid increase in crime.

As a reporter, I was invariably called to report upon a wide variety of criminal activities. However, far from being often careless examples of petty theft and opportunism, we were now entering a new era where newly organised criminal gangs, mostly from Eastern Europe, were taking crime to new and dangerous levels. I regularly heard distressing examples of how thieves would enter the homes of unsuspecting 'expats' with an intention to rob. Sometimes these crimes ended violently with victims being hospitalised or worse. A new trend was for criminals to chloroform their victims in their beds before clearing the property of all possessions that were saleable. I often wondered if the British 'expats' had finally put 'two and two' together when enjoying the boom in Sunday markets and 'car boot sales' in the area. It was quite clear to many observers as to where all the bargain household items were coming from. As in all cases of muggings and robbery, it destroyed the lives and dreams of their victims, and word was getting back to Britain that maybe a new life in the sun also had its disadvantages.

Then there was the beginning of 'reality television' programmes. Apart from well-produced programmes such as *A Home in the Sun* and similar television reality programmes that portrayed a mostly positive image of living in the sun and helped British people to finally realise that the world did not end at

Dover, we now had a new generation of freelance producers working for television companies producing 'one offs' for any network that would buy the programme. These companies were often keen to take advantage of the shock factor and negativity that, in their opinion, always produced the most interesting news items. These programmes focused upon what had gone wrong for many 'expats' and their exaggerated account of 'Builders from Hell' programmes had not helped Spain's already 'tottering' housing market.

The business of opening an estate agency had boomed, but was now beginning to take stock of itself. Now far from those heady days when Doris and Bert from Wigan could open a reasonably profitable bar in the Costas, we had moved to a situation where any Tom, Dick or Sally could become an estate agent. An empty shop space, desk and a telephone were basically all that was needed to open a new estate agency. Some of these new estate agencies were good, and served their clients well. However, many were mediocre at best and out to earn a fast euro, whilst a few were merely fronts for criminal activity and should have been closed down immediately they opened for business.

We had finally selected what we thought to be one of the most professional and well-established agents in the Costa Blanca. They had been established for many years, indeed they were one of the first in the area, the original directors were still running the business and it appeared to be professionally managed. We were not too keen on the fact that they provided their own 'in-house lawyer' for the entire transaction, but they assured us that as it was 'only a sale and not a purchase' this was the norm, and was the most cost effective and efficient way of dealing with our sale. Dealing with an outside lawyer "would delay the process" and, "We didn't want that, did we?" Yes, I recall the conversation well. It was all very convincing, but was one of our first major mistakes.

We had cash purchasers waiting, they had sold their own property and were keen to buy ours, and we were not buying a property at the same time. The 'all inclusive package' that the agents offered us came complete with a lawyer whom we had never met and knew very little about. We also became concerned that both lawyer and agents appeared to have overlooked the fact that we had a mortgage on the property and when I called the bank two days before the proposed completion meeting with the Notary, the bank was unaware of the proposed sale. The lawyer had not even been in contact with them to obtain final figures and to ensure that the bank would be represented at the meeting. The bank warned me that unless they were contacted at least two days before the meeting they might not be able to attend at such short notice. The agents assured me that this usually happened at short notice and that there would be 'no problem'. Yes, overall it seemed to be going well enough. We had met the purchasers, a likeable couple, and we felt that our villa was going to be in good hands. It was going to be a good day.

Even the four-hour wait in the Notary's office didn't seem too bad. It was even suggested that we all went for a drink in the bar next door while we waited. However, it did seem an excessive delay when compared with the ten-minute wait in the office of the Notary in Gran Canaria when we were purchasing our apartment, but these things happen at the height of the season in the Costa Blanca. When our turn came, we were surprised that our bank was not present to cancel the mortgage, but they had already warned us of the likely problem given that they had received insufficient advance notice. Apparently, it was less than twenty-four hours since the lawyer had first contacted them. The meeting was initially soured with angry words from the lawyer, who was acting for both ourselves and the purchasers, when the purchaser presented a banker's draft that would need to be countersigned. This appeared to be resolved to everyone's satisfaction with the lawyer agreeing to fund the extra bank charges himself in the meantime. Perhaps warning bells should have rung at that point in the meeting. Papers were duly exchanged, everyone signed and documents were 'bonked' with rubber stamps. The agents were given their commission cheque, we were given a banker's draft for the balance of funds due and the lawyer told us that the bank would be getting a banker's draft the following day to clear the mortgage. The Notary pointed out that the 'escritura' or house title deeds had now been cancelled, there were smiles of relief and we all shook hands. The deal had been done, or had it?

Several weeks later I checked our 'on line' banking account and was concerned to see that the mortgage account was still open and showing the same figure outstanding as it had the last time that I had checked. I gave it a few more days and checked again – only to find that a further mortgage payment had been debited from our current account. I called the bank and they told me that the mortgage was still outstanding as they had not received any money from the lawyer to clear the mortgage. Panic set in – had we been the victims of yet another Costa Blanca 'scam'? A phone call revealed that the lawyer concerned had told the bank that there would be a three week delay as the purchasers had give him 'an international cheque' which would take three weeks to clear. This was untrue, as we had both seen the banker's draft, which was drawn on a local Spanish bank. It was also very clear to us that our money was sitting in the lawyer's client's account earning him interest! Calls to the lawyer and the agent proved unhelpful – the lawyer was too busy to speak to me as he was 'with the Notary all day' and the agents did little more than to tell me how awful my bank was and how they had had problems with them in the past. In the bank's defence, I didn't think they were acting unreasonably as the mortgage had not been repaid!

I faxed a letter to the Costa Blanca lawyer, which was sharp, and to the point, pointing out the series of events and including the promise to tell everyone I could think of, including our own lawyer in Gran Canaria. I threatened to expose everyone involved, including the Notary, in the press, and this threat proved to be highly effective. Within thirty minutes, I received a call from the lawyer stating that he had just been into our bank and given them a cheque to clear the mortgage. I pointed out that his three-week delay in repayment had meant that we had to pay further interest charges on the mortgage account. I was duly accused of 'penny pinching'. Calls to my bank the following day revealed that, yes, they had indeed received a cheque, but it would have to clear before it could be credited to my mortgage account. Two days later they would 'sign off' the mortgage with the Notary and close the account. All this was around one month after we thought it had all been completed. Meanwhile, the new 'purchasers' were living in a property that they had paid for, but that was still owned by our bank and registered in our names. The implications of this arrangement were very worrying.

I learned several lessons from this unpleasant experience. Firstly, when selling, I would never go for an 'all inclusive deal' with an estate agent again, but would rely upon the lawyer of my own choosing to advise and act for me and, more importantly, one who is independent of the purchaser. I should also have asked far more questions, such as whether the bank had been informed of the meeting with the Notary. If there is a mortgage, it is essential that the bank is contacted well before the meeting to find out if they will be represented, and if not what the terms for the closure of a mortgage would be; for example, would the proceeds be held by the lawyer or paid directly to the bank? Finally, it is important to ensure the proceeds from any sale of property are in a form that can be utilised at once. Cash is always a risky business, but will bankers' drafts lead to further delays and expense? I also 'ran this problem past' another lawyer and he told me that problems such as this do happen from time to time and, whilst not common practice, if the bank cannot attend on the correct day then the cheque and deeds are left with the Notary for the bank to collect and ratify the transaction the 'day after'. Sadly, this did not happen in our case.

Like so many buyers and sellers, I fail to understand why buying and selling of property, both in the UK and Spain, should be such a difficult process. It is a major financial transaction, but one that should be a happy occasion for all involved. Purchasing and selling properties in another country with associated language and cultural differences, can also be risky unless given high quality advice and support. This experience left me wondering about the role of the Notary in the transaction that I have described. Surely there is more to his role than merely 'bonking' with a rubber stamp? Was he aware of what was going on and would he have been able to indemnify me if things had gone badly wrong? Somehow I doubt it would be quite as simple as that. As for the lawyer concerned, well I am still waiting for him to refund my additional interest charges. Indeed, a letter of apology would be welcome but, then again, 'pigs might fly'!

Ayagaures

Fataga

Firgas

Las Canteras

Las Palmas

Maspalomas Dunes

Puerto Mogan

San Nicolas

Barrie in Fuerteventura

Tejeda

Letter 25
Watching the World Go By

One of the many things that I love about living in Gran Canaria is appreciating the new lease of life that the island seems to give many of its elderly residents. You have only to wander into town and village squares throughout the island, as well as outside the many bars and meeting places, to find groups of, mainly elderly gentleman, enjoying the late afternoon and evening sunshine whilst maybe playing a game of cards or, more usually, dominoes. I do often wonder where the women are, as they are rarely to be seen during these tranquil few hours. The Canary Islands are often seen by the Spanish as a backwater of Peninsular Spain. Certainly the islands are slower to 'progress' and to integrate within modern Europe than other provinces within this large country. Incidentally, I always use the term 'Peninsular Spain' when referring to what others refer to as the 'mainland', because I learned very early on that referring to the 'mainland' tends to make loyal Canarians wince. Many do not see Spain as 'the main land' in any sense of the word; their world revolves around the seven small islands just off the coast of Africa, and Madrid is a very long way away indeed. This slowness and, in some cases, refusal to adapt to the demands of the modern world can be both frustrating, yet charming at the same time. The islanders' values such as their attitude to family life, to children and towards the older members of their families is heart-warming, and I hope will continue for many generations to come. I had initially thought that most islanders, and certainly the younger and middle-aged members of the community, would visit Peninsular Spain on a regular basis. Indeed, residents of the Canary Islands are entitled to a significant discount off the ticket price when flying to Madrid or Barcelona. However, many Canarians have never visited Peninsular Spain in their lifetimes, and have no intention of doing so. Many regularly visit the nearby sister islands of Lanzarote and Fuerteventura, maybe for a sporting event or in connection with their work or for a short holiday, but a visit to the capital city of Madrid seems to be regarded as neither necessary nor desirable. One young man in his late twenties seemed to express the general opinion when I asked him: "Why should we? We have everything we need here," was the response. This 'insular' attitude is possibly to be expected of an island community. Indeed, I recall similar attitudes when talking to residents of the Scilly Islands, off the west coast of Cornwall, or of some of the more remote islands off the west coast of Scotland.

Gran Canaria's main city, Las Palmas, is the seventh largest city in Spain and the island's airport is the country's third largest airport. As a result, communication with Peninsular Spain is very good and, one would think, would break down these long established insular attitudes. Relationships with the other six islands that together make up the Canary Islands are fascinating, and you have only to scratch gently below the surface to discover distrust and rivalries that stem from disagreements and wars over many centuries. Although the Canary Islands benefit greatly from being an autonomous province within Spain, and there are a number of differences in laws and taxation affecting these islands, the suggestion that the seven islands work closely together is a misrepresentation. It is true that Gran Canaria, Lanzarote and Fuerteventura do work closely together. The inhabitants of the smaller islands guard their uniqueness fiercely, but they do take advantage of shared facilities such as, for example, Gran Canaria's high quality hospital service when the need arises. However, relationships with Tenerife and its sister islands are another issue, and most Gran Canarian folk will pretend that Tenerife does not even exist. Old rivalries and distrust are hard to leave behind and certainly these views always come to a head during sporting activities such as Canarian wrestling. However, mutual distrust is much deeper than this, and appears to be embedded within the very soul of most true Canarians. During occasional holidays in Tenerife, I have heard disparaging comments about Gran Canaria and its people, in just the same way as I hear negative comments about Tenerife and its people whilst living in Gran Canaria. Tenerife has never been happy that Las Palmas was made the capital of the Canary Islands and so a subsequent, seemingly nonsensical agreement was put in place that gives the main town of Tenerife, Santa Cruz, equal status despite being tiny in comparison. Similar arguments emerge from time to time concerning the university in Gran Canaria, funding and political representation, such as which politician from which island should hold the prestigious position of President of the Canary Islands.

The islanders' attitudes towards family life are very strong and loyalty towards all members of the family, young or old, is an integral part of what is to be Canarian. They will adapt parts of their home to create additional space for their parents and grandparents, aunts and uncles to live in. Many a beautiful sun terrace has been ruined with the addition of concrete blocks and roofed over in a badly 'bodged' attempt, despite planning and building requirements, to provide accommodation for older members of the family. We often looked with amazement at the number of people who came and went from the small house next door to our apartment. We believed that they were all members of the same extended family all living under one roof. What Christmas and New Year celebrations they must have shared together! We often heard angry shouts and the banging of doors as well – all to be expected when so many people live in such close proximity to each other. We know from contacts in the south of the island who were working in the holiday industry that Spanish hotel management were always very wary whenever their countrymen and women booked hotel rooms and apartments for a few nights' holiday. It was not unusual for cleaners in these holiday hotels to report that a family of ten people or more was staying in a hotel room intended for only two people! Floor space would be littered with sleeping bags and blankets, and even the sun balcony and bathrooms could be utilised during these family occasions. Maybe it is carrying family life just a little too far! The concept of residential homes and care homes for the elderly is far less understood in Spain than in many other European countries, and is seen by most Canarians as avoiding one's duty and responsibility towards family members. As a result of these long-standing and traditional attitudes, there are very few facilities for those old people who are truly in need of care. Unlike the position in the UK, there are few care homes available and religious communities usually run those that do exist. I often think that there is a real business opportunity in the islands as well as in Peninsular Spain to provide such facilities for the ever-growing number of elderly 'expats' from many countries, who do not have families to care for them, and will certainly need this form of care in the future.

Most evenings when I gave our two dogs, Barney and Bella, their after-dinner walk, I passed a group of three elderly gentlemen sitting together on a bench chatting and watching the world go by. These elderly men must have been in their mid eighties – brown, weather beaten faces enjoying the last of the day's sunshine. The eldest, a rather distinguished looking gentlemen, sporting a grey moustache, looked much like an elderly version of Captain Mainwaring of the television series, *Dad's Army* and yet also reminded me so much of my own father. He was joined by a slightly younger man who had great trouble walking, and usually wore a pair of carpet slippers. This trio was completed with a man who rarely said anything, but nodded and smiled – his face was heavily disfigured, and he may well have been involved in a road accident of some kind. Barney, our Welsh Pembroke corgi, not often known for speed, usually bolted up to Captain Mainwaring who gave him a reassuring pat on the head. A bond of mutual respect and affection had developed between the pair over the previous few months. Barney had created huge amusement in Gran Canaria, and was clearly quite a talking point locally with both young and old. It was obvious that the Canarians had never seen any dog breed quite like him before and, much to Barney's great embarrassment, his presence was often greeted with roars of unrestrained laughter. His short legs, stocky long body and stumpy tail appeared to have no equivalent in Spain. Bella, our beautiful 'fruit bat', was greatly put out by all the attention shown towards her big brother, and was clearly regarded as 'just an ordinary Spanish puppy', and was mostly ignored. That was until she lost self-control. Bella had a very short fuse and tolerance was not her strong point – but that is another story. I met the elderly gentlemen during most of our evening walks. We exchanged 'Buenos tardes' and then Captain Mainwaring would make exactly the same comment, to which the other gentlemen would guffaw with laughter. It was usually along the lines of, "You have a police dog with his legs and tail cut off". Barney seemed to appreciate the joke and we walked on. Yes, it may have seemed like a tedious meeting and a pointless conversation, but it was anchor points like this, meeting the same people and a friendly comment that was helping us to feel at home, and accepted as part of the local community. It also helped me to reflect on where in the UK could a group of elderly gentlemen sit out in the evening sun for much of the year, chatting and watching the world go by. If I reach their ages, I know where I would rather be.

Letter 26
Two Fat Ladies and a Taxi

One of the busiest tourist resorts in Gran Canaria is Puerto Rico. Once upon a time it was a charming fishing village, blessed with clear blue water and endless sunshine, and home to just a few villagers. The harbour area is still a delight to wander through during the early evening when the hustle and bustle of day trippers has died down, and the mass of tourists are safely ensconced in their hotels and apartments for the early part of the evening. However, the rapid and mostly unplanned development of the tourist industry in the south of the island led to a mass of ugly hotels, self-catering apartments and commercial centres being built over the last twenty-five years or so. As a result, the town now attracts the type of tourist who is content to stay in the resort for much of the holiday and soak up the sun, whilst indulging in endless 'British style' steaks and fish and chips, ice creams and pints of lager. Indeed, 'three for the price of one' is a speciality in the resort.

I recall sitting in a bar in the town waiting to meet someone who had a news story that might have been of interest for the newspaper. There were very few people in the bar and I couldn't help overhearing a loud conversation between a rather dour, elderly lady with a broad Scottish accent and her friend who, I thought, must have originated from Newcastle. The pair had ordered two large gin and tonics and the friendly English-speaking waiter placed the two drinks in front of them, and started a cheery conversation whilst he was waiting to be paid.

"So I hope you two ladies are having a great time in Gran Canaria," he began pleasantly.

The Scottish lady sighed as she handed over a ten euro note. "Well, we're not. We have been here for three days and there's just nothing to do here. Once you've seen the harbour, that's about it."

"Oh, I'm sorry to hear that," replied the now less than cheery waiter, leaving the change on the table, clearly not expecting a tip from this pair of miseries. He walked away with a shrug, not bothering to engage in further conversation.

We had been visiting the island for the last twelve years or so and had always loved it. Indeed, it was after our very first visit when I was reluctantly clinging to the aircraft steps as we climbed on board the plane for the return flight home that I made up my mind that, one day, we would live in Gran Canaria. As a result, I am now, unofficially, one of the island's keenest ambassadors, putting many of the official tourist departments to shame as I confidently expound the virtues of this seemingly insignificant piece of land just off the west coast of Africa. I was bursting to talk to, and change the minds of, these reluctant tourists and finally could contain myself no longer.

"Hello, I'm Barrie," I began. "I couldn't help overhearing your conversation with the waiter. I live here, so if there is anything that you want to know about the island, I would be pleased to help you, if I can."

The Newcastle lady put down her glass, and smiled.

"Now, that's very kind of you, young man. I'm Emily, and this is my friend, Maggie."

I stood and shook hands with both ladies, and Maggie beckoned to the empty chair in front of her.

"Do join us. As long as we don't have to buy you a drink," Maggie added without even the glimmer of a smile. "We're pensioners and we don't have a lot of cash to spare. You're not a gigolo, are you?"

I laughed. "No, you can rest assured that, even though I may be many things, you can be certain that I am not a gigolo."

"That's all right then. There are some strange people around here. All they do is eat fish and chips and drink lager. Where's the bingo?"

This comment rather shook me. I really didn't know. Did anyone play bingo in Gran Canaria? If they did, I certainly hadn't seen them. Now, dominoes, well, that is a very different matter.

"I hope you're joking," I replied. "Surely you haven't come all this way to play bingo? You can do that at home, when it's too cold to go outside."

"That's as may be," snapped Maggie. "You tell me this, young man? What else is there to do on this barren island apart from frying in the sun? It's not a bit like Florida, is it? We love Florida."

"Have you been into the mountains yet? Have you seen the forests, the waterfalls and the pretty Canarian villages, with all the white painted houses?"

"No car," interjected Emily. "We don't drive. We like walking everywhere."

"Well then, why not take a bus? You can either go on the expensive coach tours that your tour company will offer you, or you can do it much cheaper if you use the excellent local bus service. They run nearly all day and night. Just pick up a timetable and map from the tourist information office."

"I don't ride on buses," Maggie replied in clipped tones, "I get sick on buses. Anyway, I'm told that over here passengers have to ride with chickens and other animals going to market. I'm not travelling in any cattle truck."

"Rubbish," I responded, feeling a little irritated at the negativity that I was hearing. "They are as modern, clean and efficient as any bus service in the UK. If you've no car and cannot ride on a bus, there is not much else to suggest other than a bicycle."

"Don't be ridiculous, young man. How can we do that at our ages?" glared Maggie.

By now I was feeling irritated and frustrated, and wished I had never intervened in the conversation with these two miserable women. As far as I was concerned, with this kind of attitude they deserved a bad holiday. After all, as in most things, you tend to get out of life what you put into it. Tongue in cheek, I had one more suggestion to make.

"Well, if you want a good night out with plenty of laughs and really good fun I can give you another suggestion," I began.

"And what is that?" grimaced Maggie.

"I suggest you get a taxi to the Yumbo Centre in Playa del Ingles. It is the gay Mecca of the island and indeed, Europe. Any taxi will take you there – just ask what it will cost before you go."

"What will we find in this gay place?" asked Emily with sudden curiosity.

By now, I was anxious to get away from the two ladies and head for home. I felt it was time to be a little wicked in order to test their reaction to my comments – for future research purposes, of course! Besides, thanks to this pair, I had had a boring evening so far and it needed lightening.

"Oh there's lots to discover there," I began casually. "It looks like a large multi-storey car park, but inside you have the choice of over forty gay bars, including a few for lesbians, sex shops, dark rooms, cabins, saunas – everything you could possibly need. The place has drag shows to suit every taste and there are drag queens on every corner, so don't get confused if they start chatting you up!"

Emily clearly looked shocked, and Maggie fell silent. I gathered my jacket and made my farewell.

"I do hope you enjoy the rest of your holiday," I concluded.

"Thank you, young man," began Emily, giving me a half-hearted smile. "You have certainly been very entertaining."

"What did you say is the name of that car park place you mentioned? Sounded like the name of an elephant," enquired Maggie.

"Yumbo Centre," I replied, heading for the door and hoping that I would not meet these two negative women ever again.

The following Saturday evening, David and I were sitting on the outside terrace of our favourite bar in the Yumbo Centre, when I spotted the two elderly ladies heading towards the largest of the Yumbo's many drag queen show-bars. They were laughing heartily, and Maggie was even wearing a garland of pink and yellow plastic flowers around her neck. My heart missed a beat as Emily spotted me, and they headed determinedly towards us.

"If they want to sit down with us, make an excuse, drink up and let's leave quickly," I muttered to David, who looked bemused by my sudden anxiety.

"It's Barrie, isn't it?" shrieked Maggie, standing in front of us. "Thank you for telling us about this place. We've been here every night since you told us about it. Thank you so much. We are having such a good time this week. Gay people are just so much fun, aren't they?"

If, or should I say when, the current fashion for stag and hen parties decides to move from Prague and Dublin and head towards the sun, Puerto Rico is surely the town upon where it will all happen. The ingredients are already in place. It is certainly a party town, but I personally don't relish seeing the streets awash with vomit, as I have witnessed in Prague and to a lesser extent, in Dublin. In its defence, I know people who love Puerto Rico and take their holidays in the town every year, whilst others keep well away from the town. With endless 'three for the price of one' offers on lager and a bevy of fish and chips shops to rival those in Clacton, it is remarkably good value.

On another visit to Puerto Rico whilst I was waiting outside a Chinese restaurant to cover a story, I was reminded of an incident that I had reported in the Costa Blanca. It involved a British man who had refused to pay his bill in a Chinese restaurant and then drove his car over the Chinese restaurant owner's foot. The British man demanded a takeaway at a Chinese restaurant that didn't usually produce 'takeaways'. After a long argument, which resulted in some unpleasant shouting, the restaurant finally agreed to the man's request and prepared a meal for him. When the time came to pay the bill, he offered his credit card. However, the restaurant didn't take credit cards and so the man refused to pay and left – with the meal. The Chinese owner chased the man down the street to his car – the British man got into the car, revved the engine and deliberately drove over the Chinese restaurant owner's foot and drove off. Needless to say, the restaurant owner's foot was badly injured and he needed hospital treatment. It was memories of events such as this that made me feel embarrassed to be British at times.

I had decided that the person I was waiting for was not going to turn up and I was about to leave when two rather overweight British 'good time ladies' pounced on me. You know the type – bleach blonde hair, heavy make-up – which totally ignored skin tone – complete with Pat Butcher earrings and shoes that were totally unsuitable for the uneven pavements of Spanish towns. I was well aware of their presence long before they headed in my direction. Both were laden down with carrier bags and tottered towards me bawling, "Taxi, Taxi!" I had this sinking feeling as I had a premonition as to where this was leading.

"Sorry, no, I am not a taxi," I replied. "They are just over there," I said pointing to the taxi rank just across the road.

"We must get home quickly," the even chunkier of the two replied. She seemed desperate and judging from the way she was breathing and the colour of her face, I could not help but to be concerned.

"Where do you live?" I asked hesitantly.

The more articulate of the two pointed. "Over there," and she stabbed a chubby finger in the direction of a nearby urbanisation.

"Well, if it's that urgent you had better come with me and I will drive you home," I replied, thinking that I might soon have a hospital case on my hands.

The chunky one pushed three heavy carrier bags into my hands. As we walked slowly towards my car, the more articulate one of the pair said, "You see, we have just found this lovely British Supermarket. We bought so much frozen food in there. It is great to get real food over here – not the usual Spanish muck. We just have to get it home quickly – to get it in the freezer."

I could not believe my ears. Why was I doing this? I smiled benignly, gritting my teeth. In a rare moment of quick thinking, I stopped suddenly.

"Would you mind waiting a moment? I have forgotten something," I said urgently.

I walked quickly to the nearest bar, ordered a very large brandy and coffee, and spent a very pleasant hour or two musing on the foibles of human nature. I am ashamed to say, I left the two ladies waiting – with no doubt their frozen food melting. They were gone by the time I returned to my car. Justice had been done.

John and Sue, two acquaintances from the Costa Blanca, phoned to tell me about their twentieth wedding anniversary celebration in a local restaurant that had an excellent reputation for its traditional Spanish flamenco cabaret show. John told me that the evening started off well enough, and the food and entertainment were excellent. John and Sue were seated at a table adjacent to two British couples that were seated together. Other than that, it was a good international mix with other British, Germans, French, Norwegian and Spanish couples enjoying a good night out. The group of four British diners already had had too much to drink by the time they arrived in the restaurant. They looked like trouble as soon as they walked through the door. John recounted that as the evening went on, the lager, vodka and wine were flowing and the group became noisier and more aggressive. "The language became fouler and fouler," recalled John.

During the cabaret, not only were the two men laughing and jeering, but also their partners joined in with hissing and booing.

"It was terrible," said John. "The entertainers were superb and trying their very best to ignore these rude people, and just get on with the show."

John told me that one of the men started throwing food around and only just missed one of the performers. He could stand it no more and went to speak to the manager. A few minutes later, the manager and two local police officers arrived and the group were asked to leave – to the rousing applause and cheers from the remaining diners. "I was just so ashamed of my fellow countrymen," recalled John. "We left shortly afterwards – it ruined our evening."

There are a few places on the island where, occasionally, some aspects of the tourist trade reflect those on the Spanish Costas. However, the island's tourism departments are working hard to attract a different type of tourist to the island – as the massive new luxury hotels in Meloneras, with theatres, health spas and casinos, already testify. These palaces of temptation and good living offer everything that the more discerning, and wealthier visitors, require. The downside is that the facilities that these hotels offer are so superb that tourists rarely want to visit other bars and restaurants in the area. The trend towards the 'all inclusive holiday' is growing, and many small bars and traditional Spanish and Canarian restaurants are already feeling the pinch, and a number of fine restaurants are closing down.

As far as entertainment and accommodation is concerned, the island has a lot to offer its visitors. There is something here for everyone – even the Emilys and Maggies of the world!

Letter 27
Roundabouts, Girls and 'The Fat One'

When we moved to Spain, I began to look at roundabouts in a different light. From the usually barren, weed-filled creations in the UK to attractive centrepieces that are used as a display for modern sculpture art in Spain, the differences just couldn't be more stark. Even the adventurous idea to turn ordinary UK roundabouts near busy shopping centres into something rather more attractive with floral displays in many areas, had usually led to the erection of a less than attractive sign bearing the immortal words 'Roundabout sponsored by Throne and Allcock – Plumbers. Established in 1892' and very little else, other than maybe a collection of last season's long deceased wallflowers and pansies.

No, the contrast between roundabouts in the UK and Spain just couldn't be more stark. It did take more than a couple of circuits around a large roundabout near our new home in the Costa Blanca before I was clear as to what its new sculptured art might be. When I drove by, and particularly in the early evening, there would be groups of scantily clad, and usually pretty, young women waving to passing cars. What a strange place to hitch a lift, I thought, and very dangerous too. It was only after watching the antics on this and other roundabouts for a few days that I noticed the common thread. These were not just young people trying to get a lift, not in that sense anyway, but prostitutes advertising their wares to likely clients. Certainly, from what I saw, business was brisk and doing well.

217

The hot summer turned to chilly autumn evenings and winter brought with it temperatures that often fell to a few degrees below zero, yet these scantily clad young women continued to ply their age old profession, regardless of the bitterly cold weather conditions and in the most unlikely of places. It was only after learning more about young women being brought over to Spain from Eastern European countries by local Mafia-run drug gangs for whom these desperate women worked, more or less as slaves, until age or illness finally made them no longer attractive and of no more use, that the enormity of what was happening on these seemingly attractive roundabouts became clear to me.

There were often letters and articles in local papers drawing readers' attention to the plight of some of these girls. The police tried to deal with the problem, and sometimes a patrol car would stop, papers would be shown and words exchanged. Sometimes some of the girls were rounded up and driven away in police cars, only to return to their pitch once again a few days later to continue their business.

In Gran Canaria, this human tragedy does not operate from the roundabouts. Roundabouts are a relatively modern invention on the island and, from what I have seen, neither Spanish nor Canarians are very clear as to how they should be dealt with. The roundabout is second only to the motorway in terms of the frequency and number of road accidents on the island. The problems are mainly caused by motorists approaching the entry to a roundabout at a speed that is far too fast, or when using the roundabout, swerving to the required exit without signalling, or ignoring other traffic using the roundabout at the same time. Indeed, there are also occasions when British holidaymakers go the wrong way around a roundabout, but that is a story for another time.

In the Canary Islands, the roundabout is taken very seriously by Town Halls as a focus of artistic and natural beauty.

Most are well-designed masterpieces, commissioned and funded from locally managed taxes. Cactus and other plants from the locality form areas of great beauty and interest. Some of the modern art on roundabouts in Gran Canaria shows considerable patronage of local artistic talent by Town Halls, and recognises the need to share and celebrate art with local people.

I recall one roundabout in the Costa Blanca being home to a single ancient, and rusty, tractor. Perhaps not the best way to encourage property purchases in the area, but at least someone had made an effort – of sorts. On the road to Murcia there was a sort of interlocking box-like structure on a roundabout that looked as if it about to fall over. I often tried hard to appreciate it and to see the purpose behind the sculpture, but it simply did not connect with me. Now living in the Canary Islands, my only criticism is that maybe, just maybe, some of the more magnificent modern sculpture centrepieces act as a distraction to the careful driver, and may in themselves cause some of the accidents. That is only my theory and not one that I am anxious to promote as I enjoy the displays of modern art so much. As for that British holidaymaker who went the wrong way around a roundabout, well, maybe he was just appreciating the amazing art!

It was just a few days before Christmas, Friday 22 December to be precise, and the roads were empty. I wondered what was going on as I negotiated two cactus filled roundabouts, together with one that proudly boasted an old steam engine made in that most non-Canarian of all towns, Grantham! Sadly, although that particular town is not far from my birthplace in the centre of the cabbage-filled fields of Lincolnshire, the very sight of the name of that town brings back for me, disturbing memories of a much loved or much loathed ex-British Prime Minister, depending upon which way you looked at it. It always seemed odd to me that this particular Canarian town could find

219

nothing better to install as its roundabout centrepiece, other than an exhibit from Lincolnshire.

I actually managed to drive through Vecindario's usually impossibly busy and long Avenida de Canarias – a journey that can sometimes take an hour, in minutes. However, this triumph was not to be a victory to remember. The Post Office and bank were closed, and the coffee shop that I usually visited was unusually quiet. What was going on? Was it another fiesta day that I had missed? Suddenly, the sound of a child singing numbers on the television screen in the café bar gave me the clue that I needed. It was the day of El Gordo – The Fat One, and most Canarians would be firmly glued to their television screens for much of the morning.

Canarians in the café bar were transfixed as children began to announce the winners of the El Gordo Christmas Lottery. This lottery is said to be the world's biggest in terms of pay outs as prizes, totalling over two billion euros, were announced in the televised ceremony. It is a strange event with groups of children singing from a building that was once an orphanage, carrying out the long held tradition of singing the winning ticket numbers. Over my 'carajillo', which is a strong black coffee with a generous addition of brandy, I learned that ticket holders in the town of Almazan, north-central Spain, came top with three hundred and ninety million euros to be shared between them. Lucky ticket holders in six other towns and cities also shared the spoils of that year's 'Big One'. There is a complex system of buying lottery tickets that I do not fully understand, which allows many people to buy stakes in a number. Most Canarians participate in El Gordo, and this event heralds the start of the Christmas festivities on the islands.

As Christmas draws close, the decorations in towns, villages and shopping centres are truly magnificent. A great deal of time and, no doubt, money are spent upon this period of festivity and, as I quickly learned, Canarians like nothing better than a party, particularly if it is somehow linked to religion and involves dressing up! Fortunately in Gran Canaria, unlike the rest of Spain and the UK, Christmas doesn't really start until December 6th, which together with December 8th, are public holidays, one is secular and the other is a religious festival. Any Canarian worth his or her salt knows only too well that when such days thoughtfully occur so close to each other, as long as it is not the weekend when different rules apply, it is only prudent to take the 7th off as well as a 'puente' or 'bridging day'. It is annoying for the shopper, but is fully accepted that this three day fiesta is an ideal time to start getting ready for Christmas.

Unlike the UK, where Christmas seems to start as early as September, Christmas in the Canaries only really starts during the period after the 8th December. Mind you, there is then no holding back as, gloves off, Canarian mothers and fathers can do 'battle' as well as the next nationality in their quest for the best bargain, expensive toys, electric goods and bikes and clothes for their children, families and friends!

Unlike other European countries, Christmas in the Canary Islands, and indeed Spain, appears to be more firmly rooted to the religious theme than the commercial one. It is unusual for Christmas lights to appear before December when most towns and cities will adorn their streets with coloured lights. Other traditions include elaborate Nacimiento (nativity scenes). Every town and most churches will have one on display. Some of them are very impressive and can cover a massive area. Some are animated and illuminated and draw huge crowds.

For most Spanish people, Christmas Eve is very much a family affair. The evening may start at home, but often ends up with a party in a hotel, club or disco with friends and family. Christmas Day is a fiesta day, so all banks and shops are closed, probably in order to recover from the night before! Christmas Day in Spain is one of the quietest of the year. As in many European countries, Canarian children receive gifts on the feast of the Epiphany (6 January), but more and more people are adopting other traditions and exchanging presents on Christmas day.

New Year's Eve is a major event in the Canaries! On New Year's Eve, it is the tradition to wear red underwear, but they have to be bought for you by someone else! Many towns organise street parties with entertainment and firework displays that last all night. There will be music and dancing and the wearing of the usual party outfits. At the stroke of midnight, it is tradition to eat twelve grapes – one on each stroke of the clock to bring good luck for the New Year.

The final main event for the Christmas season is the 6th January or Three Kings' Day (Los Reyes). This is the day that the Three Kings arrived in Bethlehem. This is also the most important day for children as the Three Kings, in many ways, replace Father Christmas for Canarian children. This is the time when the children can finally get to receive and open their presents. Sadly, more often than not it is back to school the following day. Many Canarian mums and dads are now realising the inconvenience of this arrangement as their children have waited all of their Christmas holidays, getting under their feet, waiting for their presents on Three Kings and they then have to return to school the following day! Increasingly, judging from the number of plastic Father Christmases adorning neighbours' rooftops, Canarian logic is shifting in favour of Father Christmas, and giving children their presents on Christmas Day, whilst retaining Three Kings as an important family and religious day. In many ways, this change of tradition is regretful, but is symptomatic of living on an island and sharing and adapting to the richness of a multitude of cultural traditions.

Letter 28
Water, Water, Everywhere

When we moved to Spain, one of our first questions was, "Can we drink the water?" It soon became clear that although, generally speaking, the water is safe to drink, it is not advisable to do so. This is due, as is also the case in the UK, to the high concentration of chemicals in the water that can give rise to stomach upsets. The considered choice was to purchase bottles of water, which were very cheap to buy in supermarkets, and so the endless chore of carrying huge bottles of water to and from the supermarket began. I was never very happy about this, mainly because of suspicions about where the water had actually come from? How was I to know it came from a local spring? Just because it was in a bottle did not mean it was high quality. Indeed a picture of 'Del Boy' from that timeless TV classic *Only Fools and Horses* with Del Trotter bottling and selling tap water from his Peckham flat was never far from my mind. Neither was I happy about the use of all those plastic bottles. Did they really contain a cancer forming substance within them, as some of the articles in the *Daily Facist* would have me believe? In any case, it was not good for the environment or, indeed, our backs as they were heavy.

The answer to this immediate problem seemed to be in an advertisement that we saw in one of the local English language newspapers. True, at the time we saw the advertisement, we did not even have a mains water supply, but we cut out the advertisement for the day when we were eventually connected to the mains system. The gadget was called a 'Water Angel' and it was intended to be plumbed directly into the mains water supply. The water was passed through a series of very clever filters, where it was de-chlorinated and all the nasty chemicals removed. It was chilled and came out of the machine tasting wonderful. It was sparkling clear, chilled drinking water – right from the tap, so to speak! The demonstration was indeed impressive.

I recall one of the few chemistry lessons that had made any impression upon me at school when I was about eleven years old. During one of these much hated lessons, I was shocked to hear a statement the unpleasant, leering science teacher had made after one of my fellow pupils had drunk the glass of water that he had given him. Although I do not recall the details of the chemical analysis involved, I do recall that he had announced, and only after the small boy had drunk every drop in the glass, that the water in the glass had been drunk by persons unknown at least seven times before. I do also remember the small boy turning a nasty shade of green before heading towards the chemistry lab sink to be violently sick. It was indeed a dramatic demonstration for an impressionable schoolboy to witness, and was responsible for my insistence that I would drink only Coca Cola for several weeks after the incident, and led to a distrust of water that continues to live with me today.

The salesman drank several glasses of water without wincing or, more importantly, without collapsing into a heap. We bought one and it turned out to be a great product, and one that we had no hesitation in moving to our new home in Gran Canaria.

We would often read, with some amusement at first, of water shortages in southern England. This always seemed to be particularly ironic as often the UK had suffered incredible rainfalls, beating recent rainfall records, and often resulting in serious flooding. However, each year there were water shortages, hose pipe bans and all of the other miseries associated with a typical British summer.

Now, in Gran Canaria it rains just a few times a year – mainly brief showers, although there are often heavy downpours for two or three days in February. Surely, water is a problem on the island? No, not at all, and the opposite seems to be the case. Even at the height of a very hot summer, during the baking hot days of the 'calima' or hot, sand filled winds from Africa, people are outside washing their cars, watering dusty, dry gardens and tubs of exotic looking plants with no hose-pipe ban in place. Workmen from the Town Halls are busy watering the beautifully tended flower beds and lawns for the tourists in the south of the island, and the seven or so golf courses on the island remain lush and green – not a brown patch of grass in sight. So where does all this water come from?

Admittedly, as we live on an island, we are surrounded by the stuff, albeit salty. In addition, there are plentiful underground reservoirs and mountain springs. The west of the island has more rainy days than the rest of the island (the main reason why this area is sparsely populated) and there are many reservoirs in the mountain areas. In addition, sea-water is desalinated to top up supplies when needed.

One of my favourite biblical stories is the one at the wedding feast when water is turned into wine (let's just hope it was a decent quality Rioja!), but how about turning wind into water? I have also always loved windmills. From the colourful plastic toys that my parents would sometimes buy me on a day trip to Skegness to the impressive structures that have graced the British landscape for so many years. Their graceful form and natural motion have always fascinated me. I grew up in fenland Lincolnshire, an area which shares an amazing similarity with the huge flatland areas and rich soil of Holland. As in Holland, the eye would always fall upon a traditional windmill somewhere on the horizon. In Lincolnshire, these windmills were used for pumping water from land reclaimed from the sea – a constant battle with nature. However, I also know that many people hate the sight of them, as yet another of man's intrusion upon a beautiful landscape. However, now that an era of limited fuel supplies is upon us, harnessing the wind to provide a cheap and sustainable source of fuel to feed our unending desire for electricity seems much more attractive. Surely the answer is to build more, and maybe also out at sea?

Visitors who care to stray away from the beaches and tourist centres of the south of the island and drive for a few minutes to a village called Pozo Izquierdo, near the town of Vecindario in Gran Canaria, will be treated to a physics lesson that they will not easily forget. Not only is it a great place for a good walk with the dogs and some fresh air, but you will be in the centre of a wind farm that not only produces electricity from the wind, but also any excess electricity produced is used to desalinate water from sea water that surrounds this island paradise.

The residents of Gran Canaria have developed a high degree of awareness of the environment and the natural world. I guess that living on an island also tends to raise a natural awareness about the conservation of scarce natural resources. Saving water, one of the island's scarcest resources due to the lack of rain, has led to extensive research in the desalination of sea water and using wind power to operate small desalination plants. The islands are not short of wind power – the Trade Winds, with their moderate speed and direction, are constant throughout the year. This technology and ideas have since been exported to many other parts of the world.

One of the main objections to wind farms has always been that they produce a varying amount of electricity. This variability of supply in the electricity grid means that there must be other power generators, such as gas-fired units, that can come 'on line' at short notice – in order to avoid wide fluctuations of power and your television or washing machine blowing up. Keeping these generators 'at the ready' is an expensive use of resources, and is often the quoted reason for not using wind powered generators.

Now this is the clever part. The desalination of water is an expensive process and requires a lot of electricity. However, scientists have found that the wind generation of electricity and the process of desalination of water can work together successfully for the simple reason that electricity cannot be cheaply stored, but water can. Using surplus electricity from wind farms such as the one in Pozo Izquierdo to desalinate sea water is the ideal solution. When there is a falling amount of surplus electricity, the number of desalination units operating is reduced. The water produced when the wind farms are in full production can then be stored relatively cheaply until required. Clever stuff, eh?

Letter 29
The Day the Sea Turned Red

After nearly a year of living in our apartment we decided that we had had enough of apartment living. Endless problems with the electricity and water supply, a non-functioning lift, as well as trying to produce a fast-growing island newspaper under such conditions, were having a negative effect upon all of us. Barney and Bella seemed happy enough with the cosiness of apartment life, but the endless climbing of four flights of stairs to give each dog their toilet break four times a day proved challenging. Yes, we were becoming fitter by the day, but it certainly did not help our tempers.

We desperately wanted to live in a house with a garden – even a small one, it did not matter. We had left a lovely villa in the Costa Blanca and the apartment was only ever intended to be a short-term measure. We started in earnest to look for a house, preferably near the sea, as well as being good value.

Although we were both quite fond of the south of the island where we had spent many happy holidays, we didn't really want to live there. It was far too close to clients and newspaper contacts that we really wanted to escape from during our time off. Also, although the summer heat of Puerto Mogan and Puerto Rico were delightful when on holiday, neither were places where we would have been happy to live when working. Our new home would have to be within easy reach of both the north and south of the island, relatively near to the airport, as well in an area representing a good mix of nationalities. We certainly didn't want to repeat the experience of living in a British community again, as that was not the original point of moving to Spain.

Eventually, after a long search, we came across some newly-built houses in a small village on the island's eastern coast. The houses were of north European, design and sensibly avoided the traditional flat roof much loved by Canarians, which we disliked. To me, it was important to have an upstairs and downstairs, complete with a cupboard under the stairs and a pitched roof! The property also had an upstairs terrace, a rear terrace as well as a small garden that would be ideal for Barney and Bella. Best of all it was only a thirty-second walk to the sea front, and I imagined many walks along the promenade with our two fluffy friends.

The houses were part of a relatively new development and there were just four left at a price that we could afford. We made a choice – basically based upon the colour of the floor tiles as they were all nearly identical. The developers were helpful and the bank even more so, and within a matter of a few weeks we were ready to sign the contract of sale and move in.

All went surprisingly smoothly until the day of the intended move. Despite using the same removals company that we had used earlier, we decided that we would move personal, valuable and easily breakable items ourselves by car a day or two before the main move by the removals company. Two days before the intended move, we had a phone call in the late afternoon asking if the removals men could come the following morning instead as they had a cancellation. Thinking that it would be better for us because of looming publication deadlines, we readily agreed.

Early the following morning, Barney and Bella were bundled into the car, to avoid confrontation with the removals men, and I drove from the apartment to the new house, leaving David to deal with the removers. It was to be my job to set up the office – the computers, telephone and fax machine in readiness for production of the next edition due a few days later.

As I drove into the village, I noticed that the wind turbines at Pozo Izquierdo had changed direction and then stopped turning. The sky was heavily laden with black clouds over the mountains – it was a bad sign and I knew we were in for a heavy storm.

A few hours later, there was the sound of a large van pulling up outside our new home and the removers were soon, very efficiently unloading the contents of the van into the house. David had followed behind them in his car, and Barney and Bella were safely locked in the upstairs spare room. They were not happy, despite being surrounded by their many toys as well as their beds, and made their views clear with a volley of barking. They knew that something was going on, and wanted to be part of the action.

A few minutes later a second removals van parked outside the house. I was looking forward to this as it was the delivery of all the large items that would not fit into our temporary apartment home, and had been held in store in Las Palmas. It contained familiar items of furniture, David's beautiful Yamaha keyboard, an antique china cabinet – a family heirloom, much loved books and DVDs and CDs, as well as garden furniture and assorted items that we had not seen since leaving the Costa Blanca. We would soon settle into our new home and start to enjoy life again, surrounded by familiar things that we were fond of, yet had not seen for a long time.

The rain started very early the following morning. We were horrified to see the heavy downpour, and although Barney was eventually persuaded to go outdoors to 'do his business', Bella steadfastly refused to budge and bolted off back to her bed – wise girl! Although Barney was totally reliable in the toilet department, Bella was not and we both knew should she need 'to go' she would without hesitation, and she would not suffer in silence. I did not have the heart to boot her outside in the pouring rain.

By eight o'clock many workers were wondering whether they should leave their homes. David left the house in his car as he had an urgent meeting with an advertiser in Playa del Ingles, but returned shortly afterwards. The roads were already awash with water and it clearly was not safe to drive anywhere. He wisely had called it a day.

Torrential rain was pouring down and already finding its way into thousands of homes through ill-fitting doors and windows, as well as flat roofs. Canarian and Spanish homes are just not built for this sort of thing. The lack of guttering on buildings meant that water was shooting straight off roofs and on to patios, paths and roads and quickly causing major flooding. By mid-morning many major roads became impassable. Cars and lorries lay abandoned at the sides of roads. Rocks and small boulders soon became dislodged by the torrent of water and came hurtling onto the roads below. The many barrancos (dry river beds) that led from the mountains to the sea, and which are a highly attractive feature of Gran Canaria under normal circumstances, soon became channels for the heavy torrents of water falling from the mountains. Huge quantities of water soon filled these channels, making its relentless way to the sea, but not before creating untold damage in its wake. Our usually blue sea had turned red from the ugly discharge that poured into it.

Cars and buildings were brushed aside as the torrent of water made its determined path to the shore. Small, simple dwellings and shops at the side of the barrancos soon became awash with water – their contents ruined as they became encased in the sticky, all enveloping mud. All the locals could do was to find a place of safety and watch the swift destruction of their homes and livelihoods. Motorways were closed, lorries overturned and large shops flooded. Villages and towns were cut off from their neighbours and became small islands in their own right. Electricity supplies were lost and many residents gave up the task of bailing out water from their homes, and headed for the relative comfort of the odd bar that was open, until it was safe to return and start the major task of cleaning up. Canarians know well the importance of the bonds of friendship with neighbours at a time of crisis.

The quiet town of Telde took the 'brunt' of the storm with the highest recorded rainfall. Reports of sightings of huge quantities of bright red tomatoes sailing down the road helped to lighten an otherwise depressing scene on television later in the evening. I shall never forget the scene of an elderly woman sitting in her living room with her few treasured possessions and photographs – surrounded by muddy water. The look on her wrinkled, worn face said it all.

We too became preoccupied with our own problems. Each of the five doors in our beautiful new home was letting in rainwater, and large puddles were appearing from beneath our new sofa in the living room, as well as from under the bed in the bedroom. Foolishly, I had left a bag containing cash and cheques collected from advertisers that was due to be banked later that day on the floor at the side of the bed. The contents were so wet and had begun to turn into 'papier mâché' and I had to hang the notes and cheques on the washing line to dry.

During the middle of the afternoon, the sun came out bringing with it a much needed comforting heat that would begin to ease the chaos that had been created. Locals stood in silence on street corners watching the unfolding scene with disbelief. Many said that this was the worst storm in eighty years. Certainly no one that I spoke to could remember worse. The day the sea turned red will not be easily forgotten.

Letter 30
Beware of High Flying Barbecues

It had started off as such a good idea. We had just moved from our apartment to a beautiful new house by the sea. Moving twice in one year was not a good idea financially, but living with two dogs in a fourth floor apartment and without a working lift had proven highly troublesome. At last we had a garden for Barney and Bella, albeit not a large one, and a space to sit outside to enjoy the sun, and to enjoy our regular barbecue, either on our own or to share with friends.

Whenever we mention barbecues to some of our friends and family, we are always met with a wry smile and a comment such as, "Whatever do you want a barbecue for? You are both vegetarians! Whatever are you going to barbecue, carrots?"

"Precisely," was the obvious reply.

All manner of vegetables can be barbecued very successfully on an outdoor barbecue, the smaller items on a skewer, interspersed with maybe onion, tofu, Quorn (a vegetable protein made from mushrooms, if we can get it) and gofio (a Canarian speciality made from maize). All such creations are usually basted with David's very tasty spicy oils and served with a selection of potato croquettes, onion rings and salads, and we have a delicious and healthy barbecue. Indeed, many a carnivorous family member or friend has been put to shame when their initial cynicism has turned to such questions as: "Can I have the recipe for that baste?" and even, "How do you make gofio into such tasty burgers?" Well, maybe one day David will produce a recipe book for healthy vegetarian barbecues, using locally grown produce.

Our new home was designed in such a way that we could see ourselves eating outside for most of the year. The area outside the kitchen door had a large foldaway canopy that would prove to be ideal for covering an outdoor dining area. Outdoor electricity points, lighting and an outside refrigerator were already in place and so all it needed was something to cook on. Indeed, this was going to have to serve as the main food preparation as well as dining area because, in common with all new properties in Spain, the kitchen was basically a shell waiting for kitchen units, sink and appliances to be fitted. All this was on order from Barcelona, and would take around two months to be delivered and fitted. It was going to be a difficult two months.

The builders had thoughtfully provided a fitted barbecue area to the back patio of our new property. All it really needed was a wire tray and charcoal. I have to confess that I am not a great lover of the traditional barbecue. As a cub scout, I could never see the point of rubbing two sticks together when I already had a cigarette lighter in my back pocket, which is why I never became a true boy scout. I guess I had missed the point of the exercise. Over many summers in the UK, I tolerated clouds of black smoke making its way across my neighbour's garden fence as yet another barbecue virgin was set to ruin my weekend in the garden. In Gran Canaria, my issue is with barbecued fish – it really is the most disgusting of odours if you don't happen to like fish – or badly operated barbecues for that matter.

What barbecue virgins don't seem to realise is that charcoal has to get hot, really hot and glowing red before you even attempt to cook food. I have witnessed barbecue virgins trying to get the thing to light with fire lighters, paraffin or worse. I have watched with horror as other barbecue virgins throw hunks of flesh onto barely warmed cinders in a determined effort to get food poisoning. I have seen hedges and fences being set alight by barbecue virgins as well as witnessing the occasional singed eyebrows or loss of body hair. Yes, and it is always the men that take the lead when dealing with barbecues, and never the women! No, I just could not tolerate charcoal. Personally, I would have been more than happy with an all electric barbecue – just as long as it was quick, clean and cooked the food. I was told that this would be a barbecue travesty and an insult to all 'barbequers' worldwide, and that my neighbours would never speak to me again if I did. In the end, we decided to settle for bottled gas.

We searched the island high and low. From Las Palmas to Puerto Rico and from San Nicolas to Arinaga – there were no gas barbecues suitable for the brick built creation on the patio. It was then that I hit upon the idea of checking the Argos catalogue website in the UK. They usually had everything. Perfect, I found a superb gas unit – exactly the right size and priced at only eighty pounds. I was returning to the UK for a brief visit to see my family, so I checked to see that they had the item in stock. I reserved one to collect from a store near the airport. It would easily be accepted as hand luggage on the return flight…

I handed over my credit card to the young woman at the Argos desk and eventually my number appeared on the collections board. Before my eyes, a large cardboard box appeared on the conveyor belt. The young man struggled to lift it and placed in on the counter. I checked the catalogue number on the box – yes, it was my barbecue. I struggled to lift it and carry it to the car. I began to imagine the scenario ahead of me. Certainly this wasn't the stuff of hand luggage. Should I just cut and run and maybe leave it behind in the store? No, I really did want the new barbecue, but why was it so heavy?

My brother had accompanied me on the shopping expedition to Argos and his eyebrows shot up when he saw what I was trying to carry. He rushed across to help me to carry it to his car.

"Are you sure this is really what you want? It's not too late to take it back."

"No, it'll be fine," I replied. "I think hand luggage allowances are quite generous nowadays. Anyway, this is just what we need," I added with supreme confidence, little knowing at the time that these comments would haunt me for a long time to come.

I have always admired those passengers who are able to travel light, look well dressed throughout their holiday and smell relatively fresh at the end of it. I have never been able to achieve this. Try as I may, my wash bag alone is usually the entire luggage allowance allocated by budget airlines.

On the day of my return flight home, I wheeled my trolley to the check in desk and I knew exactly what was going to come.

"Bit overweight are we today, Sir?" commented the grinning, spotty youth on the check in desk.

This was no doubt a well-planned line reserved for his more errant passengers. I was neither amused nor in a mood for a lengthy discussion as to why he had referred to me in the plural. I smiled benignly and muttered something about Christmas presents.

"That will be one hundred and ninety-five pounds to pay, Sir."

No, he didn't really say that, did he? I thought it would be about fifty pounds, not nearly two hundred just to get an eighty pound barbecue to Madrid! Should I leave the wretched thing with the spotty youth and cut my losses? No, I really did want the barbecue. Reluctantly I handed over my credit card.

"Have a good flight," chanted the youth whose endless grinning became a major irritation.

The arrival in Madrid airport was going to be a big problem. First I had to track down the barbecue and ensure that it hadn't been damaged, and then somehow drag it and the rest of the luggage to another check-in desk on the other side of the airport for the flight to Gran Canaria. The dreadful truth dawned. I had paid for the barbecue to be transported to Madrid and not to Gran Canaria. I would have to go through all this expense yet again! Perhaps they wouldn't notice...

The young lady at the airline desk in Madrid Airport couldn't have been more helpful.

"I will have to charge you for your excess baggage," she said with a charming smile. "You are very much overweight. Take this ticket to my colleague over there, pay her and then return here. You will have to take your luggage with you though," she added as an afterthought.

I struggled across to another young woman at another desk, dragging two large suitcases and the barbecue that seemed to be getting heavier by the minute. She looked at the ticket and then my luggage. Fortunately, she spoke very good English.

"I will charge you only a quarter of the cost to help you," she said. "That will be eight hundred euros."

Those words fell heavily on my ears. Eight hundred euros for an eighty pound barbecue? Where was it all going to end? Did I have enough spare funds on my card? I suddenly felt very hot and rather sick.

"Did you say eight hundred euros, but you said you were going to charge me a quarter of the charge?" I protested.

"Did I?" she said. "No, no, that was my bad English – I mean eighty euros."

I handed over my credit card, checked in the rest of the luggage and fled to the nearest bar for a very large brandy.

The new barbecue now takes pride of place on the patio. It fits well and cooks perfectly. Did I mention the reason for the unit being so heavy? It was because the cooking plates and grill were cast iron!

Letter 31
Veggie Burgers and Sausages

When David and I first told our friends and families that we were moving to one of the Canary Islands, it was met with some confusion and concern by some of the older members, and particularly those who had never set foot beyond the Isle of Wight. Moving to Spain was considered acceptable, but a move to one of the seven tiny islands on the globe, in the Atlantic Ocean just off the coast of Africa, did seem 'a move too far' to some. "It's still part of Spain," we protested, but no, it was clear that some thought that we were moving to some kind of 'Robinson Crusoe' tropical island, where there would be no shops and hospitals and only a few palm trees, coconuts and parrots for company.

The island of Gran Canaria itself is compact, looks a little like a dinner plate on the map, with a surface area of just one and a half thousand square kilometres, and is just below the Tropic of Cancer, some sixty miles from the Saharan coast. Much of the inner part of the island is mountainous with a scattering of small and very attractive villages at its core. The north coast has wonderful beaches for surfing and the vibrant, clean blue water of the Atlantic is a temptation to all who visit. It is the north part of the island that is the financial and business hub of the seven islands, with the city of Las Palmas at its heart. We had to be very careful to reassure those that we were leaving behind that we were only a four-hour flight from the UK and, although we were moving to an island off the west coast of Africa, it was still part of Europe. Research had shown that the island offered the full range of services that we had in the Costa Blanca. It was only in later conversations, together with photographic evidence, that doubters began to see that with the main city, Las Palmas, being the seventh largest in Spain, the airport being the third largest in Spain and both Carnival and Gay Pride being the largest in Europe, that maybe we were not going to be that isolated after all.

Indeed, the range of shops and facilitates on the island is excellent. Although Gran Canaria is the third largest of the seven islands, after Tenerife and Fuerteventura – in terms of land mass, it has the most impressive facilities of all the islands. The large commercial port and historic capital city, Las Palmas, boasts several major hospitals that have facilities that are the envy of many European countries. Patients with brain conditions and needing other necessary specialist surgery are often flown to Las Palmas from Spain for treatment. Shopping is excellent, with stores that rival the likes of House of Fraser and John Lewis in the UK. At the last count, we have four Marks & Spencer stores on the island although, sadly, none stock the usual range of excellent quality food, and an Ikea store that is hugely popular with the Scandinavians and Canarians alike. There are few things that we cannot get on the island, but we often comment that the range and variety of shopping and other facilities is often better than that we experienced in mainland Spain. Personally, I always have a craving for those wonderful Linda McCartney vegetarian sausages. Try as we may, we just could not get these on the island although a sympathetic lady from a local church did bring me a packet of them back in her suitcase after her visit to the UK!

We are even blessed, and I say this tongue in cheek, with a number of American food outlets on the island such as Burger King, Kentucky Fried Chicken and McDonalds. Perhaps this is one of the reasons why Canarian children are, in the main, obese? Maybe it is their love of burgers and fries that is their downfall? I remember watching a television interview with the Chief Executive of Burger King. He was an interesting and enthusiastic man who was extolling the virtue of his worldwide chain of eateries, because of their healthy eating menu. He assured the interviewer that whichever Burger King outlet that you happened to visit anywhere in the world, the diner would be presented with vegetarian and healthy eating alternatives. I was not quite so sure about the 'healthy' part, but it was true that I had always enjoyed a 'Spicy Beanburger' or 'Vegetarian Burger' at Burger King in the UK. I would test out the CEO's pronouncement in a branch of Burger King that had just opened in one of the new shopping centres on the island.

My request for 'two vegetarian burgers' was met with blank looks and much babble of Spanish by the two ladies serving at the Burger King counter. I repeated my request, in Spanish, for two 'vegetarian burgers and chips', adding for good measure, "We are vegetarian, no meat or fish please."

The serving lady looked even more concerned.

"How about a bun with some salad?" she enquired helpfully.

I shook my head and added, "That would be good, but with a vegetarian burger please."

"But all our burgers are made with meat."

"I would like one without meat."

"That is not possible, but I can give you a bun with salad in it."

In the end we decided that to save our helpful server more trouble, we would decline her kind offer and eat elsewhere with a mental note to write a letter to the Chief Executive of Burger King at the earliest opportunity. I never did receive a reply.

Indeed, life for vegetarians is not always easy in Spain. It is getting better, but many Spanish think that it is not possible to live without meat or fish and, in any case, tuna is a 'vegetable'. Many a time we have ordered a salad only to find it liberally sprinkled with tuna, or in the worst cases, with ham. For many years whilst on holiday in Spain, a diet of salads and omelettes was the safest option.

When we moved to the Costa Blanca, it was relatively simple to find the necessary beans and pulses in local supermarkets, and occasional treats such as Linda McCartney vegetarian sausages and burgers were reasonably easy to find in the numerous British supermarkets that were opening up along the coast. However, the real problem was our dog, Barney, the Welsh corgi who had travelled with us from Bournemouth, via a three month detour in Bognor Regis and France with David's brother. Barney was, as were all our dogs, vegetarian. As a lifelong vegetarian, I could not see the logic of being vegetarian with animal welfare principles, only to feed a dog pieces of dead animals that were usually unfit for human consumption anyway. It rather defeated the purpose of the exercise, and besides I hated the pervasive smell when those ghastly tins of meat were opened.

Barney always ate broadly the same as us, together with one of the commercial vegetarian dog-foods available in the UK, such as 'Happidog' or 'Wafcol', which he always ate with great relish. His vet always commented that he was, "A little on the plump side," but to me, in his defence, I considered him to be just 'big boned'. When we moved to the Costa Blanca, we ensured that Pickfords Removals also took several large bags of 'Wafcol' and 'Happidog' as part of the load, and fingers and paws were firmly crossed that we would be able to replace them when the need arose. Sadly, supplies ran out faster than we had anticipated, until one fateful day when we realised that at best there was only sufficient vegetarian dog food to last another week.

We tried all the supermarkets, pet shops and British food stores that we could find and, in the end, we had to admit defeat. It was not going to be possible to maintain Barney on his vegetarian diet. In despair, I wrote an article about the problem in the newspaper, and was pleasantly surprised by the response that we had from readers. It seemed that there were a number of people, like ourselves, whose dogs were on a vegetarian diet. Some, like us, were vegetarian for ethical reasons and others because of dietary problems. One helpful reader gave us the name of a sausage-like product that was intended for human consumption and was made from rice and vegetables that would be suitable. It was not expensive and looked a bit like luncheon meat. Others gave us recipes of things that we could make ourselves, whilst a most interesting email came from a man who lived in Skegness, Lincolnshire, and lived quite close to my eldest brother. His name was Martin and he was quite an entrepreneur who ran a small delivery and removals service from Lincolnshire to the Costa Blanca on a regular basis. He would collect and deliver anything and take from one place to the other – at a very reasonable cost. Martin was the answer that we had been looking for.

For about two years, Martin would collect supplies of vegetarian dog food from Skegness and deliver them to us in the Costa Blanca. We were able to give him some publicity in the newspaper, and his business began to grow successfully. I remember that on one occasion, he was able to collect and deliver a grandfather clock to my nephew in the UK, as well as bring the dog food to us. Nothing was ever too much trouble for Martin and his service was just what many British 'expats' in the Costa Blanca were looking for. By now we also had Bella, the latest addition to our family. This stray puppy, who looked very much like a jet black fruit bat, was not used to anything in particular. She had been a street dog and was lucky to find anything to keep her alive. She easily took to the new diet and our problem seemed to have been resolved.

Exactly the same problem reared its ugly head again when we moved to the Canary Islands. We broached Martin with our plan. Surely he could extend his wonderful service to Gran Canaria? To his credit, Martin looked carefully into our proposal reasoning that with a sizeable British 'expat' community it may well be worth his time and trouble. Sadly, this was not to be. Transportation costs, as well as customs issues arising from the Canary Islands being outside the EU for taxation and other issues, would lead to complications and a great deal of paperwork and expense.

Help came from our new neighbours and friends who informed us of a wonderful Canarian food product called 'Gofio'. 'Gofio' is a flour made from maize which, when boiled, would turn into a porridge-like substance. Once allowed to cool and set, this product can be cut into slices. It is a highly nutritious food, very cheap and eaten by Canarians, as both a main course as well as dessert. We heard that many Canarians would traditionally feed their dogs on it as well, and so it was time to try it on Barney and Bella. After some experimentation, and the addition of flavouring, this wonderful food product has now replaced 'Happidog' and 'Wafcol' as Barney and Bella's main diet. They adore it, as do we. We often eat it sliced and fried, baked, barbecued or grilled as burgers and sausages – in much the same way as we would cook tofu and Quorn, but at a much lower price!

Letter 32
The Rep Factor

Surprisingly, given the size of the island, Las Palmas airport is the third largest in Spain. Every day throughout the year and particularly on Mondays and Saturdays, there are endless flights to and from this busy airport. We currently live quite close to the airport and so the comings and goings are usually of great interest to us. The nature of the tourists arriving in Gran Canaria varies according to the time of the year. We have the 'Scandie season' when the 'winter birds' fly in to escape the bitterly cold winters of their homelands. The 'Wrinklies' arrive for a cheap and cheerful break in the sun, often staying for several weeks at a time. Families arrive during the school summer holidays, and gay men and women arrive over most of the year, but particularly in May to enjoy Gay Pride – now the largest gay event in Europe.

This pattern of arrival and departure brings with it much variety, as well as challenges for the island in order to keep the relevant groups well catered for and entertained during their stay on the island. The airport is always busy and this observation is not easily reconciled with the comment that I have heard from bar and restaurant owners in the south of the island over recent years. "Business is not so good. Not as good as last year. We don't know how we will survive the season." Yes, it has been the same cry for several years, yet visitor numbers to the island have increased each year, with plans to build a further runway and expand the airport. Visitors were going somewhere, but not it seemed, to the traditional tourist centres in the south. Visitors were demanding something rather better and were heading to the luxurious new hotels being built in Meloneras. These new hotels boasted excellent restaurants, infinity pools, spas, treatment centres and gymnasia. The 'all inclusive' deals could be remarkably cost effective and discouraged the average punter from leaving the hotel in favour of the cheap and cheerful 'Full English Breakfast' traditional cafés and restaurants in the town. This shift towards a new type of holiday was sad for the likes of Doris and Pete from Mablethorpe, who had sunk their life savings into buying a bar in Spain some twenty years ago, and were now looking forward to a comfortable retirement in the sun. Businesses became very competitive and were being squeezed out by the 'all inclusive' holiday packages. It was also true than many 'British' and 'Irish' bars and restaurants were, in reality, Spanish owned and run. Their overheads were often far lower and they tended to offer far better value and service than the traditionally owned German and British bars and restaurants. My heart always sank when one of our friends from the UK, who had enjoyed a wonderful holiday on the island, announced upon their departure that they wanted to move here. "Maybe to open a bar or something…" In most cases, it was often doomed to failure.

Waiting in the arrivals hall of the airport is always an emotional experience. It is here where we can see loved ones being collected by their families, partners and friends and the joy on their faces is always wonderful to see. The other side of the coin is the sadness of a tearful departure – often for unknown periods of time. It is a place of heady and mixed emotions – where holidays begin with high excitement and anticipation and often end with the sadness of a week of hellish rows with one's partner, or the worry of work and credit card debt to be faced back home. Personally, I liked watching the new arrivals with 'Guess where from?' as my favourite game to while away the time between delayed flights. I was very good at spotting which passengers had come on the flight from Madrid, passengers usually very elegant and well dressed and sporting just the hint of a tan. Passengers from Scandinavia were very easy to spot, and a stereotype certainly, but their tall, blonde good looks and pale skin was a certain give-away, as were passengers from Newcastle with their brilliant white arms and legs – body parts that had not seen the light of day, let alone sunshine, since the previous year's holiday in the sun. This was also the place to meet and chat to the tour company representatives, wearing their brightly coloured floral shirts and dresses that often reminded me of curtains taken from one of the many colourful apartments in the south of the island. These virtually pre-pubescent lads and lasses with their earnest, pale faces, clutching their company clipboards, advertised the fact that they were the latest batch of new recruits replacing the usually exhausted, and often embittered group of reps that had just returned on a flight back to the UK. The tour of duty of these youngsters was often very brief – just a few months before they were sent on to yet another destination, or maybe even retired off in their early twenties. The 'sell by date' for tour reps certainly diminished alongside the inevitable rise of the 'do-it-yourself' holidaymaker spending an hour or two on the Internet. The old adage of 'policeman looking younger as you get older' was never more of a truism than watching these young tour reps working at the airport. Most of them looked as if they had only just left school, whilst the older ones were often in some form of management role or just filling in for the occasional few hours each week. Gone were the days, it seemed not that long ago, when it was considered an advantage to have experienced staff on the island to cater for every tourist's needs. Whether the death of a family member or the way to the nearest bar, the well-dressed and knowledgeable tour rep of days gone by could be relied upon to know the answer and offer professional help. Some of the responsibility for giving help and advice that used to be borne by tour companies shifted to the British Consulate, creating other pressures such as staffing and resources. Most regular holidaymakers to any destination could usually quote at least one unfortunate experience with a tour rep, and I knew that many holidaymakers would attend the much trumpeted 'Welcome Meeting' for one reason alone – entertainment value and a free drink! Most holidaymakers had little intention of buying one of the often expensive coach trips on offer – preferring to find their own way around the island or spending the week on a sun bed with several large gin and tonics in hand. Indeed, I heard of one earnest young rep warning his guests not to try the local Canarian delicacies, but to visit the local McDonalds that he described as 'the best restaurant on the island'.

Those early pioneers of the travel industry must have been spinning in their graves. I remember the smartly dressed men and women, proud to represent their tour operator, in their smart blue blazers and cream coloured slacks who knew everything that there was to know about health and safety, local crime, sun burn prevention, currency exchange and car hire to really help to ensure that their holidaymakers had a good time. They would meet you at the airport, see you to your coach, entertain you on the journey to your hotel and then escort you into the hotel lobby to collect your room key. Throughout the holiday they would be there to guide, encourage and warn, and the holidaymaker often had a sense that these often 'larger than life characters' genuinely cared about their holiday experience. Guests would often book again immediately upon their return home for another holiday in the sun with the same tour operator, desperately hoping that the same holiday rep would still be there next time. Things change and economics dictates that the guest questionnaire thrust into your hand on the flight home is king. It is about profit margins, statistics, room occupancy and the number of 'extras' that can be sold. The 'mantra' heard by most holidaymakers from their new style tour rep is that they expect their guests 'to give them at least an excellent grade on their holiday questionnaire'. It was if their very future depended upon those reluctant ticks casually entered on the questionnaire after the drinks trolley has been trundled up and down the cramped aisle. Sadly, this was very often the case, and many reps did not even make it to the winter season. Some years ago there was a travel agent in Bournemouth where, until his death, the owner and managing director of the small company would personally allocate airline seats to his guests and wave them off as they boarded their flight. Yes, times have certainly changed in the tourism industry, and the tour representative of the past is long gone.

My mind wanders back to an encounter with an earnest young tour representative in the Costa Blanca at Alicante airport.

"You're Barrie, aren't you?" came a voice from the good-looking young man at the side of me. I nodded and smiled at the young blond man holding out his hand.

"Yes, that's right," I replied, shaking the young man's hand. "Do I know you?"

"I'm Trevor. No, we haven't met, but I've seen you here before and I recognise your photo in the paper. I read it every week. I've got an idea that you may like for a story."

I nodded and smiled, "Well, I'm always on the lookout for a good story, Trevor. If you've got time now, let's go and talk about it over a coffee."

Over a cup of coffee in the airport bar it became clear that Trevor didn't have any breaking news for me, but simply wanted a story about himself and his mates in the paper. I never minded a bit of self-publicity and self-promotion, as long as it would be of interest to our readers. Trevor's idea was that I would follow him for a day and give a 'Day in the life of a Tour Rep' account to our readers. Yes, I listened to his ideas carefully and he had some very interesting things to say, although it was clear that some of it would be a little controversial.

"My thinking is this," he began. "No one really likes us anymore. They all think we are a laugh, a lot of kids trying to do a job. It's not true. We work hard, bloody hard, we don't earn much either. The tour companies treat us like shit. They don't give us much training yet we are on the front line when it comes to complaints. They promised me my own room in one of the good hotels when I came here. All I've got is a shitty box-room that I have to share with a mate, and a bathroom on the next floor. We even have to pay for our own fucking food."

I had to admit that I was surprised at the tone of this young man's outspoken language, because I had always assumed that tour reps were rather well treated, if badly paid. Certainly, having to buy their own food as they had to remain in the resort seemed unfair.

"Well, I know you do these stories about people who work over here. So why not do something on us – or me even?" he laughed, as he swept his blond hair to one side with a single flick of his hand. "I would like it and my boss won't mind either. She's as pissed off as the rest of us, Barrie, and 'pissed as a fart' most of the time too. She's leaving at the end of the season. Wants to become a teacher. Mind you, she's got a way to go, because I don't think she's even got GCSEs and she's out like a tramp most nights!"

Trevor laughed and finally took a sip of coffee from the cup in front of him.

"So, do I gather that you want to somehow give the other side of the story, Trevor?" I asked, knowing full well that Trevor was the kind of impetuous young man who maybe had not thought everything through. Talking to any member of the press, without knowing both them and their agenda, can often be a dangerous thing.

"Yeah, too right, I do," he confided, his voice now lowering to a mere whisper. "This job used to be great. My brother did 'repping' for a couple of years, which is why I joined as well. Nowadays, the job's shit, we are treated like shit and paid like shit!"

I nodded. I would have to be careful with this one. I could see the potential of a story that would land both myself and the newspaper in a lot of trouble. There was certainly bitterness in what Trevor had to say.

By the end of our meeting, Trevor and I had agreed a plan. It was agreed that I would follow Trevor for a day in the resort with his guests. He would have to get approval from his line manager first, of course, but as long as I kept to my side of the bargain – that the day would be reported fairly, and anything that would be offensive to the company would be omitted. That was fine by me, as all I wanted was an article along the lines of, 'A day in the life of a tour representative'. Our newspaper didn't do 'controversial' articles anyway, as it was always far more profitable not to offend the advertisers!

Letter 33
Double Topping

A week later saw me standing in the entrance hall of the 'Hotel Petunia' waiting for Trevor to arrive. I had already spoken to Sally, his boss, a pleasant sounding if disorganised woman, who seemed oblivious to the potential damage that my story could cause if handled in the wrong way.

"Oh, do what you want to, dear," she had advised me. "I'm leaving at the end of the season anyway and I've had enough of this lot. There are some good boys and girls working here. Most of them do their best, but they are treated pretty badly by the company. I'd be the first to admit that. That's the main reason I'm going."

"It does all seem very negative so far. Surely there are some good things about the job that I can report as well. I want a balanced story," I continued.

"Oh, I'm sure Trevor can fill you in about the good points of the job," Sally laughed. "I warn you now Barrie that you won't be able to print some of the stuff he will tell you. I know our Trevor has quite a few little games going. As for the girls, just ask him about that. Oh yes, Trevor has plenty of perks!"

This telephone interview was not going quite as I had planned. I seemed to have stumbled into a strange twilight world that I previously had known very little about.

"Maybe I could meet you next week after I have spent some time with Trevor?"

"OK, that's fine by me, Barrie. I'm sure you'll do a good job for us. Byeee."

The line went dead. Well, Sally or no Sally, I still had my day planned with Trevor, and it was going to be most interesting.

It was already nine-thirty and Trevor had still not arrived. He was due to be at his desk by nine o'clock to deal with complaints and queries from guests. I knew that he had to sell them tickets for excursions, as well as the weekly reps' concert. There was already an angry looking elderly couple standing at the desk, and the elderly man kept looking anxiously at his watch.

"The young man said he'd be here by nine. If we leave it much longer, we shall be late for breakfast, Dorothy."

"I don't care," replied Dorothy. "I haven't slept a wink in that room. It's noisy and I want to be on the other side of the hotel. If we're late for breakfast, we're late for breakfast," she added pragmatically.

Trevor suddenly appeared, walking briskly through the front door. He had obviously just stumbled out of bed. He was unshaven and his tousled blond hair had not been combed or brushed.

"So sorry, me dearies," he beamed. "Late night, last night. Been up all night seeing to one of the guests!"

He turned to me, and gave me a broad wink. As I suddenly realised the meaning of what he had said, I stifled my snort into my clipboard. The elderly guests were totally oblivious to what Trevor was talking about. He listened to their problem, nodded reassuringly and walked over to the main desk where he spoke to the young Spanish receptionist. A babble of Spanish was exchanged, Trevor nodded and walked back to his desk and the elderly couple.

"I am so sorry, me dearies," beamed Trevor. "Please accept our apologies. I have arranged for you to be moved into another room in a quieter part of the hotel later today."

Trevor gave another disarming smile, showing his full set of gleaming white teeth. The elderly man stood and shook his hand, his wife smiled and the couple happily trotted off to the dining room for breakfast.

"Well done, Trevor," I said warmly. "You handled that perfectly."

Trevor laughed. "Silly old buggers. They pay little or nothing to come here and then want the best view in the hotel. No way. That's for the Golden Key guests."

"Yes, but you said you would move them," I protested.

"And so I have," laughed Trevor. "I have moved them to a nice quiet area overlooking the rubbish bins. There will be little noise, but it may be a bit 'whiffy' when the sun gets on them."

As the morning went on, I watched Trevor deal with a number of complaints cheerily and professionally. Yes, I did spot a lack of sincerity at times, but he did seem to be able to solve many of his guests' problems and answer their questions. I also noticed that whatever the query, Trevor always pushed the bar crawl experience, even though it was the least expensive of the excursions on offer. I asked Trevor about this during a temporary lull in the holidaymakers' visits to his desk.

"Oh, that's easy. Yes, it is a cheap excursion alright, which I lead twice a week. I take maybe twenty or thirty guests to five or six bars in the town, and as the night goes on they get plastered. It's an easy night out for me, but I make sure that my day off is the next one so that I can recover," Trevor laughed, beaming his toothy grin. He leaned towards me, "And there's the extras. That's just between you and me. Not to be reported, OK?"

I nodded and put away my notepad. I usually found this a good strategy to follow when I had an interview where people wished to unburden themselves, but didn't want it to be reported in the paper. I called it 'background material'.

"OK, fire away," I replied.

"Well, I have an arrangement with each bar on the patch. They give me one euro for each guest that I bring through their doors. They give the guests a free drink and they usually buy more anyway. You work it out, Barrie. Five or six bars a night, twenty or thirty guests at one euro each. That happens maybe twice a week."

My head was spinning as I worked out the calculations.

"Well, that works out to be a lot of money in a month, Trevor. All 'cash in hand' as well."

"Yep," beamed Trevor. "I call it my Trevor Fund. And there's double topping as well."

"Double topping? You mean tips?"

Trevor laughed. "You could say that, but the guests don't know they are tipping us. Double topping is great and helps everyone. In the late bars, I have an arrangement with the waiters to add a surcharge to all the extra drinks the guests order. By the end of the evening, the guests don't have a clue what they are paying, especially the ones who have just arrived, and so by bar five or six the surcharge is quite hefty. They're the best guests to catch. Naïve, too. They think the booze is really cheap, so they don't notice. Then we split the top-ups between the waiter and me. Simple, eh? Works a treat! It makes a tidy sum by the end of the season!"

"Trevor, that's awful. What a con! How can you treat people like that?"

I was genuinely shocked. I was aware of many scams in the Costas, but none quite as blatant as this. This guy was even justifying what he did to me.

"As I told you at the airport, Barrie, they treat me like shit, and so this way I get my own back. By the end of the season, I will have enough in the Trevor Fund to live on for the next few months. The tour companies don't bother about us, and so we just have to look after ourselves over here."

I could follow the logic of what Trevor was saying and, without moralising further on the issue, I could see where he was coming from.

"I would never have done this at home. It's just that we work all day and most nights, and you have already seen how we are treated. We may or may not get a day off. This is my way of redressing the balance in my favour."

"Do the others do this as well?"

"You bet, and worse. If we're caught we would be sacked, of course, but that is very unlikely."

"Why is that?" I enquired, anxious to pursue this line of enquiry. "All it takes is just a couple of complaints from guests."

"You ask a lot of questions, Barrie. Yes, I know it's your job. Easy, we have quite a lot on our line managers and bosses as well. If they split on us, we split on them. Bent taxi contracts, excursion back-handers. You name it and they are all into it. They have more to lose than us and so they keep quiet. Simple, eh?"

"Do you think that this is why they move you all around so frequently nowadays?" I asked.

Trevor thought for a moment. "Maybe, but it happens everywhere. We've only got to be in resort for a few days, and the local bar owners approach us. It's easy and, of course, we all talk to each other anyway, as well as those who have just left the resort."

Trevor turned to speak to his next guest who was patiently waiting his turn in the small queue of people waiting at the side of the desk.

"How can I help?" Trevor asked, beaming his most professional smile.

"Toilet's blocked again, Trevor. Can't shift it. It was the same yesterday."

"Too many curries, that's the problem, Mr. Carter," quipped Trevor. "Just go easy on the 'bog roll' next time. What number are you? I'll get it sorted. Who's next?"

"So how do you relax? What do you do on your day off?" I began, glancing at my notes on the clipboard in front of me.

"Day off? That's if Sally has remembered to give me one. If someone's off sick, or had too much to drink, we have to cover. I think I'm owed about five days so far this season."

"Yes, but it's not all work, Trevor, is it?" I persisted. "I've seen you with some of those girls. You're flirting with them all the time."

"Flirting and fuckin' most of 'em," beamed Trevor proudly. "That's what most of them come over here for. So I fucks 'em. I'm happy and they are too. I give them the holiday of their dreams," he added, almost poetically.

"So that's why you are so tired and late into work in the mornings?"

"I guess so, although I have to be professional of course. I don't go with anyone you know, only those that I like and who are discreet."

"And what about the guys? I guess the girl reps are doing the same thing with them?"

Trevor was silent for a moment, grinned broadly and then added, "You'll think I'm a right tart, but I do them too. It don't matter to me. Guys or girls, once I've had a few drinks inside me and they've got good bodies. It's all the same to me. I fucks 'em all if I likes 'em. If I can't fit 'em all in, I get some of my mates some 'totty' too."

"So, basically, you are pimping as well?" I blurted out.

Trevor clearly took exception to this comment and, for once during our interview, looked angry.

"No, not at all. I don't charge. It's just a bit of fun." For a few moments he was silent and added, "Well, sometimes they gives me presents when they leave. When you say 'pimping', does that count?"

I didn't answer and after a moment decided to change the subject.

"So what about the oldies?"

By now I was intrigued by Trevor's alarming honesty, but I already knew that I could never print this in the newspaper.

"Never old 'bears', but older women are fine. Well, maybe not too old. They tends to sag a bit, and 'saggy' tits put me off, but they are experienced and often great to train on, if you gets my meaning. Some old girls are very generous to me. One gave me a hundred euro tip last week, and another writes to me regularly from Bridgend. She even sends me money every month, and sometimes knits things for me. Helps build up the Trevor fund, Barrie. I sends her a postcard now and again, just to keep the juices flowing. She's coming again next year, but I won't be here."

"Right," I replied, my line of enquiry gradually drying up. "What would your mother say, do you think?"

"Well, as I sees it, I make 'em happy and their cash makes me happy. Gives 'em a great holiday, and maybe the last 'rogering' they will get for a while. I likes to give them a memorable holiday. My mum was always on about being generous and sharing things when I was a kid."

"Yes, I think you certainly do that, Trevor."

It was an interview that I shall never forget, although I have to confess that the article that I wrote, which appeared in the newspaper a few days later, was a mere shadow of the real thing. Yes, it focused upon the positive aspects of the job, but I had to omit the finer detail, particularly as some of the bars and tour companies concerned were our advertisers. The following week, I took Trevor out for a 'thank you' meal. He now looked more relaxed and, as always, was very good company.

"I hope I didn't shock you too much last week, Barrie? I see you didn't print everything that I told you," Trevor began, as he sipped his glass of wine.

"No, I didn't. You knew I wouldn't as well, didn't you?"

Trevor nodded. "I read some of your other stories. You sounded like a decent bloke, but I just wanted to get this off my chest. It's all true. I knew you wouldn't be allowed to print it all though."

"Did the others put you up to it?"

Trevor grinned, "Yeah, a bit. They wanted a massive exposé job doing before the end of the season. It's our way of getting our own back in this shithole."

"Look, you told me it's not all bad, Trevor. You have the sun, booze and the girls. I know the pay is bad, but there's worse in the UK."

Trevor nodded.

"Besides, what on earth did you think I could do with all that stuff you told me the other day? You knew I couldn't use it, Trevor. I am pleased you told me, but why?"

Trevor shrugged and gave me a brilliant toothy grin. "Your book maybe? Just give me a mention in it somewhere."

It had indeed been a very interesting week hearing the views and to witness at first hand the entrepreneurial spirit of one of Thatcher's children, but I somehow doubt this is what Maggie Thatcher had in mind when talking about, 'Young enterprise in modern Britain'. Anyway, this letter is dedicated to Trevor.

Letter 34
'Denuncias' and Drag Queens

When we arrived in the Costa Blanca, one of the more common words that I often heard bandied around was the word, 'denuncia'. Usually the word was uttered as the ultimate threat at a time of great anger and stress, and usually the recipient was likely to be builders, property developers or Telefonica, the Spanish telephone company – not necessarily in that order! When the word was used, one was expected to look suitably impressed and feel comforted that this hidden magical legal process would somehow solve the problem – any problem. How wrong I was...Firstly, let's have a closer look at the word 'denuncia'. It sounds much like the English to 'denounce' and could be regarded as being a very unpleasant thing to be involved in. However, this Spanish word really means 'to report' or 'to declare'; in other words, it is a police report. If you had property stolen you needed to make a report – a 'denuncia'. If your neighbour threatened to 'denounce' you, it only meant that they were going to report you – you were not likely to be pilloried in the nearby shopping centre. Well, maybe not immediately! Needless to say, 'expats' often tended to misunderstand the situation completely, because issuing a 'denuncia' was part of a criminal process and was rarely connected with civil proceedings against private companies or individuals. In the Costa Blanca, I often heard these threats being issued to builders, Telefonica, bars and restaurants. It usually made the person uttering the threat feel so much better, yet nothing was ever likely to happen in terms of retribution.

Even so, the 'denuncia' process was a useful and well considered one. I once registered a 'denuncia' when my wallet was stolen. I made the 'denuncia' by telephone to an English speaking police official in Madrid. A short time later it was sent electronically to the police station nearest to my home for me to read, agree and sign, and that was that. 'Denuncias' could be also made on the Internet in Spanish, so it is probably just as well that officials are not interested in complaints about neighbours or dog poo!

I remember one reader contacting me just after we launched the Gran Canaria newspaper concerning doubtful business practice in one of the well-known commercial centres in Playa del Ingles. Locals who knew the area would not, in the main, consider purchasing any form of electronic item from shops in the tourist areas of the south, but preferred to purchase cameras, mobile phones and all manner of electronic items in one of the major electronics stores, department stores or smaller retailers in the capital of Las Palmas, or in shopping centres in Spanish towns such as Vecindario or Telde. Sadly, with a few notable exceptions, Playa del Ingles and Puerto Rico had at that time more than its fair share of camera scams. It was an even larger problem in the neighbouring island of Tenerife, and the authorities in Gran Canaria were keen that this island did not allow such illegal business practices to continue and undermine tourists' confidence. The problem stemmed from an earlier time when many Indian family businesses, in particular, specialising in cameras and electronics products established themselves on the islands. For many years, because of considerable tax advantages, they were able to offer low priced deals to tourists from cruise ships, customers of tour operators, as well as those travelling independently. When Spain joined the European Union and with increased Internet and global trading, these retailers found that they could no longer offer such competitive prices. Competition on the islands increased with too many traders chasing a smaller number of tourists willing to pay the less competitive prices. The result was that some of the traders decided that 'conning' the tourists was the best way forward, knowing full well that in most cases tourists would not return to the shop, and in any case would be on the island for insufficient time to take any legal action. Consumer protection law was extended both in Spain, as well as the Canary Islands, to stop irresponsible and fraudulent companies, and gradually the camera scams were stopped. Tourists were often told that there were many bargains to be had on the island, and particularly for electronic goods. This was partly true, but tourists needed to be aware that although they would certainly make savings in the reduced tax charged for the items in the Canary Islands when compared to the UK and Peninsular Spain, it could be at a 'knock down price'. The equivalent of VAT (Value Added Tax), known as IGIC in the Canary Islands, was just five per cent as opposed to seventeen and a half per cent VAT in the UK and sixteen per cent IVA in Peninsular Spain. So when tourists were offered a 'massive saving' of more than ten to fifteen per cent off the usual recommended price, then there was something wrong, and alarm bells should have been ringing. No one ever really gets 'something for nothing' – and that is the first point to remember.

One tourist affected by the usual scam – let's call him John – went to a 'specialist camera dealer' as he was thinking of purchasing a video camera. John had already checked out prices for similar models in the area, and was willing to pay no more than one hundred and fifty euro for a digital video camera. The final decision came, when John passed through one of the commercial centres in Playa del Ingles early one evening. At this particular shopping centre, the shopper was greeted by several characters all shouting the usual, "Hello, where are you from?" in several different languages and who then would often hold up a camera, shouting, "video camera, video cam-e-r-a!!" This was probably the first sign that this shop was the kind that was best avoided. However, John went inside…

The shop inside was packed with glass display cases and mirrors – each and everything covered with a fine layer of dust. John wanted to buy the cheapest version of the Sony DV Handycam, and was offered a price of one hundred and seventy euro which was soon reduced down to one hundred and fifty euro. The salesperson had written out the credit card slip in seconds, and swiped John's card using the now old-fashioned carbon imprint credit card machines. Tension started to build when the shop assistant invited John to sit down by his counter and wait for 'authorisation'. The salesman then started telling John about the latest camera received in the shop while he waited. It did look like a good camera, much smaller and worked using an SD card (no tape). He showed John the quality difference on a TV. Admittedly on the TV it looked like a better output, but John was sure that he was tricking them by showing him the preview (low quality) TV output. Soon the shop assistant was tapping away at his calculator, much faster than John could see – comparing the two cameras, and again mixing up terms and language into a technical slur from his mouth. John was an IT professional in the UK, but didn't know much Spanish. Although he knew most of the terms that the salesman was using 'they were thrown at us and very fast, he basically wound us in a very exciting lie, just grounded in enough technical terms to be believable'.

John ended up buying the 'JVC branded' all-new DV camera, for four hundred and thirty-five euro, including case and did a deal on a genuine looking SD card. Suddenly, the salesperson pulled out a digital point of sale credit card reader and swiped the credit card through the machine a couple of times. He ripped up the old carbon copies and told John that the shop should keep the box, because John would never get it through customs. John wondered what he had got himself into and anxiously left the shop, clutching his new purchase. Back in his holiday apartment it was time to check the camera. John started filming immediately using the half charged battery provided, but it was dark and he couldn't see much at all... in fact he could hardly see anything. The camera didn't come with an optical zoom, which the salesman said it had, so every time the zoom went further, John realised just how low quality the camera was.

John saw the lights were off in the shop when he returned to complain, and so decided to do some more testing elsewhere. In a bar, John ordered a stiff drink to calm his nerves, and checked the contents of his black plastic bag. The camera did 'kind-of work', but 'dropped out' terribly in the dark. The manual had no JVC logo on it and there was no mention of the company anywhere. By now, alarm bells were going off in his head, but there was nothing he could do as the shop had closed early. Further analysis revealed that the JVC logo was badly stuck on the bottom of the unit, and the logo itself was printed on a red gradient (something JVC never do!). John went to the hotel lobby, and used the Internet to search the JVC website, and there was no such model listed. John could not understand how he could have been conned so easily. John commented that, 'the answer was in the unscrupulous sales tactics and the salesperson's capacity to lie so easily and profusely. He used the language barrier to hide any gaps in his web of deceit, and diverted my attention from his dodgy financial transactions'.

John went back the next morning in hope of a refund and was told that it was "absolutely not possible". When confronted with the accusation that it was a fake, the sales assistant finally agreed and said that he never actually said that the unit was a JVC (but he had!) and they were a new batch in from China. No refund was offered, but he could offer a swap, but suddenly all the cheap Handycams were out of stock, and none of the others looked worth the four hundred and thirty-five euros that John had paid. With no choice but to go for a slightly newer Handycam model, he paid a further seventy euros because 'the retail price of the unit was higher', but he did throw in a fake-branded travel case and set of five tapes. It seemed like it was the only way out and the trader was getting nasty, so John closed the deal again, hoping that this camera was legitimate.

"I took the box this time and had a stamped guarantee, but was still aware I had been totally ripped off!" Afterwards John checked the recommended retail for the camera. Sadly, it would have actually been cheaper to have bought the camera in the UK, with much less worry and from a sales person who would have known what he was talking about without lying, and proper guarantees. The incident spoiled John's holiday, and he had wasted a lot of holiday time. There were many good bargains to be had in the Canaries, but if it was too cheap – then there was probably something wrong with the deal and best avoided.

A few weeks later I had a telephone call from Tony, a friend of ours, who owned one of the large drag queen show bars in the south of the island. His elderly mother, Mary, had arrived in Gran Canaria for a short holiday and to see her son's new business. She was proud of what her son had achieved on the island, and wanted to take happy memories of her holiday and her son's new business back home to Blackpool. Mary went into the shopping centre to look for a new video camera, something small that she could keep in her handbag. By chance, Mary found herself in the same shop that John had been in a few weeks earlier. She found a video camera at a good price, agreed to the deal and paid by credit card. After a lengthy wait during which Mary was being encouraged to 'upgrade' to a more expensive model, she was finally given her new camera, without a box, but carefully wrapped in tissue paper and bubble wrap instead, "because of the customs," she was told. When Tony got home, Mary proudly opened her purchase, and mother and son were dismayed to find that it was not the branded model that

Mary thought she had purchased, but one that Tony recognised as a much cheaper model. Tony remembered the earlier report that he had read in the newspaper, and was furious that the same con had happened to his mother. Tony immediately went to the camera shop and demanded that Mary be given a full refund. This request was refused with the salesman and his boss claiming that Mary knew full well what she had purchased, and that she had merely changed her mind.

"She only bought it to take some video before she goes home. She never intended to buy it, only to borrow it. We don't hire out cameras for the day, Sir," was the response.

They had chosen the wrong person this time. Tony was furious and stormed out of the shop. Unfortunately for the shop, Tony was a man to reckon with and he would never take 'No' for an answer. Later that evening, just before his drag show opened and whilst the camera shop was still open, a group of twenty or so drag queens, in full costume and make-up, appeared outside the shop. Their chants, raucous songs and general abuse drew a large crowd and, within minutes, Tony and Mary had been given a full refund and an apology. The one thing that most people learn very quickly in Gran Canaria is 'never to mess with a drag queen'!

Letter 35
The Flying Tea Tray

Our Daewoo Matiz was a strange little car and one to which we had both become very fond. In the Costa Blanca, although the Hundai Getz was an excellent car, when we were both working, a second car was essential. We knew about all the warnings not to purchase a second-hand car in the Costa Blanca, problems that I had heard first-hand from many 'expats' who had been conned. I was in danger of becoming something of an expert on second-hand car cons, but as we couldn't afford another new car, there was little choice but to get on with finding one for ourselves, but making sure that we did our homework first. The initial search was depressing. We avoided all the British owned second-hand car dealerships in the area. Some may have been perfectly honest, but my own enquiries indicated that this was where most of the problems stemmed from. Indeed, I quickly noticed that, in the Costa Blanca, the main problem was the issue of Brit 'ripping off Brit' in all kinds of transactions – a sad indictment of the behaviour of some 'expats'. I found that second-hand cars in Spain were mostly very expensive to buy. They held their value well, and there were few bargains to be had – not in our price range anyway. Eventually, on the outskirts of a nearby small town, I discovered a Daewoo Matiz in the back of a forecourt of a Seat car dealership. This was another of my criteria – to only purchase second-hand from a main dealership – my thinking being that they had far more to lose if things went wrong. The Daewoo Matiz was a very small car, ideal for the small and busy roads in the area, economical to run and would fit perfectly alongside the Hyundai Getz in our driveway. It was not the kind of vehicle that you would choose for a long journey, and certainly not for speeding on busy motorways. Mileage was low for the year and it looked in good condition inside and out – apart from a hefty bump on the offside wing. Yet another roundabout casualty, I thought. Above all, the price was reasonable and the salesman was professional, not pushy in any way, and helpful. I asked all the relevant questions about registration transfer and tax payable to the authorities and all seemed in order. The car had been part-exchanged for a new Seat and the car had been previously driven by 'one careful lady owner' plus one other person who had the car for a short time before that. I smiled as I thought the salesman was about to tell me that the earlier owner had been a local parish priest, but he didn't. A few days later the deal was done and I drove the tiny car to the car repair body shop to have the wing repaired for around two hundred euros. Another two days and the Daewoo was sitting beside its bigger brother in our driveway, gleaming happily in the sun. I don't think some of our new neighbours were too impressed with the new acquisition. Gleaming it may have been, but 'cool' it was not, and in more than one sense of the word. Indeed, one of our cheekier neighbours referred to it unkindly as 'The Flying Tea Tray' more than once.

Overall, we were delighted with the little car, but we did find its air conditioning system less than effective. It was the middle of the summer and the journey between home and work became unbearable in the heat. Whoever was driving the Daewoo would arrive home looking like a boiled lobster. One of the reasons that we had purchased the Daewoo was that it had air conditioning, but the air conditioning unit obviously wasn't working correctly. I had tested it, and when I switched it on, the engine revs and sound changed, but there was no cool air coming from the ducts. They must be blocked or had been disconnected in some way. As luck would have it, a new business had started advertising in the newspaper. The owner had just launched a new mobile service installing and repairing air conditioning units – both in homes and in vehicles. He was keen to get some good publicity to accompany his advertising, and I was asked to write an article extolling the virtues of this new, very convenient service. One afternoon, I drove to Alex's home to talk about what his new service had to offer and to take a photo. At the end of my interview, I happened to mention my problem with the Daewoo's air conditioning to Alex.

"Probably needs re-gassing," explained Alex nodding knowledgeably, after I had explained the problem to him. "What happens when you switch it on?"

"The sound of the engine changes," I replied.

"Good. It sounds as if it is cutting in OK. Let's have a look at it."

Alex walked into the road where I had parked the Daewoo, and I opened the bonnet. He switched on the engine and listened. He then walked over and peered into the engine compartment. After a second or two, he walked over to me.

"It's a problem, Barrie," he replied seriously. "You've got a big problem here."

"Oh no, Alex," I replied. "How much is it going to cost me to get it repaired?"

Alex suddenly roared with laughter, "Nothing. It's not a repair that is needed!"

I was confused.

"Go on," I replied impatiently.

"It's not a repair that you need. It's an air conditioning unit. This car has never been fitted with one."

"But it has the switch and it even changes sound when it is switched on. Are you quite sure?"

"Quite sure, Barrie."

By now Alex's laughter had become irritating.

"Didn't you think to look for the unit?"

I drove away from Alex's home feeling very disappointed and annoyed that I had not checked the air conditioning more carefully. To be honest, I wasn't too sure what an air conditioning unit looked like anyway. Even though I wrote a first-class story for Alex's advertising campaign, I was deeply disappointed that so many of my colleagues as well as some readers quickly found out about the Daewoo and 'the missing air conditioning system'!

For the rest of the year until we moved to the Canary Islands, 'The Flying Tea Tray' ran around the Costa Blanca quite happily – with its windows open, whilst we boiled slowly inside. As I wrote in an earlier letter, thanks to Pickfords the removals company, the little car found its way into a container with our house contents bound for the Canary Islands. After we had settled on the island, we were delighted to see it once again as it was disgorged from the lorry with all of our household items. By now the car wasn't worth very much to sell, and it was better to bring it with us to Gran Canaria rather than to virtually give it away in the Costa Blanca. For the first few months, 'The Flying Tea Tray' did us proud. As the temperature in the Canaries is mostly very pleasant all year round, no longer did we need the windows down all the time. The car also seemed to come with a 'sealed fuel tank' as well. I recall only filling it a few times as a top-up with fuel that seemed to last forever. By now, the Daewoo was feeling a little like an old lady. Despite regular servicing, she no longer reacted well to fast acceleration, and so we treated her kindly and never pressed her too hard. No longer did her nickname, 'The Flying Tea Tray', suit her. One day, the time came when we had to seriously consider changing her for a new vehicle. It would be sad to see her go as she had served us well, but nothing is forever.

I was now in the market for a new vehicle. For years, I had rather fancied one of those smart jeep-like four-wheel drive buggies that were so popular, and preferably one with a soft top.

They would be ideal for some of the steep mountain roads and the odd occasion when off road driving would be necessary. I settled upon a smart new blue Suzuki. It was ideal for our purpose and there would be more space for Barney and Bella than in the Daewoo. We happened to mention this planned exchange of vehicle to one of the mechanics in the garage in Las Palmas, a big boy called Juan.

"Let me know first," he replied. "I like this car and it's just what I need to get to and from work in this busy city."

We nodded, but tried to explain that the Daewoo was a very small car and wondered if it was ideally suited to a man with a frame of his significant proportions. He squeezed inside with determination, the Daewoo groaned as it sunk to the nearside, his ample stomach pressing against the steering wheel. The seat was far too small and the greater part of Juan's bottom was hanging over the hand brake and the other buttock was hanging off the edge of the seat. No, the Daewoo was not the car for Juan. However, Juan was insistent, gave us a fair price, and one week later the deal was done, and we were saying our sad farewells to the Daewoo.

A few months later, we returned to the garage with our new Suzuki for a service. We spotted Juan working in the corner and went over to him to ask about the Daewoo. He beamed and said that he was delighted with her.

"Look there," Juan said proudly, pointing to what looked like our Daewoo sitting in the corner of the garage. Yes, it was the same registration number. It was an amazing transformation. Our previously very ordinary little car was still gleaming, but now sported tinted windows, a rear spoiler, vivid logos, smart new mirrors, two new seats and long pile carpeting. A complicated and expensive looking stereo CD system had replaced the old cassette radio, and was clearly Juan's pride and joy. He took us round to the back of the vehicle and opened the boot lid. It was a very small boot, but the rear seats had now been removed and the new expanse of space was now crammed with a high tech sound system sporting the largest woofer speaker that I had ever seen. He switched on the newly fitted CD unit and the garage, and probably most of the nearby area was filled with the most intense sound that I have ever heard coming from one car. I leapt backwards in fright – the sound was painful to my ears.

"Very good," I yelled to Juan, but I doubt that he heard what I was shouting.

"This car has the best sound system in the city," Juan beamed with pleasure at his pride and joy, as he closed the rear lid.

A few weeks later, David and I were driving to Las Palmas on the motorway, travelling at a reasonable speed, we thought, when there was a loud musical toot from the rear. We looked to our side and there was our little Daewoo, sporting its fabulous make-over, overtaking us at great speed. Juan waved cheekily to us as he overtook us and sped up the hill and was lost in the distance. Our 'little old lady' had received a new lease of life from Juan, and had justifiably reclaimed her title of 'The Flying Tea Tray'. We hoped that she and Juan would be happy together for a long time to come.

Letter 36
It's All Gone Bananas!

Gran Canaria, one of the seven Canary Islands, is situated just off the west coast of Africa. Although constitutionally part of Spain and, as a result part of the European Community, the islands maintain a distinct independent flavour based upon their close proximity to the west coast of Africa. Although Gran Canaria represents the southernmost tip of the European Union, it is regarded as outside the Community for taxation purposes. The islands are part of a European Economic Development Zone and, as a result, local taxation (known as IGIC), currently at five per cent, is the Canarian equivalent of VAT in the UK and IVA in Spain. Despite lower taxation, the cost of living is broadly the same as living in Peninsular Spain, once additional transport costs are taken into account.

Although the islands are constitutionally part of Spain and regarded as an autonomous province with their own government and president, many native born Canarians have neither visited the Spanish Peninsular or, indeed, the capital city, Madrid. Indeed, as one young Canarian had told me, "Why should we? We have everything that we need here." Indeed, many people share this view. After all there is no need to fly off to a sunny place to get an annual 'fix' of sunshine – it is already here for most of the year.

Mountains, all manner of water sports, a rich cultural heritage to explore and excellent shopping are just some of the pursuits that the islands have to offer. It is common for locals to visit neighbouring islands during their holidays or, indeed, to

272

visit their relatives in South America. It is sometimes forgotten that many Canarians fled to South America during the Spanish Civil War and that they and their descendants have always seen the Canary Islands as their home and, over the years since General Franco's death, have gradually returned to the islands to live and work. This, in part, may explain the reason why so many South Americans now live and work on the islands. Indeed, many professional people, such as doctors, dentists and accountants working in the islands originated from South America.

The heady mix of cultures that the islands now embrace are partly responsible for the colour, vibrancy and cultural richness of events such as the Las Palmas Carnival, which is unequalled in Europe. Wise central government policy of the main parties over many years have recognised the fierce, independent nature of the island people and have accepted the necessity of granting a considerable amount of local autonomy to the islands. The Canary Islands can never be compared with the Spanish Costas or, indeed, the Balearic islands. They have their own identity, heritage and culture as well as local differences in law making and ways of doing things. It would be a foolish politician or businessman who ignored these essential differences.

Warm sea currents give the Canary Islands a sub tropical climate. Fruit and vegetables that are grown, and the fish caught in the coastal waters of the islands, are found nowhere else in Spain. Maybe surprisingly, the islands' most important product, after tourism, is the banana. Away from the beaches, extensive banana plantations dominate the landscape. The variety grown in the Canaries is the dwarf banana, brought to the Canaries in the mid nineteenth century from Asia. The fruit is smaller, sweeter, and has a more intense flavour than the varieties produced in Latin America and the Caribbean, and now commonly available in British supermarkets such as Asda and Tesco. Personally, I much prefer the Canary Islands' banana to any of the tasteless varieties often available supermarkets, but then I guess I am now biased in favour of locally grown produce. Try a real Canary Islands' banana for yourself and you will see what I mean!

The banana is a fascinating subject that I have learned more about since living and working in Gran Canaria. The plant fruits only once, but a cluster of fruit can weigh up to 40 kilograms. Current high production costs in the islands means that the local produce struggles to compete with imports from the Americas. If the European Union is forced to remove protective tariffs, large-scale banana production may disappear from the islands within a short period of time. In an attempt to safeguard their future, local farmers have in recent years begun to diversify into the cultivation of other crops. These include exotic fruits, such as avocado, mango, papaya, kiwi, passion fruit and pineapple. A permanently warm climate means that other crops, such as tomatoes can supply the European market during the winter months. Vegetables also abound, and the Canary Islands are where many of the newly discovered crops from the Americas were first planted in Europe. Aside from the produce found on the mainland, sugar cane is cultivated, although this production is much less than in the past, and exotic vegetables like chayote, a pear shaped vegetable that tastes like a marrow, is grown.

Did you know that bananas from the Canary Islands were once unloaded right in the centre of what is now London's vibrant financial district known as Canary Wharf, and that this is how it got its name? Canary Wharf itself takes its name from the No. 10 Warehouse of the South Quay Import Dock. This was built in 1952 for Fruit Lines Ltd, a subsidiary of Fred Olsen Lines for the Canary Island fruit trade. At their request, the quay and warehouse were given the name Canary Wharf.

I happened to be in London during what had been the worst weeks in recent financial history in October 2008. A walk around London's vibrant financial district known as Canary Wharf revealed a slowing of pace from its usual frenetic energy.

Instead of 'the suits' importantly going about their business with plastic cups of coffee clasped in their busy hands, a new sadness was clear to see. Financial events, that became known as the 'credit crunch', meant that some of the many 'suits' dashing around the busy streets were no longer carrying plastic cups of coffee. Instead, many were now carrying their belongings in cardboard boxes out of the important looking buildings, as 'the crunch' hit yet another financial institution in the City and beyond.

So next time you 'unzip a banana', and hopefully it is a variety grown in the Canary Islands, just spare a thought for the hundreds of people, dashing around and carrying mugs of coffee in the troubled financial centre that bears its name.

Letter 37
Calm in the Correos

Earlier I gave an account of the chaos experienced by many 'expats', as well as their Spanish neighbours, in a small town in the Costa Blanca. When we moved to the Canary Islands, I fully expected the situation to be far worse. The islands, I thought, would have an even less developed postal service and anything sent to and from mainland Europe would take forever. Thankfully, in many ways, I was wrong.

All post destined from Gran Canaria to Peninsular Spain, UK and other parts of the world are routed through Madrid. This, of course, naturally means an additional delay in getting the post to Madrid and then be sorted and re-routed at the Madrid end of the operation. Fiestas, siestas and other slowdowns accepted, I am pleased to report that letters and small packages seem to arrive in the UK within three days of posting from Gran Canaria. Indeed, the reverse, from the UK to Gran Canaria can be even quicker.

Recently, David received a letter from his mother in Cornwall. It was posted on a Tuesday afternoon and the postman dropped it into our letter box at 10.30 on Thursday morning! How's that for service from the UK to the Canaries?

Anything posted by Royal Mail in the UK and, indeed, private courier companies such as DHL and Fedex seem to arrive promptly in the islands. However, post dispatched by UK's Parcelforce to the islands is quite another matter. I have many examples of items ordered in the UK, shipped by Parcelforce, only to find out weeks later that the item had been returned to the supplier. Initially I had assumed that somehow larger items were being blocked by the customs authorities in the Canaries, but after a particularly infuriating experience with an item ordered from the TV shopping channel, QVC, I discovered that the item had not even left the UK shores.

Despite the many positive aspects to the postal service in the Canary Islands, it can also have its downsides. One example of this is the small Post Office in the village where I live. It is ideally situated in the centre of the village, but for some time I have noticed that very few locals seem to use it. I think I know why.

This small village Post Office is staffed by a middle-aged woman, and for the sake of avoiding embarrassment to her, I shall call Maria. Maria is a large lady who appears to find everything in life a problem. She wears a permanent scowl, very unlike most Canarians, and however polite the greeting, she usually responds with an ill-tempered grunt. Maria's empire is a small one and the job not too onerous with the office open from nine-thirty until twelve each day and from ten o'clock to twelve on Saturdays. However, woe betide anyone wishing to send a parcel or packet that requires a dispatch slip or customs slip to be completed. Maria will scowl even more, shake her head and say she has none in the office.

The Correos in Spain has a very clever system whereby all Post Offices are connected to 'mission control' through a computer system that weighs, records and issues stamps and all manner of postal services. If a customer should happen to call upon the services of Maria on a Saturday morning, or indeed, the day before a fiesta, Maria's scowl will deepen further; she will shake her head and tell the unfortunate customer that the machine has broken. We all know that it really is a ploy to avoid completing all the necessary paper returns that must be done once the machine is in operation, but, according Maria, it is a technical fault. It is no wonder that villagers prefer to drive or catch a bus into the next large town to send their post from another Post Office.

The large Post Office in Vecindario is quite another matter. Vecindario is home to a large number of immigrants from Africa and South America and many cannot, as yet, speak Spanish sufficiently well to deal with their postal requirements. I have never known staff in a Post Office to give such care and attention to their clients and ensure that they understand the postal and banking services that they offer. Indeed, I have seen a number of customers entering the Post Office with items to send back home, unboxed and unwrapped, with the Post Office staff helping them to wrap and seal their items in the Post Office before posting. An excellent service indeed, but one that means long queues for the remainder of their customers, whilst this excellent customer service is carried out.

Anyone who lives in or has visited the tourist resort of Playa del Ingles will probably wince as they recall their own experiences in the Playa del Ingles Post Office. Although it is a large Post Office by any standards, the experience of waiting for services are not pleasant. It is always advisable to take a morning off work whenever you need to visit this office as you can be guaranteed a very long wait. Yes, there is now a 'bread ticket' system that at least guarantees a place in the queue and seats have now been provided, but it is a place where tempers grow short, much bad language is muttered from the lips of British and German holidaymakers in particular, whilst Canarians and Spanish customers stand calmly in the queue waiting for their turn. Yes, most Canarians have much to teach their British and German visitors about patience and good manners when queuing.

My own personal preference is to use the small Post Office situated right in the centre of the island's airport. My reasoning is that post doesn't have too far to travel to get to the aeroplane, thereby reducing any delays in getting it to Madrid to the absolute minimum. This small Post Office is staffed by a wonderful Canarian woman by the name of Carmen. Carmen is regarded as a treasure within the postal service circles and her knowledgeable and no-nonsense approach to the whole business of sending post is greatly admired by all who know her. Posting a parcel is a pleasure and one of calm. How different Carmen is from the grumpy Maria in our village and how I wish that Carmen would do some on-the-spot training for Maria!

Letter 38
Is Your Home Fit for a Cockroach?

I have to confess that I have given precious little thought to cockroaches in the past, but that changed as soon as we moved to Spain and the Canary Islands. You have only to mention the word 'cockroach' to some of our 'expat' friends and neighbours when a look of panic shows on their faces. I have seen grown men sweat as they recall their earlier meetings with these entertaining little creatures. I have also noticed that dinner table conversations suddenly become much fun and greatly animated when the dreaded word is mentioned. I am not sure that the words 'rat' or 'snake' have anywhere near the same effect. At least it gives a topic of conversation for those difficult times when an awkward dinner guest has little to say at the dinner table. Just the mention of the word 'cockroach' tends to liven them up considerably, although it can tend to put them off their dessert.

Until our move to Spain I had not even met one 'in the flesh' so to speak, apart from one unpleasant incident in a hotel in Tenerife, that is. An encounter with a rather desiccated member of the species in a neighbour's kitchen one morning suddenly changed all that, and I find that I now rather admire these undervalued creatures.

Until I looked them up on the Internet for a newspaper advertising-feature that I was asked to write, I did not know that there are American, German, Wood and Brown-bellied cockroaches. My task was to write a series of articles about cockroaches that would terrify readers sufficiently to contact one of our new advertisers who offered a cockroach de-infestation service – a sort of cockroach version of Rentokil in the UK, I guess. In the end, I wrote three articles that I have to admit I was rather proud of, although they seemed rather less popular with some of our faint-hearted readers. I recalled one elderly lady who, having met me at a local charity function that I was covering for the newspaper, implored me not to write anymore.

"I just have to read them, but I wish I hadn't afterwards," she told me wincing as she recalled the offending articles.

I even discovered Oriental and Tropical cockroaches on the Google reference pages – all fascinating stuff. Did you know that cockroaches even have their own website where you can watch them play? No, I thought not. If so inspired after reading this letter, you can even buy a Madagascan Giant Hissing Cockroach as a pet. Wherever they come from, they have a few things in common. They are nocturnal and live in groups. They seek cracks and crevices that are warm, dark and moist; they also live inside cardboard and paper bags. Cockroaches eat anything that is organic – even cardboard and the glue that binds books together. They need water, although some species, and there seem to be many, can live for several weeks with minimal quantities. Cockroaches prefer to remain near their food sources and shelter. Take away both and the cockroaches will almost certainly seek a more hospitable home.

Did you know that in some parts of the Far East, cockroaches are considered a fine delicacy? Fried, stewed, boiled or roasted, and they can cost a lot of money. I also heard a tragic but true story of an American lady who had a meal in one of those not so clean American 'diners'. Sadly, she must have eaten cockroach-infested food – without knowing it at the time. A few days later her gums began to swell and bleed and she rushed to the dentist. After a thorough examination, the dentist told her that her gums were totally infested with a huge number of growing cockroach eggs. The dentist asked where she had eaten, nodded wisely and then called the police. They went to the restaurant and found both live and dead cockroaches in the meat. Just also think what would have happened if the eggs in that lady's gums had actually hatched!

Experts recommend immediate action if you find that they are visiting you. Of course, our advertisers would prefer that they be called in to sort out the problem, but the best thing is to try to find the source of the infestation and use 'sticky traps' to capture the cockroaches. I also discovered that it is best to use a flashlight and dental mirror to peek behind or under cabinets. Search for living or dead cockroaches, shed exoskeletons ('skins'), egg cases and faeces. You can also find their hiding places by quietly entering a dark room and watching where they run when you turn on the lights. Oh, such fun!

On a more serious note, cockroaches are known to carry disease-causing bacteria, although their ability to transmit diseases to humans is under study. They're still a significant health concern because they trigger allergies that contribute to asthma. Finding even one cockroach warrants alertness. All cockroach problems start small, but they reproduce rapidly, so early intervention is highly recommended.

Some time ago, good friends flew from the Costa Blanca to spend a few days in Gran Canaria – a mother and daughter. When we met up the following day, it was clear that something was wrong.

"It's the bungalow," they said anxiously, looking very pale.

They had rented a small bungalow in one of the less well-maintained holiday complexes in the south of the island. When they arrived during the late evening, they were greeted by a family of cockroaches scurrying around the living room. Our friends took to standing on chairs until there was a lull in cockroach activity. When they finally managed to contact the night porter in the reception, he greeted their concerns with a shrug saying that he could do nothing until the following day.

Our friends spent a sleepless first night in their holiday bungalow, watching and listening to the cockroaches having a party with their family and friends around them.

I am also told that it is a real 'no, no' to stamp on a cockroach – you may just carry their eggs on your shoe into your home. There they will hatch – and you already know the rest of the story! Apparently, cats love to eat them, but the eggs pass through the cat and, once again, they may later hatch. The same expert also told me that extreme temperatures will kill cockroaches – but a flame thrower is going well over the top!

We do get our own occasional cockroach visitors in our present home. Usually they do not last long because Barney and Bella worry them to death, although fortunately they do not eat them. In the UK there is an expression that you are never more than a hundred yards from a rat, or is it feet? Similarly, I guess the same could be said of cockroaches in Spain. Finally, the de-infestation man told me that if we had a nuclear explosion, cockroaches would be the only living thing to survive. I am not sure if this is based upon scientific fact, but it does give some food for thought and maybe just a little admiration for these much-maligned creatures.

Letter 39
Cockroaches and Cats' Pee

Most people think that the seven Canary Islands work well together as a self-supporting homogenous unit. After all, these are a cluster of small islands in the Atlantic, and far away from the bustling metropolis of Madrid. Surely this fact alone brings the islands together?

Surprisingly, and despite politicians' claims to the contrary, nothing could be further from the truth. Memories of wars fought long ago still linger, and the fissures between the inhabitants of 'these favoured isles' have continued for many generations. True, on the surface, there are the outward signs of co-operation, but when it comes to either the political battles of which islands should get the share of available funding and grants, or the taunts between Gran Canaria and Tenerife supporters at all island football matches, it is clear that considerable mistrust and resentment between the islanders remain.

Gran Canaria and its sister islands of Lanzarote and Fuerteventura work well together. For local government, legal and medical purposes, all islanders look to Gran Canaria's capital, Las Palmas – the seventh largest city in Spain – to fulfil these essential needs. Similarly, the largest island of the seven, Tenerife, and its sister islands of La Palma, La Gomera and El Hierro look to Tenerife's capital, Santa Cruz, for much of their administrative, legal and medical needs.

The south of Tenerife has always been known as a 'British' resort, much favoured by British holidaymakers for many years, whilst Gran Canaria has always looked to German and Scandinavian tourists for its much needed income from tourism. The position changed dramatically in the last ten to twenty years when a combination of the German economy running into trouble, and changes in their taxation disclosures regarding investment in other countries, led to many Germans selling their properties and returning either to Germany or to destinations outside Europe for their second homes.

Meanwhile, the British economy was becoming stronger leading to a position that whilst Germans were selling up, the British were able to use the equity in their UK properties to buy properties in Spain and the Canary Islands. In addition, Gran Canaria, with its 'live and let live attitude' became a much favoured destination for gay men and women – both as a holiday destination, as well as an ideal place to make a new home in the sun.

I have to admit that, Tenerife, both as an island and as a holiday destination, is not one of my favourite places. Admittedly, this somewhat harsh judgement comes as a result of just three holidays on the island, which may not be the best way of coming to this verdict about the doubtful delights of this, the largest of the Canary Islands. However, as they say, first impressions do count.

I remember our first holiday to Tenerife from the UK several years ago and flying very conveniently from our local Bournemouth airport, and very good value too. After a good flight, efficient baggage handling at the airport and a pleasant welcome from a tour rep, the coach finally pulled up outside the main door of a rather smart hotel on the outskirts of Playa de las Americas. Our initial high spirits had been dampened as we had sat on the coach from the airport for nearly two hours. We and three other couples were the last drop, and so had amused ourselves patiently listening to a well-rehearsed résumé of 'What we should do' and 'What we should not do on holiday' and

'Why it was essential to attend the Welcome Meeting' by a very confident and well intentioned tour representative, who gave the impression that she would be able to tackle every possible emergency single handed.

In the hotel was a very long queue of guests checking in and out. Finally it was our turn, and after the usual formalities a surly receptionist gave us our room keys – the confident tour rep having fled long before. We made our way through the unending pathways, slopes, twists and turns indicated on the map that had been thrust at us. This hotel spread outwards rather than upwards and the weed and rubbish filled gardens and pathways that lay strewn before us did not impress us. For a relatively new hotel it was remarkably not disabled-friendly with steep slopes and steps at every twist and turn. A strong smell of cats' 'pee' became more and more overpowering as we finally reached our room.

Hesitantly we unlocked the door – we both already had an inkling of what lay before us. We looked at each other in despair. All we wanted to do was to shower, change and have a drink, but this was far worse than even our initial thoughts. Pulling the bed cover back, it was clear that the bedding belonged to a previous occupant – a 'none too clean one' judging by the stains on the sheets. The bathroom revealed a dead cockroach in the corner, and horror upon horrors, without going into detail, the previous occupant had clearly had too much curry and lager the night before!

We trudged back to the hotel reception and explained that we could not accept the room because it was dirty. The sullen receptionist, who earlier had claimed that she did not speak English, responded eloquently, "You must be wrong. The room is perfect. That is all we have available for you, because we are full."

"You have two choices," I responded, tiredness and disappointment creating a sharp response. "You will either immediately find us another room, or I will call the tour company and request a change of hotel. I will return in one hour."

Considerable mutterings, no explanation or apology, and a good two hours later produced a reasonably clean room, clean bedding and a clean toilet. This time, the cockroaches were to be seen playing outside and not inside our room. It was not the best start to our holiday, but the weather was kind, the food and drink cheap and we thoroughly enjoyed the whales and dolphin trip. That really was all the enthusiasm that we could muster for Tenerife on that occasion.

Two years later, after a particularly horrendous winter in the UK as well as a series of school inspections that all seemed to require urgent remedial action, we both badly needed a winter break. It was one evening whilst playing with the Teletext service on the TV that I found a very good value package deal from our local airport to, yes you guessed, Tenerife. It was an offer too good to miss and so, on the spur of the moment, I grabbed the credit card and booked it. The only thing troubling me was a term I had not seen before – 'allocate upon arrival'. For me, this was indeed a new concept.

I won't bore you with the withering look and numerous reasons that my long-suffering partner gave me as to why we should not return to Tenerife.

"Let's keep an open mind, it will be a different hotel. Maybe it will be in a different part of the island and, best of all it won't be raining and it will be sunny," I had tried to justify the booking with all the confidence that I could muster. Later, I discovered in the pub that 'allocate upon arrival' could be quite a good thing, as tour operators tended to put you in a better hotel than you had paid for to 'fill up rooms'. So I was told…

The coach from the airport drove down roads that I thought I recognised. I said nothing, with my fingers firmly crossed, desperately hoping that we were not going to return to Playa de las Americas, let alone THAT hotel. Sadly, it was not going to be that easy and I was not going to be that fortunate. In a cruel twist of fate, we found ourselves outside the same door of the all too familiar and much hated hotel that we had endured two years earlier. I protested to the tour rep – a humourless soul who was 'well past the sell by date of a tour rep' and who had heard it all before. "Don't worry, don't worry," she said behind her fixed, glassy smile. "This is our flagship hotel and I am sure that any problems that you had two years ago will have been ironed out by now."

Despite my continued protestations, I was left in no doubt that it was either this or nothing. We were unceremoniously dumped outside the hotel door with our suitcases, and the coach disappeared. This time we were the only ones to leave the coach. No doubt others had far more sense.

The same odour of stale cats' pee once again greeted us as we followed the weed and rubbish laden paths to our new accommodation. In silence we opened the door to our room, drew the curtains back and gave a big sigh of relief. It was clean, there was clean bedding and the bathroom smelled fresh. Maybe it wasn't going to be such a disaster after all?

For the next four days it rained non-stop. The worst rain that I had ever witnessed anywhere. It started on a journey up towards the mountains on our second morning. As we drove the rain got heavier and heavier, and we were eventually turned back by the police, because some of the roads were already being washed away and we were told it was dangerous to continue.

We returned to the hotel to find it in total darkness. There was no electricity in any of the rooms. We later discovered that the power cut only affected the part of the town with our 'flagship hotel'. No other premises appeared to be affected. By evening there was still no improvement and we made our way with a torch to reception to ask for lamps, candles and details of what was happening. The power would be off for at least the next day we were told. No, the hotel had no emergency lighting, no torches and lamps, and certainly no candles – that would be far too dangerous! It was hard to believe that this 'flagship hotel' had received any kind of certification inspection or approval upon completion without the provision of emergency lighting.

The hotel was built on a very steep slope and the chalets were all reached by narrow tiled paths, which became very slippery in wet weather. Power was not restored to the hotel for three days and by the time we left we were well used to the sound of ambulance sirens approaching and leaving our hotel with yet another holidaymaker who had slipped on the tiled pathways, and was being 'carted off' to hospital with a broken leg or arm. The local private hospital must have made a lot of money in that week! After three days we could stand the chaos no more and checked into another hotel – at our own expense.

A week later we were safely back home and in our local pub enjoying a meal. The TV was on and we were just in time to see the *Holidays from Hell* programme that was so popular in those days. Yes, there it was again – our 'flagship hotel' was featured on the *Holidays from Hell* programme. I just wish we had managed to give our input to the programme – this broadcast made it look quite pleasant!

Letter 40
Escape from the Island

Although I can think of no better place to live and work than Gran Canaria, we are not unique in wanting, from time to time, to escape and to explore the wider world beyond our sunny shores. After a year or so of living on the island I had a sudden urge to leave it for a while – not permanently, you understand, but I just wanted to go to another place. At first the feeling troubled me. Did it mean that I was not comfortable as an islander after all? Was it the beginning of a feeling that I would not settle and want to return to the Costa Blanca, or indeed, even the UK? I discussed my feelings with David, and he said that he felt just the same. It was only after discussing the issue with several of our new island friends and neighbours that we realised that this feeling was quite normal amongst newly arrived 'expats'.

"Yes, I feel like that sometimes as well," said Ruth, one of our friends. "I get the urge to travel every six months or so. I go away, feel better and then cannot get back to the island quickly enough."

Certainly, David and I have experienced exactly the same feelings. After all, there is no real reason to leave the island. We have an incredible climate and everything that we need in terms of shopping – everything is available here. We have deserts, mountains, waterfalls, sand and grass – the scenery and climate is rich and varied. I guess, however content we are, we all need a change from time to time. However, it is true that once we leave the island either on holiday or to visit family and friends in the UK, we cannot get back to the island quickly enough!

Gran Canarian residents know that once August arrives, it is almost impossible to get anything done on the island. Everything seems to close from the 15 August, and so the old adage 'if you cannot beat them, join them' springs to mind. The month of August is also further complicated by the difficulty in getting reasonably priced flights from Gran Canaria to mainland Europe. Therefore if there is a sudden urge to leave the island, it is an ideal time to visit another of our beautiful Canary Islands.

Working for the newspaper, meant constant pressures to prepare the next editions and deadlines for articles and advertising for the current edition, so holiday breaks were always difficult and needed careful planning. The quickest journey to another island where we could also take our car was to Tenerife, but the experiences of the previous two holidays were, to say the least, negative. However, time had passed and I felt that we should try again, with a positive attitude, to revisit this island. We eventually decided to avoid the south of Tenerife, and this time try out the northern area, so with some trepidation, but with a real need for a holiday break, we made the booking for the ferry and hotel.

Tenerife is the largest of the seven Canary Islands – volcanic in origin, with a neat, triangular formation that covers an area of over two thousand square kilometres. The gigantic Teide mountain and extinct volcano at a height of three thousand seven hundred metres is the highest point in the whole of Spain.

The northern part of Tenerife is greener and more dramatic than other parts of this popular island. Numerous banana plantations, vineyards, and lush colourful vegetation make it pleasing on the eye. Home of the municipalities of Puerto de la Cruz, La Oratava and Los Realejos this valley, sometimes known as the 'Garden of Teide', extends from the edge of the great volcano to the coast where there are charming villages and delightful scenery.

Although we could easily have booked air flights on the regular flights between Gran Canaria and Tenerife and with good discounts for residents, we had the luxury of a four-day break and wanted to take our car, so we booked a sailing on the Fred Olsen ferry from Agaete in the north of Gran Canaria to Santa Cruz in Tenerife. The first thing to say is don't let anyone tell you that the sailing from Agaete to Santa Cruz is 'like a bridge' with a crossing as calm as a millpond shown on the company's advertising. It is not. Our sailing was an uncomfortable one and a half hours in choppy sea conditions with many passengers suffering the effects of seasickness – ourselves included, and the return journey was not much better. If you are a poor traveller my best advice is take seasickness tablets, use acupressure wristbands or, better still, fly. On the other hand, I easily become seasick in the bath, and so I may not be the best person to judge this one!

With stomachs churning and questions regarding our sanity of returning to the 'doomed' island, we drove from the busy port and city of Santa Cruz and headed straight for Puerto de la Cruz. This is the second important tourist centre on the island, and one of the most attractive resorts on the island's north coast. We had booked last minute into a clean, yet 'tired' and poorly managed hotel, and one that I would not recommend – right next to the cemetery, we later discovered. At least it was quiet and peaceful, and the 'neighbours' did not hold any late night parties that we were aware of! After the first day, we realised that the hotel guests were mainly young Canarian and Spanish families – with some German couples, and we were the only Brits to be seen!

We wanted to explore the town and quickly found that it was charming, and ideal for tourist shopping, with good value meals in the town's squares or maybe for just wandering around the port area. The old Customs House, built in 1620, and restored in the last twenty years or so was impressive and well worth our morning visit. However, although I was easily tempted by the wealth of photographic and electrical shops, I decided to avoid those offering video cameras from as little as fifty euros. These were, of course, a scam and a sales ploy designed to get you into the shop, and, although this practice had been mostly suppressed by the authorities in Gran Canaria, it seemed that this doubtful practice was still continuing to flourish in Tenerife.

Whilst on holiday, I was keen to visit the Loro Parque animal park. I am not a great lover of wildlife parks, zoos and performing animals, but this park was advertised as being different. Would our continual disappointment with the island be extended by visiting this park? This led to some extended discussions between us, particularly when we found out the cost of entrance tickets. However, our hotel was just a short walk from the park and we decided to go with a positive frame of mind. I had also planned to write articles for the newspaper when we returned home, and when I asked if I could talk with the marketing manager of the park, we were both welcomed in as VIP guests. A substantial 'perk' of the job for us, but would also provide good newspaper coverage for this commercial animal park, and David hoped that maybe he could sell them advertising space too!

The park was established as a parrot park in the 1970s by a German businessman, Wolfgang Kiessling, and now not only housed the largest known colony of parrots from all over the world, but also many that were threatened with extinction. I was relieved and delighted to see spacious and clean accommodation for the animals, as well as some amazing shows, particularly of the sea lions that I fell in love with. The huge area around the sea lion display pool was filled with both the young and old. The layout of the park was beautiful and all the animals looked well cared for and happy, and our initial doubts were quickly forgotten. We were amazed by the 'Planet Penguin' display and we really felt we were in the Antarctic, well maybe with the exception of the moving travellators! A real treat!

So, our third attempt at a holiday in Tenerife turned out to be not as bad as we had imagined, and with some good memories to take with us when we returned home. For many years, I have collected and grown orchids, and whilst I found them challenging to grow in the UK in my conservatory, they were equally difficult to grow in Spain and the Canary Islands. However, we discovered the Orchid Garden, Jardines de Sitio Litre (Little's Place), on the edge of the town. This amazing and peaceful garden was first planned and established by the Little family and added to by the Smith family. Indeed, it has been British owned for around two hundred and thirty years. It is still a private mansion and includes Tenerife's most magnificent collection of orchids as well as the oldest Dragon Tree in the area. It was the Tenerife home of Marianne North of the Royal Botanical Gardens in Kew as well as William Wilde (Oscar Wilde's father). It was also visited by Agatha Christie and provided inspiration for the short story, *The Magnificent Mr. Quin*. We thoroughly enjoyed the Café Orquidea where we indulged in an excellent English cream tea in tranquil surroundings! Sadly the cream was of the 'spray can' variety and not the traditional Cornish 'Clotted' – but we cannot have everything, can we?

The north of the island is lush and green, but this comes at a price with three of our four-day holiday in August having some rain – mainly in the morning. We had come to the conclusion that a raincoat and an umbrella are necessary for a holiday in Tenerife, but on the plus side we had enjoyed the delights of real grass, lush vegetation and trees once again. Overall, our four-day 'escape' made an enjoyable break, but we couldn't wait to get back to Gran Canaria!

Letter 41
Where are you from?

These seemingly innocent four opening words bawled at tourists by young men and woman on street corners, or the more subtle approach of leaping out at you when you are least aware, can often lead to a disturbing encounter for many tourists visiting the main tourist centres in Gran Canaria, such as Playa del Ingles and Puerto Rico, and can sometimes lead to more serious consequences. Indeed, it is a curse that has grown into an even worse situation on our neighbouring island of Tenerife.

As well as many concerns relating to timeshare touts, our newspaper used to receive regular complaints about touts approaching tourists outside bars and restaurants in commercial centres. Often this is no more than a pleasant 'Buenos dias' with an offer to look at the restaurant's menu. Similarly, touts outside the many bars in the south shout their 'two for one offers', 'a free shot' or maybe the promise of the 'cheapest beer on the island'. These young people can often be desperate as usually their only income depends upon getting tourists inside the bar or restaurant, where they may be paid about one euro or so for their effort. Most of these approaches are good-humoured and are no more than a simple, albeit irritating, form of advertising.

A similar situation often occurs when the unsuspecting visitor lingers, even quite briefly, outside one of the many camera and electronics shops in the south of the island. Unless the tourist has a very clear head they soon find themselves lured into the very bowels of the shop where they are persuaded to purchase a video camera 'for only 50 euros'. It is often a purchase for an item that at best turns out to be a fake, or at worst the holidaymaker's credit card is used to charge for an additional, more expensive purchase. Fortunately, the situation is relatively isolated to a small number of shops in the commercial centres, although the curse is widespread in Tenerife, as well as parts of Fuerteventura and Lanzarote. I used to enjoy lingering outside such shops, but it is now something that I avoid.

The problems often come when the frustration and desperation levels of the touts concerned reach such a point that the tout becomes a nuisance, or indeed aggressive to the would-be customer. As editor of our local newspaper, I received many phone calls and emails from visitors complaining of shouts of abuse, snide and sometimes homophobic or racist comments shouted at tourists who declined to enter the premises. Sadly, the businesses concerned did not seem to realise that the very fact that it has to have a tout outside the premises plying for trade is clearly saying to all, but the most brain cellular challenged, that, "Actually we are not doing very well, we are desperate for your business, please come inside". Have you noticed touts outside the most successful and quality restaurants and bars? I very much doubt it – they have no need to indulge in this form of advertising – their reputation is worth far more.

I remember interviewing Pablo, a Canarian born and bred, and well-educated businessman. This issue had troubled him for some time although he assured me that the situation relating to time-share and bar and restaurant touts used to be far worse in the past. It seemed that the problem was that the Town Halls were not applying the laws that were already at their disposal. He told me that only a few years earlier the Canarian Government had spent a lot of money on drafting and introducing a law that was designed to curb the curse of touts. Mindful of the damage that it had done to our Tenerife neighbour, many business people on the island were very keen to see the new law applied. This new provincial law was to be applied to the islands of Fuerteventura, Lanzarote and Gran Canaria with the main responsibility for policing it to be given to the municipalities.

Pablo thought it was a good law if correctly applied. It allowed for a certain number of touts to be registered and to operate within the immediate location of the restaurant or bar concerned, with strict conditions as to what they could and could not do. A committee of five business owners from each of the commercial centres would be appointed and would apply the law and deal with any complaints arising from the behaviour and activities of such touts. Sadly, most commercial centres have not set up the mechanism needed to regulate and deal with complaints from the public, neither have the Town Halls insisted that they should do so.

Touting is the curse of many tourist resorts, not only in the Canary Islands and the Spanish Costas, but also in many parts of Europe. Presumably it is in everyone's interest that our visitors have an enjoyable stay on the island and not to return home with a bad experience and negative view of their holiday created by a small number of troublesome touts, who may be in the resort for only a few weeks.

Letter 42
Fire, Fire!

During one particularly hot summer, a forest blaze raged through the very heart of Gran Canaria. Helicopters, planes and fire fighters from Gran Canaria and neighbouring islands tackled the blaze from the air in an attempt to save over four thousand hectares of pine forest and hillside. A change in wind direction late one night worsened the problem, which was the biggest ever fire fighting deployment in Gran Canaria's history. Residents of several parts of the island affected by the fire were evacuated from their homes and villages, and spent the next few days in temporary accommodation.

The fire was started deliberately by an ex-employee of the forestry department, whose contract had come to an end. The offender was caught and imprisoned for his own safety and protection from the wrath of the islanders. Other blazes also broke out in La Gomera and Tenerife. From our home by the sea, we could see the huge plumes of smoke as well as smell the burning for many days. At night time the sky turned an eerie shade of red, and we could only pray that no lives would be lost.

I well recall the events of those tragic few days. At our home, which also served as the newspaper office, we received many calls from readers who were witnessing at first hand the drama as the events unfolded. It was the only time that I wished that we were a radio station and not a fortnightly newspaper as the immediacy of the news was so important. By the time that we published the next edition of the newspaper, the drama would long be over, yet it was touching that so many readers wanted to tell us the events as they were happening. One of our regular correspondents, Shirley, saw the drama unfold from her own villa. Fortunately, I still have the notes taken from many such phone calls:

"It's terrible and it has all got out of hand now. Building workers are trapped in San Nicolás. The roads are closed today. There is no way in or out of San Nicolás because of the spread of the fire. It looks as if it is out of control. As I sit in my house, I hear ambulances or police sirens every two minutes or so. We could see the flames late last night coming over the mountains from Tejeda from our terrace. Nobody has been allowed through this morning from San Nicolás as the road is impassable due to the smoke. Just now there are three four-by-fours and many police vehicles screaming up the valley packed with policemen with sirens blaring. It looks like a lot of police are going as fire fighters from Puerto Rico and other areas to try and help. Anyway, let's hope they do get it under control."

The forest fires will not be forgotten for many years to come, and particularly by the people who lost their homes, possessions and businesses. We learned later that many of the properties were uninsured. Fortunately, very few lives were lost thanks to the selfless bravery of the fire fighters. However, the lingering smell of smoke and charred remains hung over the south of the island for many days. Trees, plants and vegetation were completely destroyed by the raging fires. It was heartbreaking to hear the personal loss of so many people as well imagining the suffering of so many birds and animals that perished.

Our beautiful wildlife park had been destroyed and the many wonderful species of birds and animals had perished. Reportedly, park keepers had, in vain, tried to release a number of species, but it was estimated that nearly two thirds had perished because the fire had spread at such an alarming rate in the 'tinder box' surroundings. What had once been a beautiful part of the island had been completely destroyed, yet already many people were trying to reclaim what they had lost. Nearly thirty thousand hectares of land had been devastated and more than twelve thousand people forced from their homes.

A few weeks later it was heart-warming to see the island's tour operators, who rely so much upon the beauty of the island to bring holidaymakers from all parts of Europe, as well as local businesses, stand together to hold fund-raising events in aid of reforestation and emergency aid.

The island government, as well as national government, sprang into action surprisingly quickly; resulting in a visit from the Spanish Prime Minister and various other ministers, and a bill of urgent measures for the fire-ravaged areas was rushed through the Spanish Congress in Madrid. The measures approved included subsidies to repair municipal infrastructure, tax allowances, compensation for agricultural and livestock farmers, and financial assistance for those whose homes were damaged by the flames.

The fire was a serious event, and just like the flooding a few years earlier, demonstrated the unity of the island people as well as the readiness of local and national government to act in an emergency. Fortunately, events such as this are rare, but it served to remind us that even in our island paradise, we are not sheltered from the real world and that tragedy is never far away.

Letter 43
Vampire Bats in The Canaries?

The devastating fires in Gran Canaria left severe consequences, not only for the residents who had lost their homes and livelihoods, but for the flora and fauna of the island, and in ways that we could not have imagined at the time.

This was also one of only two occasions when we published a negative story on the front page of the newspaper. As the publication was mainly focussed upon tourists, we reasoned that tourists did not want to step off the plane for a long-awaited holiday, only to read about disaster and devastation. However, there was one story that was just too good to avoid.

Shortly after the fire we received a call from Maria who lived in a 'finca' or rural farm house outside Fataga, a picturesque village much loved by tourists for its traditional Canarian style of buildings. Maria and her husband, José, were the proud owners of two white horses. The two horses lived under a large wind net covering that was normally used to provide plants with protection from strong winds. The forest fires had badly damaged this net covering and about a third of it was destroyed.

Shortly after the fire, Maria and José began to notice bloodstain marks on the neck of one of their white horses each morning. These alarming marks continued with increasing frequency and, after similar staining on the second horse, Maria called her vet to check what was wrong. The vet was unsure what was the cause, but noticed that both horses had been bitten in the neck. It was after Maria and José began to cover their horses' necks at night with material, that they noticed the material was torn away in the morning leaving what appeared to be 'fang' marks in the necks of both horses. These 'fang' marks were not set wide apart, but close together – the tell-tale signs of a vampire bat. Maria and José also noticed that the horses' legs were now also being attacked after the material was wrapped around the horses' necks.

Piecing this strange jigsaw of events together was difficult, but Maria knew that the forest fires in the mountains of Gran Canaria had caused severe damage to a nearby wildlife park, and many animals and birds had perished. During the height of the fires, their keepers had released many of them in the hope that they would find their own way out of the devastation of the park. After the fire, the wildlife park appealed to local people to inform them of any unusual birds or animals spotted, and they would seek to recapture them.

José remembered seeing bats at the wildlife park on their last visit, and Maria began to investigate bats on the Internet. The size of the 'fang' cuts on the horses' necks seemed to point to vampire bats, which are close together. However, these creatures are only indigenous to countries such as Peru, Brazil and South Africa, but could have escaped from the nearby wildlife park or a private collection. However, Maria and José were surprised when a representative from the wildlife park told them that they did not have any vampire bats at the park.

Later, it was Maria who spotted about four vampire bats one night flying around the horses, but later the couple counted a total of nine bats. Maria was concerned that the bats may breed, particularly as information gathered from the Internet confirmed that vampire bats can carry rabies and that sixty-three people were known to have died in Brazil as a result of vampire bat bites. Maria noted that there were around a thousand reported cases in Brazil alone of people being bitten by these hungry creatures.

Maria and José quickly repaired the netting cover for their 'finca', which then provided safety for the horses, but Maria was concerned that they would then seek other animals or people to feed on. Maria told me that she had reported the matter to the public health department, but they said it was impossible and would not look into it further.

The developments following the publication of our story were surprising. We had two reports from readers living near Maria telling me that their dogs – both white in colour – had been attacked, and were covered in blood. I recall being accused by several businessmen in the south for promoting a 'scare story that would put off tourists from coming to the island', and although we reported the incidents to the local government department responsible, they declined to be interviewed or comment.

It was reassuring to discover that a local Spanish newspaper also decided to cover the story, as well as a national television channel. The wildlife park, no doubt mindful of possible insurance claims, continued to deny suggestions that they were responsible and even claimed not to have had any of the offending species in their park – despite readers having seen them on display before the fire. We also discovered later that, despite local and government authorities saying it was not possible, a group of bat experts arrived on the island to see for themselves! We heard nothing more and mindful of the effects on possible advertising, we dropped the story!

Finally, it is worth mentioning that whilst the TV crew were filming the bats, they too reported being attacked. All this made us very thankful that Barney and Bella were not white in colour and would not attract such unpleasant creatures. So, is it safe to go out at night in the mountains? Well, if you do, don't wear white!

Letter 44
Breaking Point

During my time as editor of the only English language newspaper in Gran Canaria, we often received telephone calls for requests for clarification of news items from the BBC. Usually this was in the form of a live telephone interview, having arranged a mutually convenient time to fit in with the appropriate news item the day before. Sometimes these calls had to take place at, what I now consider to be, a ridiculously early time in the morning to catch the early morning news items. I have to remember that I am now running on a loose derivative of 'Canaries time', which essentially means a very early start, an afternoon siesta, before resuming work later in the afternoon and continuing to maybe nine or ten o'clock. I now follow this to the letter – although ignoring the early morning part!

Much of the local news gathering was quite parochial – the usual births, marriages and deaths, the latest scandal at one of the town halls, as well as the latest wrong doing of a British (more often than not) holidaymaker. Sadly there were always a depressing number of animal welfare issues to be included as well. Suddenly, the Canary Islands appeared under the spotlight due to its ever growing illegal migrant issue, which was now becoming worthy of headline news.

Usually BBC interviews would be related; an increase/fall off in tourism numbers, drugs and alcohol, the 'Brits abroad' as well as Spanish building scandals – of which there were few that I was aware of in the Canary Islands. This time it was a very different subject matter – an ongoing human tragedy concerning illegal migrants from Africa landing on our shores and then, as was their intention, on to a better life in mainland Europe. My interview began as follows:

"Boatloads of desperate Africans on rickety fishing boats are turning up on the beaches of the Canary Islands nearly every day carrying their gaunt and exhausted human cargo..."

It was estimated by Mauritania, that only around sixty per cent of the migrants that leave Africa actually arrived in the Canary Islands, with the remaining forty per cent perishing on the five day sea journey in flimsy, wooden fishing boats. These were the lucky ones.

We regularly received information from readers about yet another boatload of would-be migrants landing on our shores. In each boatload, there were many who did not survive whilst others arrived badly dehydrated and very ill. It was a situation that was proving to be a human tragedy for the migrants as well as the Canarian authorities, who were ill equipped to deal with this unfolding crisis. The Red Cross, volunteer workers and government employees did their best to care for the sick and dying, many were looked after in hospitals whilst the fitter ones were looked after in camps newly set up for the purpose, until the Spanish Government decided what to do with them.

The fishing boats (known as cayucos) could carry anything between seventy and one hundred and fifty people crammed side by side. However, many of the cayucos were well equipped and a few even had handheld GPS systems. Some had two or three forty-horsepower engines with barrels of diesel loaded below the makeshift wooden decks. Food and water appeared to be minimal, but among the putrid remnants left behind when the passengers were taken ashore were life jackets, gas cookers, pots and evidence of rice, onions and biscuits. Migrants landing in the Canary Islands often had to be treated for dehydration and sun burn, but other arrivals were relatively fit.

I told the story of one fishing boat that turned up on Maspalomas beach having set out with eighty 'passengers' on board, but arrived with only a handful of those still alive. This horrendous human tragedy had been unfolding for many months, so why was it that only now the world appeared to be interested and listening?

One of the reasons was that the number of people arriving was three times higher than three years earlier. Similar problems were also being faced by governments in Italy and Malta as well as Peninsular Spain – so the Canaries were not alone. It had also reached the level where resources on the Canary Islands had reached breaking point and there was concern as to how tourism would be affected by this developing issue.

Visits to the Canary Islands by Government ministers and Spain's Prime Minister, José Luis Rodríguez Zapatero, were at last showing that Madrid was aware of the problem and trying to help. The European Union had long promised maritime patrols around the Canary Islands and along the West Coast of Africa, but it was too little too late.

After many more flimsy boats had landed on the shores of Gran Canaria, and with many more landing in Tenerife, the European Commission said that it would do more to help deal with the large influx of migrants. This decision was in response to a new appeal for help from Spain. The EU had already launched a small operation to turn back boats carrying migrants from Cape Verde, Mauritania and Senegal to the Canary Islands. However, Spain said that the operation was not big enough and took too long to get started. Indeed, at the time of Spain's representations to the EU, only one Portuguese ship had joined the Spanish effort. An Italian ship broke down 'en route', and a Finnish aircraft had yet to arrive.

At last the position appeared to be changing. The EU Commission asked all member states to show more solidarity with Spain and to increase the amount of money available for border control, and to strengthen the role of the new EU border agency, Frontex, which involved air and sea patrols along the coast of Cape Verde, Mauritania and Senegal. A similar operation was planned in the Mediterranean to intercept migrants from North Africa to Italy and Malta.

A number of other countries also agreed to provide experts to help to identify migrants. A Frontex official said that help from experts was necessary, because migrants tried to avoid repatriation by concealing their nationality. It was estimated that over five thousand migrants had been repatriated so far that year.

Patrol boats, planes and helicopters from Spain, Italy, Portugal and Finland began to operate off the shores of Mauritania, Senegal and Cape Verde in a bid to stop the immigration at source. If they located and identified any illegal boat within twenty miles of the African coast, they were immediately returned. If found outside that zone, the boats were escorted the extra two thousand kilometres or so to the Canary Islands.

There were also local rumours that the 'cayucos' boats whose passengers arrived in a relatively good state of health after between eight to ten days at sea would have had help from bigger vessels – either towing or dropping them off within striking distance. However, the authorities were unable to prove this theory.

Many of the would-be migrants from North Africa and sub-Saharan Africa were well aware of the risks. They knew that many of their family and friends would not survive the journey, but they still risked their lives in the forlorn hope that they would be able to enter Spain illegally and make a living, or make their way north to other European countries. Their desperation accepted no boundaries. It was both a humbling and very depressing period in news gathering and reporting.

Letter 45
Too Much of a Good Thing?

I confess to having a weakness for red wine. At UK prices the temptation was never quite as strong, but for me this has been one of the real benefits of moving to Spain in general, and Gran Canaria in particular. A plentiful supply of good wine – almost on tap – most of which is remarkably drinkable and exceptionally good value, just warms the 'cockles' of my heart!

I well recall two pieces of very useful advice that one of our neighbours gave us upon our arrival in the Costa Blanca. The first was, "Never to believe what anyone tells you – find out for yourself." That was a good piece of advice, as how often have you been given conflicting advice about what to do in your new country? Listen to advice, ask lots of questions and find out more for yourself.

The second piece of advice was the most useful, "Never pay more than one euro for a bottle of wine!" I didn't believe it, but yes, it is quite possible to buy a perfectly drinkable bottle of 'plonk' for around that figure, and quite a decent bottle for under three euros. It was only after spotting three bottles of wine in our bin after only one day in our new home in the Costa Blanca that I realised that a brake would have to be put on our alcohol consumption! "All things in moderation," I heard my mother's reprimanding voice! Well, we all tend to over indulge from time to time, don't we?

Most people appreciate wine for its delicious and complex taste. There are countless different types of wine, each pairing mouth-wateringly well with certain combinations of food.

Personally, I like most of the Spanish Riojas, but tend to prefer Navarra and La Mancha wines that are less popular and cheaper. This immense variety means, if you had enough money, you could live a lifetime without drinking the same wine twice. All very well, but how does this affect your health?

Wine, like any other item of food and drink, should be taken in moderation. Just like eating eight pounds of chocolate a day is unhealthy, and fifteen bags of crisps a day is not a good idea, so would drinking eight bottles of wine a day. Wine, like anything else overdone, can harm your body in large quantities. The key is moderation.

Assuming a glass of wine is drunk with dinner every day, what benefits will this wine bring to your body? I recall reading heart-warming research showing that wine helps to reduce coronary heart disease. This is known as 'The French Paradox' because doctors couldn't work out why the fat-loving and heavy cigarette-smoking French weren't dying from heart attacks. Wine, it turns out, was the answer.

What is wine doing? The wine is altering the blood lipid levels. It lowers the total cholesterol count, and raises the high density lipoprotein levels – it keeps the blood vessels clean. Research as far back as 2001 showed how polyphenols in red wine keeps the arteries clear. More recent studies show that wine helps to fight cancer, as it contains a chemical called resveratrol that helps to suppress cancer. The red grapes that go into red wine also have bioflavonoids, which are antioxidants and help prevent cancer to begin with. As a stress fighter, wine is also shown to help cancer patients by relaxing them and helping them to fight their disease.

Studies also show that wine helps to prevent strokes. Scientists conclude that the alcohol breaks up blood clots and increases 'good' cholesterol in the bloodstream, and this keeps the arteries clean. This helps with the common stroke, but not the rarer stroke, which is sudden bleeding in the brain.

Wine is a calming influence, something which may seem incidental but should not be forgotten. The fact that dinner on the terrace in the evening is accompanied by a drink that helps the body relax and unwind can help the mental transition between work and play. Also, people fighting other illnesses can combat them better when calm and focused. Alcohol, like any other food item, can be used properly, or can be used to excess. Indeed, I have recently seen research in that most hateful of daily UK tabloids that seems to contradict the benefits of such a perfect beverage, but as we all have a choice in life, I choose to completely ignore that one!

Finally, I should add that at all costs do avoid those ghastly cartons of wine – retailing in local supermarkets for around sixty cents. They may look like a bargain, but really most are fit for use only as a substitute for lavatory cleanser and certainly not intended for your stomach! Cheers!

On a more serious note, I am well aware of the devastation that over-indulgence of alcohol can bring to individuals as well as their families and friends, and this is the downside of living in a country where alcohol is cheap and plentiful. I recall receiving an email from one reader who wanted to share her problem with our readers and I was moved by its both sincerity and honesty.

Helen was an alcoholic. She was also a mother and a grandmother. She was just one of the crowd who nobody noticed. She left her country to live in Gran Canaria for a change of climate and environment, and not for of the price of alcohol! When Helen first arrived she had been sober for less than two years. Ten years earlier, she had been in a treatment centre for alcoholics, and after a couple of years of sobriety, she found out that she could control her drinking. This wisdom did not last long. She was soon back where she started and within a few years, Helen had to seek help again. Out of curiosity, I agreed to meet Helen in a juice bar in a nearby town. I was surprised by her appearance, as she was nothing like I expected her to be based on a couple of emails and a telephone conversation.

Helen told me that there is no such thing as a typical alcoholic. They come in all sizes and types, from good or bad homes, educated or ignorant, believers or agnostic, intelligent or not. Women, men, even children. The majority of them work, many in high positions, others are retired or disabled and some live on the street. The one thing that they all have in common is that one drink is never enough. Maybe in alcohol they find something that, in the beginning, improves their personalities, usually self-esteem, courage, ability to express themselves or to get rid of shyness. Some find this need to go on drinking right from the first drink, others gradually or a little later. However they start drinking, in the end, they always end up drinking more than they meant to and more than enough. Over a fresh orange juice, Helen told me:

"To discover and admit that you are an alcoholic is a very tough process. We go to great lengths to make excuses for our drinking and constantly convince ourselves that we can stop tomorrow. To find that we cannot put on make-up or shave in the morning, because our hands are shaking and we need alcohol just to steady them, is not an enjoyable experience."

Helen went on to explain that an alcoholic does not like to go to sleep at night knowing that he has no alcoholic drinks in his house or wherever he is staying. He hides bottles in unusual places, but often forgets where, when he needs them. He will go out in any weather, at any time of the night, do almost anything to make certain that he has enough in the morning to be able to 'function' or to feel 'normal'.

"I felt that my life was over if I could not take a drink ever again. A vacation was when you could drink freely at all times. Later, my daily life was about drinking, although I was working and kept a home. At home, after work, and in the end also before and during work, a bottle helped me get through the day. I only

311

felt 'normal' after having had a few. I often drove with my grandchild in the back seat, and was never sober those days. Talking to people, I was careful not to breathe over them."

The last time that I spoke to Helen she was still attending Alcoholics Anonymous meetings, sharing her experience and feelings with other alcoholics. It makes her feel stronger to talk to others who are in the same situation and have to accept that they cannot take a drink. They often have a laugh as well as an occasional tear, but the common factor is wanting to stop drinking and improve their lives. The only condition for attending the meetings is to want to stop drinking (or taking drugs).

I recall a number of tragic stories on the island over the years that I have been here. One involved a young man, Colin, a known alcoholic, who went on yet another late night drinking binge. He eventually returned to his apartment and was never seen alive again. Colin's body was only discovered several weeks later when neighbours called the Town Hall complaining of "a bad smell in the upstairs apartment". Tragically, no one had even missed him.

Young holidaymakers are also particularly vulnerable when they visit the island. A lively nightlife, cheap and easily attainable alcohol and drugs lead to a potentially tragic mix. I remember one eighteen-year-old British teenager who, for a bet, and egged on by other holidaymakers as well as the barman who should have known better, was persuaded to drink a whole bottle of vodka. Later he died in hospital from alcohol poisoning.

Those who really want to stop drinking can get help and support in Alcoholics Anonymous meetings in Gran Canaria, but this is often only in the Spanish language. We regularly see residents and tourists who have had too much to drink and cannot control themselves. Those are only the tip of the iceberg. A big part of the drinking is done at home before going out or just passing out at home. I learned a lot from my conversation with Helen and realised that some people can hide their addiction from others for years, whilst others have it printed on their foreheads.

Letter 46
Bonnie and the Tomato

The World Health Organisation had confirmed that the Torrevieja area was one of the healthiest climates in the world, and this fact was well promoted by holiday tour companies and by sales promoters to potential British purchasers of properties in the Costa Blanca. Many 'expats' moved to the area because they were suffering from arthritis, asthma and other bronchial conditions, and many moved specifically to the Costa Blanca in order to gain some relief from pain. If this climate is so good for us, then surely it must be good for our pets?

Bonnie was a sixteen-year-old golden retriever from Manchester. From the age of seven, Bonnie suffered from severe arthritis. She found it difficult and painful to walk and her joints were very swollen. She was on constant medication and her family and vet were very concerned about Bonnie's future. Bonnie was slowing down and, because she was in some pain, did not enjoy the long walks that she used to. It was clear that Bonnie was no longer the happy, playful dog that she used to be.

Bonnie's owners decided to move to the Costa Blanca and Bonnie's future was discussed thoroughly with her vet. Initially, the vet was sceptical about Bonnie travelling so far from home at the ripe old age of fourteen. However, Monica a nursing sister, was well aware of the health benefits of the Costa Blanca, and reasoned that if it was good for humans, then it would be good for Bonnie too!! Once the couple had bought their villa in the Costa Blanca, Bonnie was driven to Spain from Manchester, in order to avoid the possible trauma of an air flight.

Bonnie settled remarkably well in her new home, and appeared to be very content with her new life in the sun. Within two weeks of arriving in Spain, her condition noticeably improved. She began to enjoy walks again and seemed altogether a much happier and livelier dog. Amazingly, her joints were no longer swollen, she moved freely, loved long walks, and retrieved toys and balls thrown for her.

"She behaves like a two-year-old," said Monica.

It was clear that she was no longer in any pain, nor was she on any medication. The Costa Blanca had given Bonnie a new lease of life!

David and I often used to look after Bonnie when the family returned to the UK to see family and friends. We always enjoyed looking after her and she and Barney became good friends, although Bella was less sure of this 'grand old lady'. One example of Bonnie's tolerance was that she always allowed the family cat to sleep between her front paws at night. I am sure this would be the stuff of nightmares for Barney and Bella!

Sadly, Bonnie died shortly after our move to Gran Canaria. Old age had finally taken its toll on the old girl, and she died peacefully. She was greatly missed by her human family and all who knew her, as she was an intrinsic part of their lives and, in so many ways, helped her human family to settle well in their new country.

It was when we moved to Gran Canaria that we spotted many lorries and vans bearing the immortal name, 'Bonny'. Yes, I know it is spelled differently from dear Bonnie, the golden retriever, but whenever we see those lorries carrying boxes of tomatoes to the port, we always think of her. Tomatoes are an important part of the Canary Islands economy, and I urge readers to purchase as many tomatoes from the Canary Islands as possible during the winter months, because they really are the best!

I recall attending one of the really 'fun fiestas' that takes place in the small Spanish town of Buñol, in the province of Valencia, each year. A record forty thousand people took part in the annual 'La Tomatina' – a festival of tomato-hurling that leaves people and buildings covered in red juice, pips and skin.

Five trucks had delivered over a hundred tons of the fruit for the hour-long combat which had attracted foreign tourists, among them British, French, Argentinean and Japanese, as well as locals, and many wearing a minimum of clothing. I hid well out of the scene of the main action – just in case, but with my camera at the ready!

Tradition states that on the last Wednesday of August, at eleven o'clock in the morning trucks move down the central street of Buñol, which has a usual population of around nine thousand people, to the town square depositing their squashy load as they go. On the stroke of noon, the signal was given and for the next hour, people hurled tomatoes at each other, until a gunshot signalled the end of the fiesta.

The aftermath of La Tomatina puts any blood-injected, horror film set to shame. Don't count on recognising your friends, or them recognising you for that matter. However, within hours, the town was transformed back to its former state. Shopkeepers took down their tarpaulins, and everyone helped to hose down the town and return it to its former 'tomato-less' glory. Combatants washed the signs of battle away in the local river or under hundreds of temporary showers. The fronts of buildings were then hosed down, looking brighter than ever after their shower.

So how on earth did this gastronomically obscure tradition start? I don't think that there is a patron saint of the tomato, but the tradition was born way back in 1945 when some locals got carried away in a restaurant food fight. Nowadays, it all seems a very good excuse to use the excess tomato produce, have a great party and have lots of fun – something the Spanish always do very well!

This was perhaps the most curious and fun-filled fiesta that I had ever experienced and I can assure readers that no one is safe from a surprise attack from a ripe tomato thrown by enthusiastic teenagers with an accurate shot! Yes, I too was splattered, but thankfully I was wearing old clothes and my camera was already safely back in its case. It could have been so much worse!

Letter 47
Hepa Filters Are Us

Some readers may wonder why I have dedicated one of my letters to my Dyson vacuum cleaner. Those of you who are already 'expats', either living in Spain or elsewhere will, I am sure, readily understand the necessity of having some familiar inanimate things around you. For me, these necessities boil down to just three items, a Corby trouser press, my beautiful Roberts radio and our Dyson vacuum cleaner.

Readers who have already moved permanently overseas will surely also recognise the trauma that I am about to describe. "What exactly shall we take with us?" became the focus of many an increasingly urgent discussion as the removal date approached. Removal costs are high at the best of times, but surely this was the time to recognise that the new cylinder lawnmower that sat so proudly in the garage was not going to be needed in Spain, nor indeed, were blankets, heavy duvets, vacuum flasks and the like. We had exactly the same problems to resolve as everyone else, but one thing was for certain, Dyson would be coming with us.

Dyson, our vacuum cleaner, was already eight years old at the time of our move. Those of you who have owned a Dyson will no doubt recognise the feeling that 'I will never have anything else' as well as an understanding that the verb 'to hoover' is now long since dead. Over the years, I have also learned that Dysons are rather like Marmite – you either love them or hate them. "Heavy, expensive things," some would say.

"It's just a gimmick, give me the good old Hoover any day," protested others.

Yes, in our UK home, Dyson reigned supreme with its "suck to end all sucks" reputation, and a capability to clean that was awesome. Yes, you've guessed, I am one of large fraternity of worldwide Dyson fanatics. Friends and neighbours would visit Dyson soon after his arrival and cry with amazement, "Look, no bag!" and "What a brilliant hypergenic hepa filter!" whilst we looked on admiringly like proud parents.

Kitchen tiles, woodblock flooring and shag pile were all dealt with ease and we were sure it would do equally well with the marble flooring in our new villa in the Costa Blanca. The big day came and Dyson was duly bubble-wrapped, and carefully placed in a large Pickford's box. The next time we would see it would be in Spain.

A few years later, and after sterling service of dealing with dust, dirt and builders' rubble, Dyson was again made ready to travel. Dysons were rare in the Valencia region at that time, although we did manage to find a 'hepa' replacement filter in El Corte Ingles Department Store in Alicante on one occasion. Our good friends at Pickfords once again came to collect Dyson, whilst we made our way to Gran Canaria. It would be six months before we would have Dyson once again with us, and had to cope with a cheap 'Carrefour special' that made me curse every time I used it.

Dyson lived happily with us in our Gran Canaria home for two years. It dealt with dog hair, dust and dirt with ease – marble tiles, rugs and wood flooring were all taken in its stride. It was so easy to take Dyson for granted as it sat in the cupboard under the stairs when not being used.

Then, disaster struck. Dyson began to make the noise of a large cement mixer and its awesome suck was reduced to that of a pensioner with dentures. Did this mean the end for Dyson? Anxiously, we asked in several local electrical shops, but the answer was the same. A sombre shake of the head, and a nod in the direction of a new range of shining new Dyson look-a-likes at the back of the store. We experienced great joy when we discovered one in El Corte Ingles in Las Palmas, but it didn't really look like our trusty faithful. It was a sad, flash purple imitation of the real thing. We wanted our beautiful yellow and grey model back in action.

One evening, I had an idea. I typed in 'Dyson Spain' in Google on my PC and up popped a Dyson website – in Spain! The following morning, I telephoned the number and a helpful lady answered in Spanish. I began to explain the problem in Spanish, but it was not easy describing a machine that would not suck anymore to a complete stranger, when I was at the early stages of learning the language. Recognising my difficulty, Pilar then began to speak to me in English, and listened most carefully as I described the problem.

"Ah," she sighed as I gave her the model number. "That was one of the very best. It was a wonderful machine. It must be fourteen years old now."

"Was? Does that mean… the end… you cannot do anything to save Dyson?"

"No, no," Pilar laughed. "Just pack it carefully and our courier will be along to collect it tomorrow, and take it to our service engineers in Gran Canaria. They are in Aguimes. We will look at what is wrong, and tell you how much it will cost. We will then repair it, and send it back to you just like new. Señor Dyson will live on for many more years."

A week later, Pilar called again, "We have your Dyson, and we have looked at it. It needs new brushes, a new hose and new filters. It will cost one hundred euros, including delivery, to put right. We will replace anything that is faulty, and it will be returned to you as good as new."

Several days later, a courier arrived at the door. It was Dyson! Very carefully we removed the layers of bubble wrap and packaging. It was our Dyson – bright yellow and grey – looking like new, just as Pilar had described! Was it really our trusty Dyson? The scratches on the plastic had disappeared, the marks on the casing had gone – it just stood there glaring at us as if to say, "Switch me on then! Let's get started!"

It was our Dyson – it had exactly the same voice as when it was new, and its suction was unbelievable. Our home is once again as clean as a new pin, and with not a dog hair in sight! Bella scurries off to her basket whenever she sees it, and I am convinced that she thinks it will suck her up if she gets too close! As for Barney, well he just looks at it with an air of indifference, and wanders off wondering what all the fuss is about.

Letter 48
The Queen's Birthday Party

Writing and publishing a newspaper is hard work, and I think if we had realised how much it would eat into our lives, both in terms of our time as well as our home, I doubt we would have accepted the challenge given to us quite so readily. As well as our dining room being used as the newspaper office, the telephone seemed to ring constantly. There was always a barrage of emails from readers to reply to, and we rarely had a day off. I took perhaps a naive view that if readers cared enough to write to us with a comment, concern, praise or, indeed, criticism, they at least deserved the courtesy of a reply – albeit a short one. We were both determined to stick to our original principles, but it often came at the expense of our personal health and well being, despite the overall enjoyment and fulfilment that the job gave us.

Occasionally, we would 'take the day off' and head for the mountains, but this was always with a view to taking photographs and writing an article for the next edition. Indeed, I often joked about it, but it was true that I always had at least three newspaper editions on my mind – the one that I was in the middle of producing as well as the next two, and I often would awake early in the morning after dreaming of appropriate headlines, feature stories and new articles. Yes, the newspaper had taken over our lives.

On the positive side, we would sometimes be wined and dined by a new advertiser, wanting to make a good impression and hoping to receive a good restaurant review, cover the opening of a new shop or maybe a review about a new cabaret show. As they say, "There is no such thing as a free lunch," and we had to be careful about what we accepted, because we had no intention of misleading readers, nor did we wish to upset advertisers. Indeed, it was amazing how many 'friends' we made during this period, although the term 'fair weather friends' now occasionally springs to mind.

One particular event meant a great deal to us both. We received an invitation from the British Consulate in Las Palmas to attend the Queen's Birthday Party in Madrid. It was addressed to us personally and not as representatives of the local newspaper, which meant even more. I had not realised before, but Queen Elizabeth's Official Birthday in June is also celebrated at British Embassies throughout the world, with British Ambassadors hosting the event. In was a kind and much appreciated invitation. We always did what we could to help promote and publicise the services of the British Consulate in Las Palmas. In our view, they were doing a good job for British 'expats', as well as for British tourists to the island. In many ways, it was a thankless task, because their own role had changed so much in recent years, and many people seemed to have unrealistic expectations of what the Consulate could do for them. We would occasionally receive complaints from tourists who, having run out of money usually through their own fault and sometimes theft, that the Consulate would not buy them their ticket home, or somehow fund them until their crisis was over. This is not the role of the present day Consulate service, nor can they use taxpayers' money to do this.

The resources and staffing of the Consulate service appear to have reduced in real terms over the years by not increasing sufficiently to match the rising numbers of independent travellers, and the consequent demands upon their services. However, the services that they do offer are invaluable to British passport holders who get into trouble with the police, lose their passport, are jailed or hospitalised. Many a distressed holidaymaker has been grateful for the help and support from the Consulate; for example, when their partner has died on holiday or they have had a family crisis.

There was no doubt that attending the party in Madrid was going to cause some problems for us. Firstly, it was going to take place during publication week, which meant that, at best, we could only manage one night away from home. We would have to work extra hard to ensure that the paper was ready to publish before we left the island. There was also the question of the dress code. It was obvious that new suits would be needed. As I wrote in an earlier letter, when I left the school inspection service for a new life in Spain, I had dumped all my suits, black shoes and briefcase into the Oxfam recycling bin, fully intending never to wear a suit again. After spending most of my working lifetime up to that period wearing a suit and tie for work, I swore I would never wear one again. Indeed, for those readers who have to wear formal clothing for work, I cannot stress enough the freedom and well-being that one feels when abandoning suits and ties for ever! It is the very best of retirement gifts.

The problem was that now I had no suit to wear. Well, I did have one – a white one, which was more suited to a visit to a casino than a party to honour the birthday of Her Majesty. A trip to the local equivalent of a House of Fraser or John Lewis department store saw me exit the store proudly with a smart new grey suit, snappy tie and even a new shirt to match, since I found that none of my old long-sleeved white shirts would fit – no doubt due to excesses of red wine and restaurant reviews!

It was a beautiful evening and our taxi drove us through the suburbs of Madrid to an area that looked and felt very much like the expensive suburbs of London on a warm summer evening. Tree lined roads, graceful mansions and even grassed lawns told us that we were entering the 'better part of town'. Our taxi swept into the driveway of the Ambassador's residence and we were ready to party.

It was all a little surreal. After being ushered through a large drawing room and past a collection of photographs of Her Majesty, as well as photographs of the British Ambassador to Spain and her family, we met the Ambassador herself, standing very regally on the steps leading to the rear garden. We were then formally introduced to the Ambassador, her husband and her son, and then ushered down the steps into the garden. It looked rather like a very well-groomed vicarage garden. At its centre was a beautiful well-manicured lawn – the like of which I had not seen since leaving England. A combination of English roses and native growing Spanish plants seemed comfortable bedfellows. Elderly, tall trees and huge bushes graced the edges of the main garden and set inside the tall hedging were entrances to a number of other, more private gardens and, of course, the obligatory swimming pool. A military band was positioned on the terrace and was playing uplifting music that I suddenly had the urge to march to, but refrained from doing so.

There seemed to be hundreds of suits, dresses and large hats on the lawn, all holding glasses of wine and nibbling 'bits and pieces', no doubt really called 'canapés'. We gratefully accepted a glass of wine from the smart, ever-attentive waiters but, as vegetarians, ignored the 'bits and pieces' as we were unsure what they were! We noticed a large Jaguar trade stand proudly displaying a number of Jaguar cars at the side entrance, as well as a fish and chip van standing alongside a table of 'tapas' delicacies. It was just a little bizarre, I thought, as the band struck up a version of that all time hit, *Greensleeves*.

We spotted our friend, the British Consul from Las Palmas, in the distance and eventually managed to squeeze our way over to him. He greeted us warmly and introduced us to a number of his colleagues. We learned that the newly appointed Ambassador had insisted that the event be self-funding with donations and sponsorship from industry and similar interested UK businesses represented in Spain. Ah, so this was the reason for the fish and chip van and the Jaguar stand, I thought. The band played on.

Suddenly there was a drum roll, the Ambassador and a suit from the House of Lords (I'm still not sure who he was, but he looked very important) appeared on the balcony. The music stopped, the Ambassador made an excellent speech in both Spanish and English, glasses were charged and we raised a toast to Her Majesty Queen Elizabeth. It all was very moving, until I spotted that an elderly looking 'suit' in front of me had drunk rather too much, and had, whilst talking, splattered some of the contents from both his mouth and his glass over my new suit. I gave him a frosty stare, but he merely gave me a friendly wave. It was good to be with so many interesting people gathered in one place at the same time, and we were soon involved in some fascinating conversations. If only I could have published some of the stories that I heard, but, of course I knew better than to betray confidences!

It was a wonderful evening and certainly one that we would remember for a long time to come. At around ten o'clock – rather early for the end of a social evening in Spain, I thought, the Ambassador and her family disappeared inside the building and waiters busied themselves collecting empty glasses, and certainly stopped offering to top them up. This was the cue to begin to leave. I spotted the elderly looking 'suit' once again, accompanied by a much younger woman. I thought I had seen the elderly 'suit' somewhere before... They both nodded and smiled, which this time I acknowledged, although I was still feeling a little peeved about the splattered mix of wine and chip stains on my new suit.

Not wishing to outstay our welcome, we made our farewells and wandered back to the front driveway where there was a queue of guests awaiting taxis. It looked as if we were in for a long wait, but the evening was warm and it was no hardship to stand in the night air for a while admiring other grand properties and listening to the banter of happy conversation in the queue.

"Mind if we join you?" came a voice from the elderly suit, pushing in at the side of us. The couple behind us didn't seem to mind, and so I smiled and nodded.

"No, not at all. Have you enjoyed the evening?" I enquired politely.

"Bloody good evening!?" spluttered the elderly suit, swaying from side to side on the pavement. "Not enough booze mind, but what can you expect from one of Her Majesty's functions?" he burbled in a strong Australian accent.

It was at that moment that I suddenly realised where I had seen this elderly man before. It was comedian Barry Humphries' (of Dame Edna Everage fame) alter ego, the comical yet totally revolting Sir Les Patterson, who played the part of the spluttering cultural attaché for Australia! This man looked, behaved and spluttered in exactly the same way. I looked at David and it was clear from his expression that he was thinking exactly the same thing as myself. The likeness was uncanny.

"Anyway, got some of my own, sport," grinned the elderly man, showing an uneven set of teeth – not without gaps, and pulled out a generously sized hip flask from his inside suit pocket. "Want some?"

"No, I won't, but thank you all the same," I replied. David too shook his head as the old man offered the battered, well-used flask to him. A strong smell of alcohol wafted across our faces, replacing the fresh night air.

At last it was time for our taxi – the next one would be ours and as we saw it speeding towards us, the Sir Les 'look-alike' spluttered.

"Tell you what. Why don't we share the cab? We can split the fare," he beamed his toothy smile once again.

"That's a good idea," added the young woman, speaking for the first time since we had met the couple.

Neither of us could face a journey of an undetermined length with the Sir Les 'look-alike' reeking of booze, and I also noticed the grimace upon David's face.

"No, that's quite alright. We are not in a hurry. You take it and we'll get the next one."

"You sure," spluttered the Sir Les 'look-alike', taking another swig from his hip flask. "Thanks, so much."

The unlikely couple clambered into the cab and it sped away in the distance.

"Phew, that was a close one," I sighed with relief.

"Well done, young man," came a voice from behind, hastily suppressing a laugh as I turned towards him.

I turned to see a smartly dressed portly gentleman whom I had been talking with earlier. He was a Consul from another part of Spain.

"Yes, I had begun to think we had companions for the evening," I replied, genuinely relieved at the departure of Sir Les and his hip flask.

"He always gets like this at these functions. Always brings along his latest secretary to look after him, but always ends up the worse for wear."

"Who is he?" I enquired, desperately wanting to find out more about the colourful guest.

"Oh, you would never think it, but he's the Australian cultural attaché to Spain!"

Letter 49
"Let go and trust me"

It had been an exciting and challenging three years. We had been given considerable trust and responsibility, and it was not something that either of us had entered into lightly. We had launched a new newspaper in Gran Canaria from almost nothing, and had quickly learned that what was suitable for the Costa Blanca newspaper was not well suited to the Canary Islands. Instead of producing a newspaper for mostly retired British 'expats' in the Costa Blanca, we were now catering for a heady mix of tourists from many European countries, as well as a much smaller group of British 'expats'. We also were quickly reminded that as well as entertaining and informing straight holidaymakers and residents, we now had a large group of gay, lesbian and transgendered readers to consider. It was a huge challenge for us, and after the first few editions, we were confident that we were well on our way to getting the balance about right. The feedback from readers was, in the main very positive, and we quickly decided to drop the television pages that were so popular in the Costa Blanca, but were regarded as 'space fillers' in Gran Canaria. No doubt this was due to the fact that receiving British television in the Canaries was very difficult and expensive, as there were none of the cheap 'micro mesh' television re-transmission services that were so prevalent, if illegal, in the Costa Blanca.

It became a real community newspaper, of which we were very proud. We would often receive well-written contributions from readers, together with their thoughts and insights about life in the Canary Islands, which we were usually pleased to publish. Emails, phone calls and letters were coming into our cramped office from all over the island, and even from holidaymakers when they had returned home. The newspaper was equally popular with Scandinavian holidaymakers, and we even had a good response from German holidaymakers and residents. We did our best to reply to any messages that we received, as I was once told that you can always tell how popular a newspaper is judging from the number of letters sent in by readers for the letters page. Apart from the first edition, there was never any problem in filling that particular page, with most of our correspondents being supportive of our efforts and, thankfully, with very few negative comments coming our way. David dealt with some very interesting and hard-working business people who were trying to launch and make a success of their businesses, and we were confident that both he and our small sales team did their best to help them. There were strong links with the local churches, radio and television stations, tour operators and the various Consulates on the island. Everyone seemed to know and like the newspaper, and we could proudly claim that, "It is everywhere."

As in all jobs, we had our frustrations, of course, but they were few and, at least, we didn't have to travel too far to go to work! Our main problem was lack of time off to see our families and friends in the UK. Whenever we did take a week off work, there would be several weeks of manic preparation beforehand, trying to ensure that the next issue was ready to go to print. Upon our return home, our first job was to deal with queries and issues arising from the sales team during our absence, and it was always several weeks later before we managed to get back to normal life. We were always concerned about what would happen in a crisis, such as a family illness, because we knew full well that there were no contingency plans to cover such eventualities. As head teachers in the UK, we were both used to having emergency procedures and contingency plans for all eventualities, and this lack of any was worrying. I remember returning from one UK holiday, and it was two weeks before we had time to empty our suitcases. I also recall one insensitive comment from the company that, "You should take holidays separately and then we wouldn't have this problem."

We lacked a caller office for readers and clients, and it was often embarrassing when readers or advertisers wanted to visit to discuss advertising or articles. I recall one telephone call from a police officer asking to call at our office to interview us about one of our stories. We had to make excuses and meet the police officer in a local bar instead, but he didn't seem to mind too much! I think he was used to it.

The newspaper was growing fast and making a decent profit at last. We always knew that it would take between two and three years before a new business such as this could begin to make an acceptable profit and, even though David had brought the paper into profitability after about eighteen months, we were now confident that it was sustainable. We were in discussions with the company about adding an additional sixteen pages to our existing forty-eight pages after the Christmas edition, as we were already having considerable problems in placing all the new advertisements in the existing space, whilst maintaining the all important balance of editorial content. The future was looking very good, but we were getting very tired.

I have often noticed in life, that when faced with a problem, the right answer somehow always turns up. Often it may not be the answer that we are looking for, but the problem tends to be solved in one way or another. Our resolution of the problem came in the form of being made redundant!

The storm clouds of world recession had been gathering for some time. We had already noticed this from the slowing down of property sales, warning comments from professionals on the island, and the consequent reduction in property advertising.

There was already a new 'cautiousness in the air'. We commented upon this to one of the owners of the newspaper during one of his infrequent visits to the island. "Recession, what recession? There is no recession," was his swift response. I think, looking back, we knew then that from this admitted state of unpreparedness that problems were surely due to follow. I also remember some fateful words uttered by our employer during our last telephone conversation with him, "Just let go and trust me!"

We had not been paid for nearly three months, and it was becoming clear that there were problems looming on the horizon. It was on St Valentine's Day that, over a cup of coffee in a hotel foyer, we were told that our services would no longer be required. We could continue as self-employed staff if we wished, but we would no longer have contracts of employment. Apparently, it was going to be more cost effective to edit and administer the newspaper from the Costa Blanca, and we would no longer be needed as Editor and, in David's case, Sales Manager and Administrator of the company on the island. Maintaining our existing Costa Blanca contracts was the only condition that we had stipulated in agreeing to move from the Costa Blanca to Gran Canaria to launch the newspaper, and so we declined the offer.

I remember, now with some amusement, the elderly couple that had sat in silence on the next table behind the one that we were sharing with our ex-employer. As the elderly couple prepared to leave, the old gentleman walked over to me and put his hand on my shoulder.

"I am so sorry for you both," he said, quietly. "I do hope it works out well for you."

His wife nodded sympathetically, and they both wandered out of the hotel.

Sadly, after several weeks of promises and waiting to be paid, it became clear that neither the salaries owed to us, or the redundancy payments that we were entitled to, were to be voluntarily forthcoming from the company, and we had a difficult few months paying our mortgage and other living expenses. Eventually, our lawyer instructed us not to have any further communication with the company, whilst they did battle on our behalf. We had also been told by our lawyer not to have any communication with anyone connected with the company, be it readers or clients, and this led to a period of isolation for us that, in many ways, we were grateful for. On the day when the legal papers were due to be presented to the court in Las Palmas, our claim was met in full – paid in cash to our lawyer's bank account and just one hour before the appointed time! It had been a difficult process dealing with legal matters, courts and tribunals mostly in Spanish, but it was a very good test as to how well our Spanish was improving.

Our friends on the island, as well as friends and family in the UK, were very supportive and I was particularly grateful for the wonders of the Skype telephone service for the availability of free telephone calls to the UK. We were taken out, had meals cooked for us and received many supportive telephone calls from friends on the island. It was certainly a time when we found out who our 'true' friends were. We knew many people on the island because of the jobs that we did, and it was interesting to discover that as soon as they realised that they would no longer benefit from their 'friendship' with us, we heard no more from them. I guess this is human nature, and this lack of contact from some did not really surprise us. I have always taken the view that you are a fortunate person indeed if you can count the number of 'true' friends on the fingers of one hand. We also managed to resist the temptation of listening to, and entering into gossip, about the newspaper and our ex-employers – nothing would be gained from this kind of thing, and we did still have many happy memories of some good times. We wished the paper well, but now it was time to move on.

We busied ourselves with 'cleansing' the newspaper from our home. Many trips to the rubbish bins followed, as well as a large box containing company property being sent by courier to the Costa Blanca. Repainting, hanging new pictures, rearranging furniture all followed and, at last, we had our 'dining room' back in action, but this time as a study. We washed curtains, emptied and tidied cupboards, set new plants and, basically, did all the kinds of jobs that people do when made redundant or face retirement. Barney and Bella now had us to themselves, and they had many more exciting walks than previously. They seemed very pleased with the new arrangement that we would now be at home all day to play and entertain them.

For the first few weeks of our enforced retirement, my mind was still full of the newspaper that had occupied me so much over the last few years. I would still wake early in the morning having dreamt of the next three editions, main features and headlines. It was very clear that we badly needed to have a holiday to unwind and then later a visit to the UK to see our families and friends.

One of the countries that I had wanted to return to for many years was Italy. I had been there as a teenager and had wonderful memories of Sorrento, the Amalfi coastal area and, of course, Pompeii. We decided to travel to Madrid, a city that we both loved, and then on to visit Rome for a few days. We had a wonderful time in Madrid, spending nearly a whole day in the Royal Palace which was magnificent, walks in some of the beautiful parks, visiting museums and, of course, shopping. I am a great believer in the therapeutic value of 'retail therapy' following a crisis, and Madrid was certainly the place to do it.

Sadly, we found Rome to be hugely disappointing. We know that many love the city, but it was not for us, and by the end of our visit, we couldn't get out of the country quickly enough. We found it to be noisy, dirty and threatening, and the people we met to be generally unhelpful and unfriendly. We tried desperately to get a train out of the city to visit some well-advertised gardens in the countryside, but no one seemed prepared to help us. Even the tourist information office at the central station impatiently demanded that we speak Italian, which is really not the point when helping tourists to make the most of their visit to a new country. We had wanted to visit the Vatican, which we attempted on at least four occasions, only to find long queues of people, standing in what looked like cattle pens, in the hot sun awaiting their turn to hand over quite a lot of money before they could enter the building. The place was awash with 'pick-pockets' and as David already had his wallet stolen previously, I didn't want another problem to deal with, and so we left. We never did get into the Sistine Chapel, and I doubt that I ever will be inclined to revisit the place again. A week or so after we arrived home the Italian government announced that troops would be put on the streets in Rome and two other cities that were causing problems. I can now see why. On the more positive side, the pasta and pizzas were, of course, excellent!

Letter 50
Saying Goodbye and Moving On

I won't pretend that losing our jobs was not a shock, as well as a great disappointment. Although not entirely unexpected, given rapidly declining economic conditions, it was the first time in our lives that we were unemployed. At first, it seemed strange not to have the daily work routines pressing upon us as well as the endless deadlines, telephones calls and emails to deal with. We kept ourselves very busy, catching up with all the many jobs that were outstanding since the move to our new home. Also, at last, we were able to take full advantage of the many opportunities that our beautiful island offered us. It was now possible to sunbathe, explore the island, take long walks with Barney and Bella, as well as going shopping. Indeed, even supermarket shopping became enjoyable as it had been so long since we had both been able to do it. During the previous two years, it had become almost impossible to visit the supermarket and so, every Sunday, I would compile an order for groceries from the supermarket 'on line' and it would be delivered to us the following day, for an additional charge, of course.

Now that we had a significantly reduced income we had to be careful with our spending and we found that by shopping locally, buying fresh vegetables and fruit at our local village market and avoiding purchasing anything from the tourist areas, we could save ourselves a considerable amount of money. We still had the occasional meal out – not two or three times a week as previously, but avoided the tourist restaurants, and only went to where the locals ate. The difference in prices, although not unexpected, were considerable. Looking back, I feel that the experience was a very positive one and we learned a lot about household budgeting!

Another benefit from being unemployed was that we now had the time to do the things that we wanted to do. Several years earlier, whilst on holiday in Fuerteventura, I had started writing a novel. This was something that I had wanted to do for many years, and I had a number of stories inside me just waiting to get out. I wrote the first three chapters of the novel during that holiday, but then forgot about it because of pressure of newspaper work. Now I finally had the time to continue where I had left off and before I knew what was happening I was well on the way to completing my first novel, 'Journeys and Jigsaws'.

The time had come for our long planned visit to the UK. It was wonderful to be able to plan it carefully and to ensure that we would see as many family and friends as possible during our two-week stay. The worry of producing the newspaper early to cover our absence had disappeared, and we could at last enjoy the break. Two weeks off the island was the maximum time away that we had set ourselves, because we didn't want Barney and Bella to be in kennels for too long. We had every confidence in the kennels that the dogs stayed in, and both always seemed very happy to go there when we had previously managed to get a weekend away. The only problem was that Barney was always a lot plumper when he came out of the kennels than when he went in. The predicable routine then followed – we would place Barney on strict diet for the next few weeks until we were able to feel his ribs once again! Bella never seemed to put on additional weight – no doubt due to her usual state of hyper activity.

The visit to the UK was a great success and we managed to visit our friends in Newcastle, where we arrived at its calm airport, Lincolnshire, Cornwall, Bristol, Bournemouth, Portsmouth and London, returning from Gatwick two weeks

337

later. It was good to spend time with our family and friends again and, as usual, we ate too much, drank too much and spent far too much money in the process! However, it was very good therapy and we felt so much better by the end of the visit. I was, as usual, shocked by the rapid increase in prices since our last visit, as well as worrying changes in the High Street shops, there was even talk of Woolworths disappearing! Favourite shops such as Dixons, Cowardines and The Pier had disappeared and there were now growing numbers of empty shops appearing in the high streets of all the towns that we visited. A soup-bowl full of tasteless coffee for three pounds fifty in one of the trendy new multiple coffee outlets, despite me asking a spotty youth for 'a small one', was quite ridiculous as were the cost of train and bus tickets. There was also a new growing trend, that I had not noticed before, of suits dashing around town first thing in the morning carrying polystyrene cups of steaming hot coffee to their places of work. Surely they had kettles at their workplace? I have now come to the conclusion that is the acute need to do something with unoccupied hands. Before smoking became an cardinal sin and, quiet correctly, totally socially unacceptable it was possible for idle hands to 'smoke a fag'. Maybe, with that possibility now gone, idle hands now turned to carrying plastic cups instead. Well, it is just a theory.

How I dislike Gatwick Airport! We would try to avoid it whenever possible, much preferring the more civilised and relaxed atmosphere that regional airports such as Newcastle, Bournemouth, Exeter and Bristol could offer. I have had many a disagreement at Gatwick Airport, and refused to be treated as 'fodder' for a processing plant operated by 'Jobsworths' where customer service is a very low priority! Still, to be honest, flights to and from Gatwick were cheaper than any other airport and, under our new budgeting regime, were cost effective. Yes, I had the usual disagreements about excess luggage and pointed out, without success, that the new weight restrictions recently imposed to 'save fuel' barely covered the weight of my wash bag, let alone sufficient clothing for two weeks! The argument was to no avail and I had to graciously hand over the cash, but I had enjoyed making my point to a look-alike from the Catherine Tate TV Show at the check in desk, although she still added an insincere "Have a Nice Day", which she must have known would make my blood curdle.

Although we had enjoyed a wonderful visit to the UK we couldn't wait to get back to Gran Canaria. The island really had become home to us and we were so excited about collecting Barney and Bella from the kennels the following day. We could already hear Barney barking loudly as soon as we parked outside the kennels – he always recognised the sound of the car engine. Once inside, we saw Barney happily playing with other dogs in the large open exercise area in front of their night quarters. He looked really happy as he sped over on his short legs to greet us. He looked 'well', which in Lincolnshire has actually nothing to do with one's health, but which really means that 'you look fat'! He looked happy and barked with joy, as we made a fuss of him. Bella was nowhere to be seen until we suddenly spotted a flurry of black fluff at the far end of the field. She was playing a game of chase with three other dogs and had not even seen us. We called her, her ears shot up and she dashed over to greet us as well, squeaking and yapping as she usually did when she was excited. As we left, Barney looked behind him to all the other dogs who were standing watching him at the edge of the play area. He seemed to be saying his 'farewells'.

We were pleased to be home, and Barney and Bella slept solidly for the next day or two, only stirring for their food or to go out for a walk. They both seemed just as exhausted as we were. Over the next few days there was work to be done in the garden, as well as catching up with some paperwork, but thankfully there was no newspaper to worry about. After a week or so we noticed that Barney had begun to cough. At first we thought that it was fluff, or something that he had chewed or caught in his throat, but the cough became deeper and more regular. Although he looked healthy enough, with bright eyes and a cold nose, we decided to take him to the vet – just in case. I thought that he may have caught 'kennel cough'. Our other dogs had occasionally had this from time to time, and it usually cleared up after a couple of weeks, sometimes needing medication and sometimes not. Our vet, Manuel, examined him carefully and nodded, "Yes, it is kennel cough." He continued to examine Barney carefully and, looking concerned said that he would like him to have an x-ray.

The x-ray revealed that as well as kennel cough, Barney had an enlarged heart. Manuel looked concerned as he gave us the medication that Barney would need and said very little other than to return a few days later for another examination. Meanwhile, we were to call him if we became concerned. We did become very concerned as Barney seemed to becoming increasingly breathless, and the inconsistent breathing alarmed us greatly. After a couple of days we returned to see Manual again. He gave him further medication and this seemed to help greatly and Barney began to look much better. We began to take him for walks again – just short local ones at first, and later further afield in the car. He really enjoyed these and was eating well. Apart from toilet accidents, which was never like Barney, he almost seemed back to his old self.

It was one morning during the following week when I was working on my novel that Barney came and sat beside me in the study and suddenly licked my hand. I thought this unusual at the time, because Barney usually stayed in his basket until coffee time – he was always a late riser. I stroked him and made a fuss of him. At coffee time, I always had a slice of toast spread with Marmite. Marmite is one of those things, rather like Blackpool, that you either love or hate. I always gave Barney and Bella a soldier of toast each – Barney would drool and gulp his down

340

immediately, whilst Bella was never that keen, and gingerly licked the Marmite off the toast before finally eating it some time later.

David and I sat on the patio with our coffee, and myself with toast and Marmite. Bella sat beside us waiting for her treat, whilst Barney sat in the corner nearby looking at us with very sad eyes. "He's not well this morning, is he?" I commented to David. David shook his head and I gave Barney his Marmite soldier. He ignored it and turned his head away. We agreed that we would take Barney to the vet immediately after coffee, and I began to clear away the coffee mugs and to get ready for the visit to the vet. Suddenly, I heard a couple of brief moans from Barney who was still sitting in the corner of the patio. His eyes said all I needed to know and I noticed that he was sitting in a puddle of urine. I called David and he gathered Barney up in his arms and hugged him. Barney died peacefully in his arms.

We were both devastated. As I said in an earlier letter, those readers who are dog lovers will, I am sure know the awful feeling of loss. It is just like losing a much loved member of the family. Barney was only nine years old when he died, and we both felt cheated that we did not have longer with him. During those nine years Barney had dominated our lives and he had been with us through so much. He used to accompany me to school, school inspections, our move to Spain and then on to the Canary Islands. He was the one constant in our ever-changing lives. He was a strange dog in so many ways, loveable and intensely loyal, but was stubborn, often grumpy and knew his own mind. He had an intelligence quite unlike most dogs that I had known and often, when I looked at him, he seemed to fully understand what I was thinking. It was often uncanny, and we both loved him very much. We buried him in the garden and planted a red rose tree by his side.

Of all the events during that year, losing Barney was the worst and made us value what we had even more. We still had our beautiful 'fruit bat' Bella to fuss over and it was thanks to this crazy little dog that we still managed to smile, laugh and, indeed, to get through the rest of the year. Saying goodbye to those things that you love is always a difficult yet a necessary process of life. Looking back, we were grateful that our busy lives with the newspaper had come to an end, and that we were both happier and healthier for it. Losing Barney was a great shock, but we have so many happy memories of him that will be with us for ever.

So, what of the future? I am often asked if we will stay in Gran Canaria, go back to Spain or, indeed, return to the UK. At the present time, I honestly do not know. All I can say is that we are both believers in 'not going back', but always to move on positively in life. As I walk along the seafront with Bella trotting by my side, I count my blessings that we live in such a beautiful place with its turquoise blue sea, clear blue sky and incredible weather. Moving to Spain had been the right thing to do and our new country has been welcoming to us and given us so many new opportunities and experiences that we would not have had otherwise. I am proud to call our little island in the Atlantic, our home.